A FAN'S GUIDE TO NEO-SINDARIN

A Fan's Guide to
Neo-Sindarin

A Textbook for the
Elvish of Middle-Earth

by Fiona Jallings

NEMVUS

CreateSpace PB	ISBN 978-1546961253
Lulu PB	ISBN 978-0-9974321-6-9
Hardcover	ISBN 978-0-9974321-5-2
E-book	ISBN 978-0-9974321-1-4

ed. 1.0

Table of Contents

Introduction

Welcome, linguistic traveler, to the Neo-Sindarin road! I, Fiona Jallings, am happy to be your guide. Please pay attention to where you place your feet; this road isn't the smoothest of walks. There is a narrow trail of stones forming the center of the path. They were laid by a master craftsman, but only when he felt like it, and he kept changing his mind on the design and cut of the stones. As your guide, I'll keep you on the path, and help you avoid the worst of the mud. Three cheers for The Professor, and *Aphado nin*![1]

---

[1] "Follow me!" in Neo-Sindarin.

0.1.1 What is "Neo" Sindarin?

Sindarin is the language as Tolkien made it. Neo-Sindarin is the fan-extended version of Sindarin.

Tolkien didn't finish Sindarin. He got close with Quenya, but Sindarin is in pieces, only developed as far as he needed it for a few scattered translations. There is a plentiful vocabulary and a fairly complete phonology and historical phonetic development, but only a little grammar. Much is left to speculation. Anyone translating in this language must use a collection of hypotheses and speculations about what Tolkien was getting at. The translations in the *Lord of the Rings* movies are most definitely Neo-Sindarin, and translations in Sindarin alone are extremely limited.

There is no standard Neo-Sindarin. Everyone has their own pet theories and their own selection of others' theories that they've decided to use. What I am presenting here is NOT the definitive Neo-Sindarin, it's just my version, and if other people use other theories or disagree with my theories, they are not necessarily wrong.

0.1.2 Goals of this Book

This is an introduction to the scholarship and usage of Neo-Sindarin as it exists in the dark corners of the internet. It's impossible to really speak Sindarin, as we know so little about it and can do so little, even with our reconstructing. I hope to give you the tools to go forth and do research on your own, and come to your own conclusions.

I've attempted to design the lessons in a way that people unfamiliar with linguistic or grammatical terminology can follow along with relative ease. When linguistic concepts come up, they'll be carefully defined for you. Because of that, this book also functions as a beginner's introduction to linguistics.

My use of Sindarin has centered around Role Play and Fan Fiction. Because of that, my version of Neo-Sindarin has a lot of focus on dialects.

Casual, modern use of Neo-Sindarin has not been the focus of its development, and I won't tell you which dialect you ought to use. That's up to you and your *lámatyávë*.[2]

0.1.3 Conclusions

This is not Tolkien's Sindarin. This is a language that grew out of the nerdy corners of the internet. In this Sindarin, we can utter thoughts that Tolkien never would have conceived. We can talk about our *pelengoen*,[3] and what we watched on *palangened*.[4] We can share intimate secrets in bed; we can describe our daily lives. By using it, we have made this language our own. *Se i Edhellen 'wain.*[5]

Expect new editions often. Every once in a while, a scrap of paper gets published where Tolkien scribbled some notes about Sindarin. These little scraps often revolutionize everything we thought we knew. Constantly editing this textbook is a necessity.

Through this course, I hope you will come to fall in love with Neo-Sindarin as I have. Good luck with your studies![6]

0.1.4 Review

1. What is Neo-Sindarin?

2. Does anyone own Neo-Sindarin?

3. What do you want to say in this language and why?

---

[2] "Linguistic tastes" in Quenya.

[3] Cellphones

[4] Television

[5] This is the New Sindarin.

[6] If you're interested in another Neo-Sindarin translator's advice for newbies, I suggest reading an essay by Carl F. Hostetter called "Elvish as She Is Spoke." http://www.elvish.org/articles/EASIS.pdf. This essay functions as a thesis statement for much of Neo-Sindarin scholarship, and highlights the difficulties we face as translators.

0.2 Invitation

If you'd like to get more practice using Sindarin or would like to chat with other people studying Sindarin, join the community at the *Realelvish Academy*. Check out the free online class there using this textbook. On the website, you'll find quizzes and a series of short vignettes for practicing your translation skills. *Govano ven!*[7]

https://academy.realelvish.net/

---

[7] Join us!

0.3 Acknowledgements

Special thanks to:

My wife Sophia for the cover art and supporting me through this project

My friend Julia Lindquist for the illustrations

Faravenel Faramiriel and Paul Strack for your helpful comments and encouragement

Mark Rosenfelder for helping me edit this mess

My students for teaching me how to teach

And my cat Muior for sleeping on my toes

Chapter 1: Background

This chapter is all about what you need to know before you can start learning Neo-Sindarin grammar. It contains an explanation for the mysterious asterisks you'll find all over Neo-Elvish translations and a set of brief internal and external histories of the language.

1.1 About Fan-Made Words

Before we go any further, allow me to introduce you to how fan-made words in Neo-Sindarin texts are marked and how they will be handled in this book.

1.1.1 Asterisks

If you've browsed the internet, looking for Neo-Sindarin translations, you may have noticed a lot of *asterisks all over the place. There is a specific reason for that, and it starts with an in-joke of sorts. In linguistic annotation, an asterisk placed at the start of a phrase indicates that it isn't grammatically correct or not attested, according to speakers of the language. In Neo-Elvish translations, if an asterisk is in front of a word, that word was made by fans, not Tolkien. Therefore, it means "fans made this word, it might be wrong, use it with caution."

There are some types of fan-made words that we don't bother marking and just assume to be fan-made.

- Any conjugated verb. We have so few examples of them that you can just assume any conjugated verb is a hypothetical form and not a conjugation that Tolkien provided us with. If the verb root is fan-made, it will be marked with an asterisk.

- Any mutated words. Mutation is a grammatical process in Sindarin that changes the beginnings and endings of specific words. We only have partial charts from Tolkien describing which sounds turn into what, and the rest is hypotheses by fans.

- Any plurals. Tolkien never clearly and completely described how plurals in Sindarin work. The system we use has been carefully cobbled together over the years through careful research in Sindarin's phonological development, but it's still a fan-made system.

- Pronouns. Everyone has their own theories about how the Sindarin pronoun system works, because we don't have any thorough description of them by Tolkien, and what we do have is quite contradictory. Each person's system is slightly different, built from slightly different sets of cherry-picked data. Pronouns must be used so often that we don't bother marking them as fan-made, and just assume that whatever system is being used should be taken with skepticism.

- Late Noldorin words that have been 'normalized' into Sindarin. Late Noldorin is almost the same in phonology and historical development as Sindarin, so many words can be borrowed without changes. Some words do require small changes. But, these changes tend to be so minor the word is still easily recognizable, and most Sindarin dictionaries include Sindarinized late Noldorin vocabulary, so we don't bother to mark those words as fan-made.

- Numbers beyond 12, since Tolkien only provided us with the first 12 in Sindarin.

1.1.2 Where do you draw the line?

After all of this, you may be wondering what fan-made words are built from, and if you can use them while considering yourself serious about Tolkien-linguistics. The answer is: It's complicated, and everyone draws the line a little differently. Many, many an argument has been borne in the conflicts over this line.

Some people[8] want to use the languages as Tolkien had conceived them only around the time of the writing of *Lord of the Rings*. Some

---

[8] I used to be in this camp myself.

people[9] go by the motto: later stuff is better. Some people[10] just focus on different eras and try to translate using only the vocabulary and grammar available in that era. Some people[11] borrow and Sindarinize vocabulary from all eras and languages in the Tolkien-mythos. Some people borrow real-world vocabulary, though that is rare and usually confined to things like the names of places, languages, and technology from our world. There is a lot of diversity here, and the way to know whether you want to use a certain fan-made term is to know its background. Any good Neo-Sindarin translator will include notes in their translations explaining where and how their fan-made terms were created.

Words should never be made up from nothing. It's a huge taboo in our community. The only Tolkien-conlangers that can get away with doing this are the Neo-Orcish and Neo-Dwarvish conlangers. There is so little of those languages that was described by Tolkien that you're given free rein to do as you like there. But in Neo-Sindarin? Be prepared to do a lot of research!

As for me, personally, I have a two-directional approach that lets me have the largest possible plausible vocabulary. First - later is better. If I can find a later word or root that Tolkien made for the concept, I'll use that instead of an older one. Second, I'll reach as far back as I can, as long as I can build a plausible ancient root for a word that doesn't conflict with other ancient roots. This is what the vocabulary in my lessons is based on. As for you - make up your own mind on where to draw the line. It's not my place to decide that for you.

1.1.3 How are the new words made?

Other than borrowing late Noldorin vocabulary and making compound words out of existing Sindarin words, most words are built from two sources: The Common Eldarin ancient roots, and Quenya. Many Neo-Sindarin scholars view borrowing from any earlier languages as the limit where the fan-made words get too risky. Early Noldorin, for

---

[9] This is how most Neo-Sindarin translators proceed.

[10] Aglardh http://middangeard.org.uk/aglardh/ is a great place to find people trying out translations like this.

[11] This is a really common practice – though the further you get from Sindarin, the less confident people are in such translations.

example, is very different from Sindarin, and the methods that Tolkien used to make the words was different, so trying to make a Neo-Sindarin word from those is quite difficult. Coining Neo-Sindarin words is tricky, and only recommended for experienced Neo-Sindarin translators.

Fan-made words aren't used to replace words that Tolkien made, ever. They are used when there is a gap in the vocabulary. Even then, we go to great lengths to avoid having to do it. There is a generally agreed upon modus operandi in the Tolkien conlang community when it comes to fan-made words, and it is this: **Paraphrase first, derive second, reconstruct third, otherwise give up.** It's the order that you approach any translation problem where the translation isn't immediately clear. To put it in other words:

1. Find another way to say what you mean.

2. Derive a new word from existing words in the language you're using. This could be making a compound, or using affixes to modify an existing word.

3. Reconstruct a new word by taking a word from another of Tolkien's languages and trace it back to its roots, then walk it through its phonological development until you reach the target language. This should only be attempted by experts.

4. Recognize when there just is no way to complete a translation. For example, I was asked for a translation of a statement that contained a lot of modern scientific terms and concepts, and I had to turn it down. The language doesn't have words for such concepts, and I'm not sure where to even begin. The Sindarin language is built to fit a medieval culture that believed there is an ocean of water floating in the sky that Eärendil is sailing back and forth across, and that the stars are glowing crystals floating in that ocean. And math? You can do some simple math in Quenya, but in Sindarin, there are so few numbers that it's just about impossible. It's better to turn down such a request than have someone tattoo nonsense permanently onto their body.

1.1.4 In Conclusion

Fan-made vocabulary is a hot-button issue in Neo-Sindarin circles. The best way to approach it is to be as clear as possible about when you're reconstructing and when you aren't. Reconstructed words should be carefully marked and annotated, especially since not everyone will be familiar with the same set of fan-made words.

Conflicts over this will inevitably come up. Like in all conflicts, do your best to not make it personal, and understand that this issue isn't a simple one. We're dealing with an imaginary language here, a hypothetical of a hypothetical of a hypothetical, so there is no right or wrong answer, and any judgments you make will just be opinions. Do your best, and recognize that everyone else is doing the same.

1.1.5 Review

1. What does an asterisk mean in linguistic notation?
2. What does an asterisk mean in Neo-Sindarin?
3. Which 5 types of words are always automatically assumed to be fan-made?
4. Who can make words up from nothing?
5. Which approach do you think is best to filling the gaps in vocabulary?
6. Name 3 different ways to fill vocabulary gaps.
7. What are the 4 steps to take when dealing with a vocabulary gap?

1.2 The History of Sindarin

When looking at the history of Sindarin, there are two types of history to examine. The first is the history Tolkien imagined for the language, which is called the Internal History. The other is called the External History, the changes and revisions that Tolkien made to the language as he developed it.

1.2.1 Internal History

Among the elves who awoke on the shores of Cuiviénen, three tribes emerged. There were the faithful Vanyar, the studious Noldor, and the ones that we're here to study, the most numerous tribe, the musical Teleri.

Abandoned on the eastern side of *Belegaer*, the Great Sea, dwelt a group of *Telerin* Elves who called themselves *Edhil*. The *Noldor* who came upon them later called them the *Sindar*, the Grey Ones. It was in that land, named *Beleriand*, that a unique Elven language was born: *Edhellen*, called *Sindarin* by the *Noldor*.[12]

In Beleriand, the language of the Sindar slowly diverged into dialects. What was **maltin** (golden) in the ill-fated far north was **malthen** for the wilder elves in the far south and **mallen** in the western and central regions of Beleriand, including Doriath.

The Sindar prospered for many ages in the dark of the world, before the sun and moon were made, but then came the dawn. A wave of marauding orcs wiped out the Northern elves and burned their way through Beleriand. Following the sun on its eastward trail, the Kinslaying Noldor, who were banished from *Aman* for murdering the peaceful Telerin Elves of *Alqualondë*, came to Beleriand. Unlike the Sindar, the Noldor came prepared for war, with weapons and knowledge of their uses. The Noldor were welcomed as saviors at first. When the King of Beleriand, ruling from the guarded realm of *Doriath*, discovered the

---

[12] The Noldor are the ones who are interested in writing histories, so this language is usually described from their perspective, using Quenya terms and not the native Edhellen terms.

crimes of the Noldor against his kin, he forbade the use of the *Noldorin* language, *Quenya*.[13] He ordered all peoples in his kingdom to shun those who spoke Quenya openly. The Noldor were forced to learn Sindarin.

When foreign tongues pronounce words new to them, they change the words a little, and add many of their own. What was **De fael**[14] in Doriath was **Le fael** to the Exiles. This new dialect of Sindarin I will call "Exilic Sindarin," while the older version of Sindarin, the dialect of the King in Doriath, was considered the purest, highest form of it. This "pure" Sindarin I will call "Doriathren Sindarin." Because of the Noldor's bloody history, Exilic Sindarin carries with it a stigma for Doriathren Sindarin speakers.

Then Doriath fell into ruin. Almost all of the Noldorin strongholds in Middle-earth fell as well, sending the Elves fleeing further from Aman, deeper into Middle-earth. With the help of Men, Morgoth, for whom Sauron was just a Lieutenant in his army, was cast into the void for all eternity. The Noldor eventually settled in Eriador to wait out their banishment.

The surviving Sindar, most of whom dwelled in Southern Beleriand, fled all the way to their Telerin cousins on both sides of the Misty Mountains: the Denwaith[15]. With them they brought their language, and the Denwaith adopted it as they adopted their Telerin kin into their forests. They changed the language slightly again, but not much. The Woodelven name **Legolas** was **Laegolas** in the other dialects. This I will call "Woodelven Sindarin."

The humans who had helped defeat Morgoth were given their own island in the middle of Belegaer that was called Númenor. They spoke their native tongue, *Adûnâyê*[16], alongside Sindarin, which they learned from the Noldor. They also used Quenya for matters of law and naming royalty. Eventually they rebelled against the Valar, demanding to be made immortal like the Elves. Instead, their isle was sunk beneath the sea and the survivors who hadn't taken part in the rebellion fled back

---

[13] This is known as the Ban of Thingol. You can read up on it in *The Silmarillion*, Chapter 15: Of the Noldor in Beleriand.

[14] "You are generous." It's a way to say "Thank-you."

[15] Referred to as **Nandor** in Quenya.

[16] Commonly referred to as Adûnaic in English.

to Middle-earth. They called themselves Elf-friends because they valued Elven language and culture, and many of them took Elven names. The Elf-friends established the two Númenorean kingdoms: Arnor, from which Aragorn is descended; and Gondor. What was **Rochan** to the Elves was **Rohan** to the humans. The dialect of Sindarin that they speak will be called Númenorean or Gondorian Sindarin in the lessons.

And here we are at the beginning of the Third Age of Middle-earth, with many dialects to choose from. This textbook covers the known and inferred differences between the dialects of Sindarin. The dialects that we know the most about, and that will be covered in the textbook are the dialects of Doriath, the Woodelves, the Exiles, and the Gondorians. Studying these four dialects covers most of the speech of the Sindarin speakers, and I will take care to mention the differences between them as we go along.

1.2.2 External History

Tolkien loosely based Sindarin on Welsh, a language that he loved dearly. If you've studied Welsh, or indeed any Celtic language, you will see a lot of familiar features in the grammar and pronunciation. But there is a lot more to the history of Sindarin than just its primary influence.

Let's travel back in time, back to the trenches of World War I when the first version of *The Silmarillion* was being written.[17] Around the same time, Tolkien wrote two manuscripts: *The Gnomish Grammar* and *The Gnomish Lexicon*.[18] This language was not envisioned as the language of the Sindar. As the name "Gnomish" indicates, it was for the Noldor. "*Noldor*" means "Wise ones," and "Gnomish" comes from the Greek word for "knowledge." In the language itself, it was called "*Goldogrin*."

The next version of the language we call "Noldorin." It appeared in the 1930's. This language was much closer to Sindarin, almost identical, in fact. It's so close that some of Neo-Sindarin grammar and vocabulary

---

[17] Published as *The Book of Lost Tales* Part 1 & 2.
[18] Both published in *Parma Eldalamberon* #11 with notes that Tolkien was adding to the manuscripts in *Parma Eldalamberon* #13.

is borrowed from Noldorin, with only minor adjustments. *The Etymologies*[19] is a document listing the ancient roots and the words derived from them in the various languages, and it comes from this era.

By the time *The Lord of the Rings* was sent off to the publishers in the 1950's, Tolkien had decided that the Noldor would speak a language much more similar to that of the Vanyar, who lived in the same place, so Quenya became the language of both the Vanyar and the Noldor, with the differences between their speech reduced to a dialectal level. Then he discarded the languages that he had the elves of Beleriand speaking, Ilkorin and Doriathrin, and with a few tweaks here and there, made Sindarin.

After writing *The Lord of the Rings*, and getting many letters requesting information on the languages, Tolkien decided to make a guide to the non-English words, phrases, and passages in the book. He never finished it, and we only see a much-slimmed down version in *Appendixes E & F*. The unfinished manuscript, *Words, Phrases, and Passages in The Lord of the Rings* was published in *Parma Eldalamberon* issue #17. This text remains the greatest source of Sindarin grammar and vocabulary, and it wasn't published until 2007. The shockwaves of that publication are still felt in Neo-Sindarin, even now.

Unlike Quenya, which has had detailed descriptions of its grammar published for decades now, there are still documents about Sindarin being published to this day that revolutionize everything we thought we knew. Many old websites and books lack the data from these later publications, so you have to be careful and check when a resource or translation you're using was published to make sure it includes the latest information. This means that Neo-Sindarin changes drastically from publication to publication. The last publication to do this as I write this is *Parma Eldalamberon issue #22*, which transformed the future tense and 1st person pronominal verb suffixes.

1.2.3 Review

1. Who gave the Edhil the name "Sindar"? What language is this name in?

---

[19] Published in *The Lost Road and Other Writings*, with a series of notes, corrections, and additions published in *Vinyar Tengwar #45 & 46*.

2. Where did the Sindar live for most of their history?

3. What dialects developed in Sindarin before the Noldor came?

4. What drove the Noldor to learn Sindarin?

5. Which dialect of Sindarin holds the most prestige?

6. Which dialect of Sindarin is the Woodelven dialect based on?

7. Who were the Elf-friends?

8. What languages did the Númenóreans speak?

9. What language did Tolkien base Sindarin on?

10. What was Sindarin called before it was Sindarin?

11. Who was the language for? What made Tolkien change his mind?

12. Why does Neo-Sindarin change so much faster than Neo-Quenya?

Chapter 2: Pronunciation

We'll start this chapter with a very basic primer on how to read and write the International Phonetic Alphabet (IPA), to prepare you for doing phonetic transcriptions of Neo-Sindarin. Then we'll learn how Neo-Sindarin is spoken, as well as some of the phonetic differences between the dialects. After that we'll cover how to pronounce multi-syllable words and phrases.

2.1 IPA Guide

If you are taking my Sindarin course and are not a linguist, you will find this short guide to basic usage of the International Phonetic Alphabet (IPA for short) useful. Otherwise, skip this.

2.1.1 Why IPA?

I use it in my lessons because:

- It is internationally recognized as a way to describe pronunciation.
- It is the most accurate way to depict how words are pronounced outside of looking at the sound waves themselves.

Before switching to this system, I tried using the phonetic alphabet in American dictionaries but found it inadequate because there are sounds in Sindarin that don't exist in English. Before that, I tried to use typical English letter combinations, but this was even worse. As clear as I tried to be, there are multitudes of ways to pronounce any set of letters in English. This is why I ask you to use IPA instead of the dictionary system or English spelling. I tried, and it just didn't work.

Now that you know **why** I expect you to use it, let's learn **how** to use it.

2.1.2 The IPA Charts

The IPA's letters are listed in two charts: one for vowels, the other for consonants.

2.1.2.1 The Columns of the IPA Consonant Chart

Consonants are listed by where in the mouth they are found, and how they are made. Take, for example: the "p" of "pet," the "b" of "bet," the "f" of "fret," the "v" of "vet," and the "m" of "met." All of these sounds are labial, that is, made with the lips. They are in the same column.

Labial: Sounds made with the lips. Some sounds can be made in two places at the same time, like /w/.

Dental: Sounds made either between or off the backs of the teeth.

Alveolar: Sounds made using the alveolar ridge behind your teeth.

Palatal: Sounds made using the roof of your mouth.

Velar: Sounds made using the back of your mouth.

Glottal: Sounds made using your throat.

2.1.2.2 The Rows of the IPA Consonant Chart

Now take this example: the "t" of "tack," the "p" of "pack" and the "c" of "cake." Those sounds are made the same way, and they are in the same row, the Voiceless Stops.

Stop: The air is stopped, then released.

Fricative: The air is pressurized, making a hissing sound.

Affricate: The air is stopped, then released as a hiss.

Nasal: The air is pushed through the nose.

Approximant: The air is barely obstructed. These sounds are the closest to being vowels - so close, they often aren't distinguishable.

Lateral Fricative: Like a fricative, but the place of constriction is at the side of the tongue, not the top.

Lateral Approximant: Like an approximant, but with the constriction at the side of the tongue.

Trill: The air is stopped many times at a very rapid pace.

2.1.2.3 The IPA Consonant Chart

Here is a chart of all of the American English consonants.

The two biggest categories of how sounds are made are the voiced and unvoiced sounds. Voicing is the vibrating in your throat that you feel when you speak. If you whisper, your throat won't vibrate at all. You'll be speaking "voicelessly."

Consonants		Labial	Dental	Alveolar	Palatal	Velar	Glottal
Stop	-voice	/p/		/t/		/k/	
	+voice	/b/		/d/		/g/	
Fricative	-voice	/f/	/θ/ "ba**th**"	/s/	/ʃ/ "sa**sh**"		/h/
	+voice	/v/	/ð/ "**the**"	/z/	/ʒ/ "fi**ss**ure"		
Affricate	-voice			/ts/	/tʃ/ "**ch**at"		
	+voice			/dz/	/dʒ/ "e**dge**"		
Nasal	+voice	/m/		/n/		/ŋ/ "si**ng**"	
Approximant	-voice	/ʍ/ "**wh**at"[20]					
	+voice	/w/		/ɹ/ "**r**ed"	/j/ "**y**ell"		
Lateral Approximant	+voice			/l/		/ɫ/ "litt**l**e"	

And here is a chart of all of the Sindarin consonants for comparison.

Consonants		Labial	Dental	Alveolar	Palatal	Velar	Glottal
Stop	-voice	/p/		/t/		/k/	
	+voice	/b/		/d/		/g/	
Fricative	-voice	/f/	/θ/	/s/		/x/	/h/
	+voice	/v/	/ð/				
Nasal	+voice	/m/		/n/		/ŋ/	
Approximant	-voice	/ʍ/					
	+voice	/w/			/j/		
Lateral Fricative	-voice			/ɬ/			
Lateral Approximant	+voice			/l/	/ʎ/		
Trill	-voice			/r̥/			
	+voice			/r/			

---

[20] The sounds /w/ and /ʍ/ are labio-velars, and are articulated in two places at once.

2.1.2.4 The IPA Vowel Chart's Columns and Rows

Vowels are categorized in four ways. In the chart, each column lists if they are "rounded" or not. "Rounded" refers to the puckering of the lips, like in the "u" of "Luke."

The columns refer to front/center/back—where the tongue is positioned when they are articulated. Compare the "ai" of "bait," the "u" of "butt" and the "oa" of "boat." You should notice that your tongue is going farther and farther back into your mouth with each word.

The rows list how far open the jaw must be to make the sound. Your mouth opens more as you move from "beat" to "bait" to "father."

The rows also indicate how tense or lax the muscles are in the mouth. This corresponds to the tongue being slightly closer to the middle of the mouth as well. This is the difference between the "i" of "bit" and the "ea" of "beat."

2.1.2.5 The IPA Vowel Chart

Here is the chart of English vowels.

Vowels		Front -round	Center -round	Back +round
High	Tense	/i/ "beat"		/u/ "Luke"
	Lax	/ɪ/ "bit"		/ʊ/ "look"
Mid	Tense	/e/ "bait"		/o/ "broke"
	Lax	/ɛ/ "bet"	/ə/ "butt"	/ɔ/ "caught"
Low	Tense	/æ/ "brat"		
	Lax		/ɑ/ "father"	

Here is the chart of Sindarin vowels.

Vowels		Front -round	+round	Center -round	Back +round
High	Tense	/i/	/y/		/u/
Mid	Lax	/ɛ/	/œ/		/ɔ/
Low	Lax			/ɑ/	

As you can see with the large number of differences between these charts, using systems designed for describing English just won't work for Sindarin.

2.1.3 Using IPA

So, now that we know what these symbols mean, how do we use them? It's actually quite similar to using the Latin alphabet. You simply list the sounds in the order that they occur. Let's try this on a few words. I've transcribed these in the General American dialect, so these might not line up exactly with how you pronounce them.

"funny" /fəni/	"away" /əwej/	"sheep" /ʃip/
"guy" /gɑj/	"change" /ʧenʤ/	"horrible" /hoɹɹɪbəɫ/
"day" /dej/	"learn" /ləɹn/	"evil" /ivəɫ/
"laugh" /læf/	"fear" /fiɹ/	"hammer" /hæməɹ/
"bring" /bɹɪŋ/	"wonder" /wəndəɹ/	"society" /sosɑjɛti/
"brain" /bɹen/	"people" /pipəɫ/	"slipping" /slɪppɪŋ/

Note the use of // around the words, indicating that this is a phonemic transcription in IPA.

However, these are not the only aspects of pronunciation that you need to learn to describe. There are also vowel length, stress, and syllables.

2.1.3.1 Describing Vowel Length in IPA

Here are the symbols for marking vowel length made nice and big:

Long Vowel   Extra Long Vowel

Vowel length isn't phonemic in English (meaning that we don't use it to differentiate between words), but it does exist.

Say these two words carefully to yourself:

> "beat" and "bead"

They are transcribed like this, with the vowel length marker directly following the vowel it's lengthening.

> /bit/ and /biːd/

The colon is used to show that the vowel is spoken for a longer period of time. There are other symbols for showing the length or shortness of a vowel, but they don't apply to English. Sindarin has three vowel lengths, so you'll have to pay attention to that. Here are the three vowel lengths in Sindarin:

> "bâd" /bɑːd/   "hwá' /ʍɑˑ/   "san" /sɑn/

2.1.3.2 Syllable Boundaries in IPA

Another thing IPA covers is syllable division. Instead of dashes or bullets, it uses periods. Here is the wordlist with syllable divisions added.

"funny"/fə.ni/	"away" /ə.wej/	"sheep" /ʃip/
"guy" /gɑj/	"change" /ʧeːnʤ/	"horrible" /hoɹ.ɹɪ.bəl/
"day" /dej/	"learn" /ləɹn/	"evil" /i.vəl/
"laugh" /læf/	"fear" /fiːɹ/	"hammer" /hæ.məɹ/
"bring" /bɹɪŋ/	"wonder" /wən.dəɹ/	"society" /so.sɑj.ɛ.ti/
"brain" /bɹeːn/	"people" /pi.pəl/	"slipping" /slɪp.pɪŋ/

The reason for worrying about syllables is to find where the stress is placed and how to break up consonant clusters.

2.1.3.3 Syllable Stress in IPA

Stress is how loudly a syllable is spoken. In English, we have to worry about two types of stress: primary and secondary.

Primary Stress   Secondary Stress

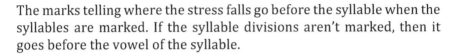

The marks telling where the stress falls go before the syllable when the syllables are marked. If the syllable divisions aren't marked, then it goes before the vowel of the syllable.

The above one (') marks the primary (loudest) syllable, and the below one (ˌ) marks the secondary (second loudest) syllable.

Once again, let's look at our revised wordlist.

"funny" /'fə.ˌni/	"away" /ˌə.'wej/	"sheep" /ʃip/
"guy" /g'ɑj/	"change" /ʧ'enʤ/	"horrible" /'hoɹ.ˌɹɪ.bəɫ/
"day" /d'ej/	"learn" /l'əɹn/	"evil" /'i.ˌvəɫ/
"laugh" /l'æf/	"fear" /fiɹ/	"hammer" /'hæ.ˌməɹ/
"bring" /bɹ'ɪŋ/	"wonder" /'wən.ˌdəɹ/	"society" /ˌso.'sɑj.ɛ.ti/
"brain" /bɹ'en/	"people" /'pi.ˌpəɫ/	"slipping" /'slɪp.ˌpɪŋ/

And that's it. Now you know about IPA. There are actually many more possible symbols than just the ones found in this lesson, hundreds more in fact. These are just the ones that you need to worry about. Anything that a language can use to differentiate between words can be described with IPA, from pauses to pitch. We only need this little sliver of it for English and Sindarin.

2.1.4 Conversation Practice: Choose an Elven Name

You'll use this name in the lessons' conversation practice, since it is better to have a name[21] that will work with Sindarin's grammar. All of these names are genderless.

---

[21] These names all can be found on my website, Realelvish.net. There are thousands more to be found there, if you find yourself in need of more than this short list.

Arahael	Noble and Wise	/ˈa.ra.haɛl/
Baralin	Fiery/Eager Eyed	/ˈba.ra.lin/
Calaer	Sea Light	/ˈka.laɛr/
Cammaen	Skilled Hand	/ˈkam.maɛn/
Cellin	Spring/Stream Song	/ˈkɛl.lin/
Dúvain	Beautiful Night	/ˈduˑ.vajn/
Elhael	Wise Elf	/ˈɛl.haɛl/
Faethurin	Secret Soul	/ˈfaɛ.θu.rin/
Gaerlin	The Sea Gleams in their Eyes	/ˈgaɛr.lin/
Gollor[22]	Wizard	/ˈgɔl.lɔr/
Haengil	Distant Stars	/ˈhaɛŋ.gil/
Himel	Cold Star	/ˈhi.mɛl/
Hwingel	Giddy Joy	/ˈʍiŋ.gɛl/
Iorist	Ancient Lore	/ˈjɔ.rist/
Lammaen	Clever Tongue	/ˈlam.maɛn/
Lingel	Song Joy	/ˈliŋ.gɛl/
Meneginc	1000 Ideas	/ˈmɛ.nɛ.giŋk/
Mormeril	Black Rose	/ˈmɔr.mɛ.ril/
Nengel	Water Joy	/ˈnɛŋ.gɛl/
Ningannel	Tears of a Harp	/niŋ.ˈgan.nɛl/
Noril	Fire Radiance	/ˈnɔ.ril/
Olodhin	Dream of Silence	/ˈɔ.lɔ.ðin/
Olorod	Mountain Dream	/ˈɔ.lɔ.rɔd/
Rhossolas	Whisper of Foliage	/ˈr̥ɔs.sɔ.las/
Rívallen	Golden Crown	/riˑ.ˈval.lɛn/
Rothurin	Most Secret	/ˈrɔ.θu.rin/
Saelcheneb	Wise Eyed	/ˈsaɛl.xɛ.nɛb/
Tirnel	Star Gazer	/ˈtir.nɛl/
Thangur	True Heart/Counsel/Conscience	/ˈθaŋ.gur/
Thurimir	Secret Gem	/ˈθu.ri.mir/
Triwath	Slender Shadow	/ˈtri.waθ/

---

[22] This is an NG- word, which you will learn about in chapter 5.

2.1.5 Review

Sound out the IPA, and write the English word you think it represents. There might be more than one correct answer. These are all in the Northwestern General American accent, since that is what this writer speaks. (Hint: try saying the word out loud, that really helps!)

1. /ˈhɑ.lo/ _____
2. /ˈhɑ.bɪt/ _____
3. /ˈslɑj.mi/ _____
4. /ˈkəm.fəɹt/ _____
5. /kˈæt/ _____
6. /lˈet/ _____
7. /ˈʧæ.lɪnʤ/ _____
8. /ɹˈið/ _____
9. /ɹˈiθ/ _____
10. /əv/ _____
11. /ˈʃɑj.ni/ _____
12. /ɹˈid/ _____
13. /ˈtɹɛ.ʒəɹ/ _____
14. /lɪŋ.ˈgwɪs.tɪks/ _____
15. /ʍɛn/ _____

Write the words in IPA. The answer key shows the answers in North-western USA English, but sound the words out in any dialect that you speak.

1. Rope _____
2. Cake _____
3. Simple _____
4. Feeling _____
5. Real _____
6. Unfinished _____
7. Moonraker _____
8. Jewels _____
9. Defeated _____
10. Shingle _____
11. Leisure _____
12. Wrong _____

13. Fifth _____

14. Japan _____

15. Riddle _____

16. Whether_____

17. Catch _____

18. They _____

2.2 The Sounds of Speech

There are four sorts of sounds that we need to learn: vowels, diphthongs, vowel-consonant combinations, and consonants.[23]

If you'd like to hear these sounds, visit https://realelvish.net/pronun-
ciation/sindarin/ which has recordings to practice with.

2.2.1 Vowels

Accents on vowels denote extra length on the vowels. Hold the vowels
longer. In music this is shown with a tenuto (-) over the note. The circumflex accent (ˆ) is held longer than an acute accent (´). In IPA, the
Sindarin circumflex accent would be shown with (:) and the Sindarin
acute accent would be shown with (·).

A / Á / Â

Pronounce them /ɑ/, in the back of your mouth, like the A in the word
"father."

> **râd** path → /rɑːd/

E / É / Ê / Æ[24]

Pronounce them /ɛ/. It sounds like the E of "better."

> **gem** sickly → /gɛm/

---

[23] The majority of this lesson is just paraphrasing what Tolkien wrote in *The
Lord of the Rings, Return of the King*, Appendix E. There are similar pronunciation guides in the back of *The Silmarillion* and *The Road Goes Ever On*. Hope-
fully this is easier to understand, and more precise. Tolkien was frustratingly
vague on the phonology of his languages.

[24] You won't find Tolkien using this symbol in Sindarin. This is a fan-short-
hand to indicate an E that used to be an A. It's pretty rare, but you might come
across it occasionally. I don't use it.

I / Í / Î

Pronounce them /i/, in the front of your mouth, as in the word "machine." The Sindarin I also acts like the consonant Y before vowels.[25]

> **lind** tune → /lind/

O / Ó / Ô

Pronounce them /ɔ/ as in the word "la**u**d." Make an O with your lips. If you're a west-American dialect speaker like me, you don't have this sound. It feels like an A with an O's lips, or an O with the back of your mouth open a bit more than normal.

> **nordh** oak → /nɔrð/

Œ [26]

This is pronounced /œ/, as in the French word "b**œu**f." To make this sound, make the inside of your mouth like the Sindarin (E), and your lips like the Sindarin (O). This sound is only found in Archaic Sindarin. In later Sindarin, it has become an (E).

> Early: **cœryn** globes → /kœryn/
> Late: **cœryn** globes → /kɛryn/

U / Ú / Û

Pronounce them /u/ as in "br**u**te." Put your lips in the shape of a kiss.

> **rûth** anger → /ru:θ/

Y / Ý / Ŷ

Pronounce them /y/ like the French U, as in "l**u**ne." To make this sound, make your mouth in the shape of the Sindarin (I). Then, shape your lips

---

[25] Information from *The Road Goes Ever On* appears to contradict this, but the working theory of fans is that the quality of the vowels Tolkien was trying to describe was the length of time that the vowels were said, not whether they were lax or tense. Therefore, no contradiction! This idea is supported by Tolkien's flawed attempts to speak his languages. He seems to be *trying* to give the vowels the same qualities no matter their length, but he often ends up slipping up, and his English accent shows through.

[26] Despite not existing in the later dialects of Sindarin, œ can be used to indicate an E that came from an O, and it's used this way occasionally.

the same way you shape "U" in Sindarin. Or, take the easy road out and use the Gondorian pronunciation, and say it /i/ like the Sindarin "I" above.

> Elf: **ylf** cup → /ylv/
> Gondorian: **ylf** cup → /iʝv/

2.2.2 Diphthongs

A diphthong is two different vowels or a vowel and an approximant that have been smushed together and are treated like a single long vowel. Diacritics[27] never appear in Sindarin diphthongs.

AI

Pronounce this /ɑj/, as in the word "tw**i**ne."

> **said** private → /sɑjd/

AE

Pronounce this /ɑɛ/, almost exactly the same at (AI) above, just glide into an (E), not an (I). The Woodelves don't have this diphthong, and instead pronounce it like an (E).

> Non-Woodelf: **faen** white → /fɑɛn/
> Woodelf: **faen** white → /fɛn/

AU

Pronounce this /ɑu/, as in the word "**ou**ch." Make sure that you pronounce both the /ɑ/ and the /u/. To many English speakers, this will sound like there's extra emphasis on the U.

> **raud** noble → /rɑud/

AW

Pronounce this /aw/, as in the word "**ow**l."

---

[27] A diacritic, or accent, is another symbol that's attached to a letter, like the ^ on ô or the ~ on ñ.

> **raw** lion → /rɑw/

EI

Pronounce this /ej/, as in "**ray**."

> **bein** beautiful→ /bejn/

OE

Pronounce this /ɔɛ/, as in the word "**boy**."

> **goe** terror → /gɔɛ/

UI

Pronounce this /uj/, as in the word "**gooey**."

> **muin** dear → /mujn/

2.2.3 Consonants

Like vowels, consonants can be lengthened. A lengthened consonant will be written with two letters instead of just one.

Asterisk

Asterisks mark fan-made words, and thus, have no impact on pronunciation at all.

> ***rên** he remembers → /rɛːn/

'Apostrophe'

Apostrophes mark where a letter, usually a G, has been dropped. They have no effect on the pronunciation of the words, and should not be included in phonetic transcriptions of words.

> **'ost** dread → /ɔst/

I

Before a vowel at the beginning of a word, (I) is pronounced /j/ and used as a consonant, as the Y in the word "**yellow**." If there is an accent on the (I) you always pronounce it /i/, as you do for the vowel.

> **ial** call → /jɑl/

C

Pronounce it always as a /k/, as in the word "kill."

> **cîl** renewal → /kiːʝ/

G

Pronounce it always as a /g/, as in the word "give."

> **gell** joy → /gɛʝʝ/

F

When it's at the end of a word, say it as a /v/ as in the word "slave." The rest of the time, it's pronounced /f/.

> **falf** seafoam → /fɑlv/

L

Pronounce it as a /l/, as in the word "leer." When it comes between E or I and a consonant, or at the end of a word after E or I, it is pronounced /ʝ/ with the middle or tip of the tongue touching the palate behind the ridge behind the teeth.

> **lest** girdle → /lɛst/
> **pel** fenced field → /pɛʝ/

LH

Pronounce it /ɬ/, a voiceless L. That means, you shape your mouth the same way that you would when making the L sound, but only air will come out, and it will sound a little like a TH or an SH.

> **lhing** spiderweb → /ɬiŋ/

MH / Ṽ [28]

Pronounce it /ɱ/. To make it, bite your bottom lip and make an M-sound. This sound is found only in Archaic Sindarin and Doriathren Sindarin. In the other dialects, it's pronounced as a V.

_____

[28] MH is sometimes used to indicate a V that came from an M, but that's a pretty rare usage. I don't use it this way.

Doriath: **lâmh** / **lâṽ** she licks → /lɑːm̃/
Elsewhere: **lâf** she licks → /lɑːv/

R

Pronounce it as an /r/; roll it as in the Spanish word "perro." If you can't roll an R, like me, make an H sound with your throat closed a little. It should make a rolled A sound, or a French /ʀ/. It'll be a little like gargling water.

rem net → /rɛm/

RH

Pronounce it /r̥/, a voiceless R. That means, you shape your mouth the same way that you would when making the rolled R sound, but only air will come out, like a trilled H.

rhach curse → /r̥ɑx/

PH

Pronounce it /f/, as in the word "**ph**one." It's used to mark the /f/ sound in places it rarely occurs, like at the ends of words.

salph broth → /sɑlf/

CH

Pronounce it /x/, as in the name "Ba**ch**." Say it in the back of your mouth, it should feel a little as though you are hocking a loogy, or gargling without anything in your mouth. The Gondorians had difficulty making this sound, as apparently, it isn't found in Westron. Therefore, they simply turned (CH) into an (H) before a vowel, thus the word "Rohan" instead of "Rochan," and (CH) becomes (C) everywhere else, thus "Orcrist" instead of "Orchrist."[29]

---

[29] This information actually comes from detective work. It is incompletely mentioned in *Lord of the Rings,* Return of the King, Appendix E, where it simply says that the CH is pronounced as an H by the Gondorians. Hidden away in the *Unfinished Tales,* Part Three: The Third Age, II Cirion and Eorl and the Friendship of Gondor and Rohan, Note #49 we get some more detail. To quote: "...the people of Gondor, unless learned, represented [the CH sound] by *h* in the middle of words and by *k* at the end of them." But, this still doesn't

Elf: **bach chall** hidden item → /bɑx xɑll/
Human: **bach chall** hidden item → /bɑk hɑll/

TH / Þ

Pronounce them /θ/, like the TH in the word "no**th**ing."

thôl / **þôl** helmet → /θɔːl/

DH / Ð

Pronounce them /ð/. We make this sound in the word "**the**" and "bli**the**."

sîdh / **sîð** peace → /siːð/

HW

Pronounce it /ʍ/, as in the word "**wh**ite." It's a really airy W that has been lost in many dialects of English. You can hear it if you listen to old recordings from the 30's.

hwest breeze → /ʍɛst/

NG / Ñ [30]

Pronounce them /ŋ/, as in the word "si**ng**." It can occur at the begin-ning and end of a word. It's difficult for English-speakers to say at the beginning of a word, but with some practice, it can be done. Start by making the /ŋ/ sound by itself. After a while of that, you can start put-ting it at the beginnings of words.

ngîl / **ñîl** stars → /ŋiːʲ/
fang beard → /fɑŋ/

---

explain names like "Orcrist." So, amidst this vaguery, I think I've come up with a phonetic rule that covers all of the examples.

[30] Tolkien didn't do this in his orthography of Sindarin. Fans do this because in some contexts at the beginning of words an NG is pronounced /ŋg/ because of **Prestanneth**, something you'll learn about in later chapters. I don't usually use this shortcut, but I will in this book when it'd be ambiguous how to pro-nounce it.

The rest of the letters are pronounced as we pronounce them in English.

2.2.5 Conversation Practice: Greetings and Introductions

We'll start with phrases that have one-syllable-long words, since that's all you know how to pronounce at the moment.

Here are some simple greetings:

- **A!** - This is an interjection to show mild excitement or surprise. It's useful as a casual greeting as well.
- **Ai! / Ae!** - This is an interjection that shows high excitement from a strong emotion, like surprise, terror, elation, euphoria. It's also useful as a greeting. It's less casual than "**A!**" is, but still fairly casual. Woodelves wouldn't use **Ae** because the diphthong AE doesn't exist in their dialect. Like Legolas' terrified exclamation in Moria when he realizes they are facing a balrog, they'd use **Ai** instead.

Here are some phrases for handling introductions.

- **Ma len?** "Who are you?" In Doriath, they'd say "**Ma dhen?**" instead.
- **Im...** "I am..." literally this means "oneself is..." but it's how you would introduce yourself.
- **... a de...** "...and he/she is..."

For example, you could say:

> **Ae! Im Lammaen, a de Triwath. Ma len?**
> "Hello! I'm Lammaen, and she is Triwath. Who are you?"

2.2.6 Review

Write the phonetic transcriptions of the following words into IPA.

1. **alph** swan _____
2. **bŷr** follower (non-Gondorian) _____
3. **bŷr** follower (Gondorian) _____
4. **caw** top _____

5. **chae** distant (non-Gondorian, non-Woodelven) _____
6. **chae** Distant (Woodelven) _____
7. **chae** Distant (Gondorian) _____
8. **dîl** Stopper _____
9. **duin** River _____
10. **erch** Prickle (non-Gondorian) _____
11. **erch** Prickle (Gondorian) _____
12. **fîr** Mortals _____
13. **gae** Dread (non-Woodelf) _____
14. **gae** Dread (Woodelf) _____
15. **geil** Star _____
16. **gwing** Spray _____
17. **helch** Bitter cold (non-Gondorian) _____
18. **helch** Bitter cold (Gondorian) _____
19. **hoedh** Tombs _____
20. **hwîn** Giddiness _____
21. **iôn** Son _____
22. **limp** Wet _____
23. **lhaw** Set of ears _____
24. **maur** Gloom _____
25. **ñoll** Wise _____
26. **nûr** Sad _____
27. **paich** Juice (non-Gondorian) _____
28. **paich** Juice (Gondorian) _____
29. **raef** Net (Non-Woodelf) _____
30. **raef** Net (Woodelf) _____
31. **rhoss** Whisper _____
32. **sí** Now _____
33. **sûl** Wind _____
34. **taen** Slender (Non-Woodelf) _____
35. **taen** Slender (Woodelf) _____
36. **talf** Hand/palm _____
37. **thent** Short _____
38. **'waith** People _____

2.3 The Rhythm of the Words

Stress is saying a syllable louder with more emphasis than other syllables. In English we memorize where we place stress in each word,
making it part of how we recognize and reproduce words. For example,
say the words "digest" (as in "The Reader's Digest") and "digest" as in
"to digest breakfast." The Sindarin system is much different. Sindarin
has rules dictating where the stress falls in a word, based on the phonological structure of the word.

2.3.1 Consonants in Multi-syllable Words

Some of the consonants are pronounced slightly differently when inside words, rather than at the beginning or end of words, which is all
we have been studying until now.

The following sounds never appear inside a word in Sindarin, and if
you see that combination of letters, then you know that they are two
separate sounds.

> (RH) like in **Gaurhoth** (horde of werewolves) → /gaurhɔθ/
> (LH) like in **Edhelharn** (Elfstone)   → /ɛðɛlharn/
> (HW) like in **Gladhwen** (Laughing Maiden)   → /glaðwɛn/

Inside a word, (I) before another vowel doesn't make it a consonant, it
behaves like the vowel (I).

> **Gilthoniel** (Starkindler) → /gilθɔniɛl /

Inside a word, if you have an (I)/(E)+(L)+Consonant combination
(only in that order, first the (I) or (E), then the (L), lastly the other consonant), the (L) is pronounced /l/ as it is at the end of a word after (I)
or (E). However, simply following an (I) or (E) isn't enough make the
(L) a /l/. It must be followed by another consonant for it to happen.

> **Tellen** (sole of the foot) → /tɛllɛn/
> **Belthas** (strength)   → /bɛlθas/
> **Thela** (spearpoint)   → /θɛla/

Pronounce (NG) with both the N and the G, like in the word "fi**ng**er"
when it is in the inside a word.

Bango (to trade) → /baŋgɔ/

2.3.1.1 Exercise

Transcribe the words into IPA. For this exercise, don't worry about where to place stress-marks or how to separate syllables. We'll cover that after this.

1. **Gódhellim** Noldor _____
2. **Perhael** Samwise (Woodelf) _____
3. **Elhael** Wise Elf (non-Woodelf) _____
4. **Teiliassef**. We played a game. _____
5. **Rochwaith** Horse-Folk (non-Gondorian) _____
6. **Nediathon**. I will count. _____
7. **eiliant** rainbow _____
8. **meldir** male friend _____
9. **Lathradasseb**. We eavesdropped. _____
10. **apharch** very dry (Gondorian) _____
11. **Fangorn** Treebeard _____
12. **Angwedh** Iron-chain _____
13. **Glamdring** Foe-hammer _____

2.3.2 Dividing the Syllables

Syllables are determined by vowels and diphthongs. There is one vowel or diphthong per syllable.

> **awarth** abandonment   → /aw.arθ/
> **uiail** twilights   → /uj.ajl̪/
> **periain** hobbits   → /pɛ.ri.ajn/

Unless there are two consonants next to each other, syllables end with a vowel or diphthong between them. Then you split these two consonants apart: you put one at the end of a syllable, and the other at the beginning of the next. These rules don't apply to the last syllable in a word, since the end of the word is the last syllable. For the behavior of the very beginnings and ends of words, go back to 2.2.

Onod Ent → /ɔ.nɔd/

Ennorath all of Middle-earth → /ɛn.nɔ.rɑθ/

Estent very short → /ɛs.tɛnt/

If there are 3 consonants between the vowels/diphthongs, you know that the word is a compound, and you put the middle consonant with whichever word it came from. At this point you don't know enough to know what the words are, so I'll help you out with that for now.

Andram → And-ram (Long-wall) → /and.rɑm/

Ninglor → Nin-glor (Water-lily) → /niŋ.glɔr/

Lanthir → Lant-hir (Fall-river, i.e. "Waterfall") → /lant.hir/

2.3.2.1 Exercise

Transcribe the words into IPA. For this exercise, don't worry about where to place stress-marks. We'll cover that next.

1. **Gódhellim** Noldor _____
2. **Perhael** Samwise (Woodelf) _____
3. **Elhael** Wise Elf (non-Woodelf) _____
4. **Teiliassef.** We played a game. _____
5. **Rochwaith** Horse-Folk (non-Gondorian) _____
6. **Nediathon.** I will count. _____
7. **eiliant** rainbow _____
8. **meldir** male friend _____
9. **Lathradasseb.** We eavesdropped. _____
10. **apharch** very dry (Gondorian) _____
11. **Fangorn** Treebeard _____
12. **Angwedh** (Ang-gwedh) Iron-chain _____
13. **Glamdring** (Glam-dring) Foe-hammer _____

2.3.3 The Placing of Stress

Stress is extra emphasis put on a syllable. I'll show stress by putting an apostrophe as primary stress mark (') before the stressed syllable.

In Sindarin, the trick to understanding how stress works is to look only at the last three syllables. The stress can only be placed on the second-to-last and third-to-last syllables in a word.

If the word is 2 or 3 syllables long then the first syllable gets the stress.

> **Balan** Vala   → /ˈba.lan/
> **Gwanunig** twin → /ˈgwa.nu.nig/

If it is longer than 3 syllables, the third syllable from the end gets the stress.

> **Aronoded** Uncountable → /a.ˈrɔ.nɔ.dɛd/

If one of the following syllables with special attributes is <u>the second-to-last syllable</u> in a word, it gets the stress instead.

1. Accents (Acute and Circumflex)

2. Diphthongs (AE, AI, AU, AW, EI, OE, and UI – just like we learned in Lesson 1.)

3. Multiple Consonants (This only counts if the "special" syllable ends with a consonant and the following syllable begins with a consonant. They can be two of the same or several different consonants, but they must end one syllable and start the next one. Remember that CH, DH, PH, and TH each only count as one consonant.)

These types of syllables are called "heavy" or "long" syllables because they take more time and effort to say. Therefore, stress is drawn to the heavier syllables. In Sindarin, only if the heavy syllable is also the second-to-last does it pull the stress away from the third-to-last.

> **Forodwaith** Northmen   → /fɔ.ˈrɔd.wajθ/
> **gobennathren** historical → /gɔ.bɛn.ˈnaθ.rɛn/
> **alírui** undesirable   → /a.ˈliˑ.ruj/
> **Gwathuirim** Dunlendings → /gwa.ˈθuj.rim/

2.3.3.1 Exercise

Transcribe the words into IPA, taking care to mark syllable boundaries and stressed syllables.

1. **Gódhellim** Noldor _____
2. **Perhael** Samwise (Woodelf) _____

3. **Elhael** Wise Elf (non-Woodelf) _____

4. **Teiliassef**. We played a game. _____

5. **Rochwaith** Horse-Folk (non-Gondorian) _____

6. **Nediathon**. I will count. _____

7. **eiliant** rainbow _____

8. **meldir** male friend _____

9. **Lathradasseb**. We eavesdropped. _____

10. **apharch** very dry (Gondorian) _____

11. **Fangorn** Treebeard _____

12. **Angwedh** (Ang-gwedh) Iron-chain _____

13. **Glamdring** (Glam-dring) Foe-hammer _____

2.3.4 How Words Interact

First off - this section is somewhat speculative. Tolkien never went into detail about how phrases would be pronounced, so these rules are our educated guess work.

The words we'll be looking at interact with the words following them, often changing the beginnings of the following words and changing the ends of the words themselves. This process is called **Prestanneth** (mutation), and you'll learn about it in detail in later chapters. As a preview, we'll focus on the places you'll see it most often.

Words that cause Prestanneth are prepositions and certain pronouns.[31] In these examples, I'll use **i(n)** which means "the," **an** which means "to/for," **a(h)** which means "and," and **ni(n)** which means "me."[32] The (parentheses) around some of the letters indicate that Prestanneth often makes that letter vanish completely.

"The" **i(n)** never receives stress, but it does become part of the beginning of the following word. In fact, many people write it with a dash

---

[31] The bit about pronouns a pet theory of mine that not everyone agrees with, so take it with a grain of salt.

[32] **Nin** is being used as the example for the oblique pronouns like "us/you/him/her/it/them." There are so many, it's not feasible to list them all at this point.

between "the" and the following word to indicate this close relation-ship. I don't, but if you find it helpful, go ahead.

The pronouns can receive stress, but in a sentence, I usually stress them less than words like nouns and verbs. When I write the pronun-ciation of these sentences, I often give the pronouns secondary stress.

If any of these words precede an NG/ÑG, MB, or ND, pronounce as though it's between two vowels. If one of these words ends in an -N and the word they are before starts in a G, they are pronounced the same way.

> **I ngellyr / i ñgellyr** the wizards → /iŋ 'gɛɹ.lyr/
> **Ni *ñgollar**. They're teaching me. → /ˌniŋ 'gɔl.lar/
> **Añ galad** for light   → /aŋ 'ga.lad/
> **I ndîr** the men   → /in 'diːr/
> **I mbair** the homes   → /im 'bajr/

2.3.4.1 Exercise

1. **In gwoen** the geese _____
2. **A ñûl** and sorcery _____
3. **Ni ñohenathol**? Would you please forgive me?

   _____
4. **I ndaim** the hammers _____
5. **I mbechyr** the pedlars _____

Before a vowel, **i** acts like an (i) at the beginning of a word, becoming a /j/. The only exception is words already beginning with (i). Then the two (i)s combine to become a long (i). If the (i) was a consonant (i), then the consonant (i) separates from the word it was on and makes "the" a long (i).

> **I 'olf** the branch   → /jɔlv/
> **I alfirin** the alfirin-flower → /'jal.fi.rin/
> **I iôn** the son   → /iˑ 'ɔːn/
> **I ist** the knowledge   → /'iˑst/

Ah and the only other word like it, **oh** "about, concerning," behave in an interesting way before vowels. The -H, which is deleted or silent before consonants, attaches itself to the beginning of the word starting in a vowel. It is otherwise impossible for an H to come at the end of a Sindarin word, as such Hs were lost long ago.

> **Ah orod** and a mountain → /ɑ ˈhɔ.rɔd/
> **Ah iell** and a daughter → /ɑ ˈhi.ɛl̬/

2.3.4.2 Exercise

1. **i iaw** the corn _____
2. **ah iaw** and corn _____
3. **i ivor** the crystal _____
4. **ah ivor** and a crystal _____

2.3.5 Conversation Practice: Greetings, Farewells, and Intros 2

Now that you know how to pronounce longer words, you can learn some longer greetings.

- **Galu!** "A blessing/Good fortune!"
- **Mae govannen!** "Well met!" A casual greeting. Don't use with strangers!
- ***Maedol! / *Galdol!** "Welcome!"
- **Na vedui!** "At last!"
- **Êl síla erin lû e-govaned 'wîn.** "A star shines on the hour of our meeting."
- **Suil anlen!** "A greeting for you!"

And here are a few Farewells:

- **Cuio vae!** "Live well!"
- ***Novaer!** "Be good!"
- **Galu!** "A blessing/Good fortune!"
- **Boe annin mened.** "I must go."
- **Fer-dandolo!** "Return soon!"

And some longer ways to introduce yourself:

- **Ma i eneth lîn?** "What is your name?"
- **Ma i eneth dîn?** "What is his/her name?"
- **Ma in enith dîn?** "What are their names?"
- **... i eneth nîn.** "... is my name."
- **Im ... estannen.** "I am called ..."
- **... i eneth-e-mellon nîn.** "...is my friend's name."
- **... i eneth-e-ben hen.** "...is this person's name."

2.3.5 Review

Write the pronunciation out using the International Phonetic Alphabet (IPA) symbols I used in the lesson. They are the symbols put in /slashes/.

Separate syllables with periods, as I did in the lesson.

Mark the stressed syllables.[33]

1. **aderthad** reunion _____
2. **aduial** evening _____
3. **aearon** ocean (non-Woodelven) _____
4. **aearon** ocean (Woodelven) _____
5. **ah adanadar** and father of man _____
6. **ah iathrim** and Elves of Doriath _____
7. **am bâr** to home _____
8. **an dagnir** for a killer _____
9. **añ garaf** for a wolf _____
10. **annúnaid** Westron _____
11. **bauglir** oppressor _____
12. **cenedril** mirror _____
13. **dringo** to beat _____
14. **edhellen** Elvish _____
15. **fim-brethil** Slender-birch _____
16. **galadhremmen** tree-woven _____
17. **galu** good luck _____

---

[33] Review how to do this in 2.1.3.3.

18. **gelir** happy person _____
19. **girithron** December _____
20. **guruthos** shadow of death _____
21. **hwiniol** twirling _____
22. **i 'aladh** the tree _____
23. **i iell** the daughter _____
24. **i ñannel** the harp _____
25. **i phelaith** the surfaces _____
26. **i ithron** the wizard _____
27. **i ñen-draim** the hewn stones _____
28. **ínias** annals _____
29. **lhewig** ear _____
30. **mellyrn** Mallorn trees (non-Gondorian) _____
31. **mellyrn** Mallorn trees (Gondorian) _____
32. **ñilher** Star-lover _____
33. **Ni ñeril**. You advise me. _____
34. **Ni phedir**. They speak to me. _____
35. **Ni ñgawasser**. They howled at me. _____
36. **pelio** to spread _____
37. **rhúnen** eastern _____
38. **rochben** horse rider (non-Gondorian) _____
39. **rochben** horse rider (Gondorian) _____
40. **talraph** stirrup _____
41. **thend-rim** Grey-Elves _____
42. **thoronath** eagles _____
43. **teithannen** written _____

Chapter 3: Syntax

Before learning how to inflect words, we're going to learn syntax - the order that words are put in. Sindarin, unlike Quenya, depends heavily on syntax for keeping track of parts of speech and what modifies what, much as English does. Because learning new syntax structures is quite hard, we're learning it at the beginning and will be practicing it throughout this book.

3.1 Articles, Adjectives, Adverbs, and Prepositions

Think about all of the ways we take simple words and modify their meanings. Take "man" and add an article. Now we have "the man." Take "the man" and add an adjective. Now we have "the bold man." Take "bold" and add an adverb. Now we have "the very bold man." Take "very" and add another adverb, "occasionally." Now we have "the occasionally very bold man." Each addition modifies the image being made for you. This lesson will describe the syntax, or word order, of the various things you tack onto nouns in Sindarin.

3.1.1 Articles

Articles are a little more complex in Sindarin than in English. In Sindarin, there are singular and plural words for "the." They are:

Singular "the"   **i**
Plural "the"   **in**

There are no indefinite articles (words for "a" or "an"), because indefiniteness isn't marked in Sindarin.[34]

drambor   a fist
i dhrambor   the fist
in dremboer   the fists

3.1.1.2 Prestanneth

The word for "fist" in Sindarin is **drambor**; so why would it become **dhrambor** when **i** was attached? It is because of an interesting part of Sindarin grammar: mutation. **Prestanneth,** as it is called in Sindarin,

---

[34] The articles are well established in Neo-Sindarin, and have been for a long time. For more information, I suggest Helge Fauskanger's article "Sindarin - the Noble Tongue" http://folk.uib.no/hnohf/sindarin.htm#Heading9 or "Summary of the Sindarin Grammar" by Ryszard Derdzinski http://www.elvish.org/gwaith/sindarin_grammar.htm#article or David Salo's book *A Gateway to Sindarin* pages 149-152.

changes the consonants at the beginnings and ends of words. Tolkien made specific rules governing which consonants change into which sounds when, which you will study in full later. I will provide the mutated words for your homework until then.

There are two types of mutation that are used with "the."

- **in** causes *Nasal Mutation* because it ends in an N. Mutation often makes the -N vanish.
- **i** causes *Vocalic Mutation* because it ends in a vowel.

These two types of mutation are the most common, and you'll end up getting very, very familiar with them.

Throughout the lessons, I will use "lenition" to describe a particular type of mutation. The sound changes it causes are the exact same as Vocalic Mutation, but they happen for grammatical reasons, not because the word that is causing the mutation ends in a vowel. Lenited words don't have any vowel-ending words causing them to change.

3.1.2 Adjectives

Adjectives in Sindarin are fairly easy to spot. Many of them have one of these adjective suffixes on them:

1. **-eb:** Often found on nouns turned into adjectives, like the word **aglareb** "glorious" from **aglar** "glory."
2. **-en/-n:** Often a sign that the adjective is also a past participle; like the word **dannen** "fallen"from **dant** "fall."
3. **-ol/-el:** Usually found on adjectives that are also present participles; like the word **hwiniol** "twirling" from **hwinia** "twirl."
4. **-ren/-len:** This suffix doubles as the suffix for the name of a language because of its connotation of something being "of" the noun it is attached to; like the word **edhellen** "elvish" from **edhel** "elf."
5. **-ui:** Most often found on nouns and verbs that have been turned into adjectives; like the word **erchammui** "one-handed" from **er+cam** "one+hand."

6. **-weg:** Found attached to verbs, meaning that whoever is described by this adjective does that action a lot; like **madweg** "gluttonous" from **mad-** "eat."

This is of course, not an absolute rule. I just wanted to point out that these are the most common endings to Sindarin adjectives; but there are a lot of exceptions, and some nouns will end in these letters as well. Thus Sindarin is very different in this respect from Quenya, which has much more easily spotted adjectives, as most of them end in **-a**. Sindarin lost the majority of its vowels at the ends of words, therefore many of the adjective-making affixes were lost as well.

When an adjective modifies a noun, it follows the noun. Adjectives become plural when their nouns are plural. This is called "adjective agreement."

In English, words like "the/my/our/your/his/this/that/those" are determiners. The determiner "the" can't be used alongside any of the other determiners. But, in Sindarin possessive pronouns, interrogatives, and demonstratives are all determinative adjectives. That means in Sindarin, it's perfectly grammatical to say something like "the my shoe," while in English that makes little sense. There is a slight difference in meaning when you leave out "the" in Sindarin. It'd be like saying "a(n) __ of mine."

cîr + glân	= **cîr 'lain**	(<u>white</u> ships)
cair + dîn	= **cair <u>dhîn</u>**	(a ship of <u>yours</u>)
i + cair + sen	= **i gair <u>hen</u>**	(<u>this</u> ship/the <u>this</u> ship)
i + cair + man	= **i gair <u>van</u>?**	(<u>which</u> ship?/the <u>which</u> ship?)

The beginnings of **cair, caran, glân, dîn, sen,** and **man** all changed because when an adjective modifies a noun, it is lenited. "White" **glân** became **glain** because it became plural with **cîr** "ships."

We don't have any examples of multiple adjectives on a single noun, just an adjective and a possessive pronoun.[35] What I suggest is to treat them the same. Lenite both of them. The possessive pronoun (and I

---

[35] This can be found in *Vinyar Tengwar* issue 44, page 21, line 6 of Tolkien's Sindarin translation of the Lord's Prayer.

assume, the demonstrative/interrogative adjective as well) would go last.

find + caran + cîn = find <u>garan</u> <u>gîn</u> (<u>your</u> <u>red</u> hair)

3.1.2.1 Exercise

Nouns	Lenited Adjectives
dog **chû** (from **hû**)	good (singular/plural) **vaer** (from **maer**)
rat **nâr**	your **gîn** (from **cîn**)
horses **rych**	wet **nenui**
birds **aew**	fast (plural) **gelig** (from **celeg**)

Translate these phrases.

1. The good dog _____
2. Fast horses_____
3. Wet rat _____
4. Your wet dog _____
5. Good fast birds _____

3.1.3 Adverbs

Unlike adjectives, there is no common suffix or marker to be found on Sindarin adverbs; except that some adjectives have become adverbs.

There are two types of adverbs. The first is the independent words. They follow the verbs they modify or go at the beginning of the sentence. They are lenited when they follow their verb, just like adjectives. If they follow other words directly behind the verb, then they aren't lenited.

neri + lim   = **neri <u>lim</u>** (to run <u>quickly</u>)

edro + si   = **edro <u>hi</u>** (to open <u>now</u>)

si + aníron glired = **<u>sí</u> aníron glired** (<u>now</u> I want to sing)

3.1.3.1 Exercise

Verbs/Sentences	Lenited Adverbs
they loom **Brastar**	now **hí** (from **sí**)
hide **Delio**	yonder **ennas**
we are terrified **Grogab**	above **am**
I eavesdropped **Lathrassen**	today **hîr** (from **sîr**)

Translate the following sentences.

1. They loom above. _____
2. Hide yonder!_____
3. We are terrified today._____
4. Hide now! _____
5. Today, I eavesdropped. _____

The second type of adverb is prefixed directly onto the verb. They made the verb undergo Prestanneth. Once again, the Prestanneth rules are quite complex; so I will be sure to mutate the words you need beforehand.

> fer- + minno = **fer**-vinno (to enter **soon**)
> go- + linno   = **go**-linno (to sing **together**)

3.1.3.2 Exercise

Adverb Prefixes	Mutated Verbs/Sentences
again **ad-**	we laughed **alólef**
easily **ath-**	y'all wished **iestassedh**
thoroughly **tre-**	I'll heal **nestathon**
always **ui-**	they played a game **deiliasser** (from **teili-asser**)

Translate the following sentences.

1. We easily laughed. _____
2. They played a game thoroughly. _____
3. I'll heal thoroughly. _____
4. Y'all wished again. _____
5. We always laughed. _____

Adverbs also modify adjectives. The adverb precedes the adjective it modifies. The adverb lenites the adjective. [36]

| edregol + muin | = <u>edregol</u> vuin (<u>especially</u> dear) |
| mae + c'ovannen | = <u>mae</u> g'ovannen (<u>well</u> met) |

A blind spot we have is what to do with an adverb that is modifying an adjective that is in turn, modifying a noun. What I do is lenite the adverb to show the connection between it, the adjective, and the noun, but, since we have no examples to work from, it could just as easily be that the adverb wouldn't be lenited.

We also don't know if an adverb would become plural with an adjective that is modifying a plural noun. I don't make adverbs plural, but I could be wrong on this point.

| yrch + dae + gwaur | = yrch dhae 'woer |
| | OR yrch dae 'woer (very dirty orcs) |

---

[36] All of what we know about how adjectives and adverbs interact is based on **mae govannen**, which has a tricky past. Tolkien went through several different ways that the phrase could have come about. For years, we assumed that it was simply the adverb **mae** and the past participle of **govad-**. But, in *Parma Eldalamberon #17*, we see that Tolkien wanted this phrase to have a worn-down by time and many tongues feeling to it. He came up with two different ways to do this. The first was to have the verb start with a C. He came up with a few different verbs - **cova-** and **covad-**. But in *Parma Eldalamberon #17* pages 16-17 Tolkien wrote: "*This won't really do.* The explanation of the word as containing Sindarin √BAN 'meet', come up against, prefixed by *go* (<Common Eldarin WĀ, WO) is obviously right." Thus, he settled instead on having the verb be **govan-** and that it would stay being **mae govannen** by being **mae ci govannen** first, then the phrase getting worn down until it became **mae govannen**, like this: **Mae ci govannen > mae gi 'ovannen > mae g'ovannen**. Think of it like the greeting "Howdy!" in southwestern American English. It used to be "How do you do?" but was worn down into a much shorter phrase. So, does the adverb before the adjective cause lenition? We're not actually sure.

3.1.3.3 Exercise

The nouns in this wordbank either have no distinct mutated form or don't need to be mutated.

Nouns	Lenited Adverbs	Lenited Adjectives
mother **naneth**	very **dhae** (from	smiling **raen**
father **adar**	**dae**)	kind **vilui** (from **milui**)
sister **muinthel**	especially **edregol**	generous **fael**
brother **muindor**	still **eno**	cheerful **'ladhweg**
	long-time **anand**	(from **gladhweg**)

Translate the following phrases.

1. The still generous mother_____
2. The especially kind father_____
3. Long-time cheerful brother _____
4. Very kind sister _____
5. Still smiling brother _____

3.1.4 Prepositional Phrases

Prepositions are interesting tools in our arsenals. They tell us how something connects or relates to an action or something else. In English, they take the form of a preposition followed by a noun phrase like this:

- By a plane
- On a plane
- Like a plane

Prepositional phrases can modify both nouns and verbs. For example, you can say:

- The child on a plane
  and
- I play on a plane

In Sindarin, they carry out the same functions as in English.

When building a prepositional phrase you start with a preposition, since, after all, it is in the "pre-position."[37] Sindarin has two types of prepositions, one that has "the" included in its meaning,[38] and the other that doesn't.[39]

> **Erin gond** on the rock
> **Po i 'ond** on the rock

Prepositional phrases can behave like adjectives, following the nouns they modify, appearing after any adjectives that may be attached to the noun. When they are carrying out this role, the preposition is lenited.[40] Prepositions can't become plural to match a noun that they follow, however.

> **hên   bo 'ond vi   dhuin vi dawar**
> child on rock   in   river   in forest
> *A child on a rock in a river in a forest.*[41]

Prepositional phrases can also behave like adverbs, following the verbs they modify, and following any other adverbs, pronouns, and other verb-adjacent words connected to the verbs. If it directly follows the verb, the preposition is lenited, just like an adverb would be.[42]

---

[37] Yes, there are languages that have postpositions instead of prepositions. One such language is Japanese.

[38] You see this in a lot of Romance languages like Spanish, "del" meaning "of the."

[39] See Helge Fauskanger's article "Sindarin - the Noble Tongue" for more information about this interesting feature of Sindarin grammar. You can find the article here: http://folk.uib.no/hnohf/sindarin.htm#Heading9

[40] This is demonstrated in Tolkien's translation of the Lord's Prayer into Sindarin. There we have the prepositions **po** and **mi** attested in their mutated forms, **bo** and **vi**.

[41] The non-mutated forms of the words are **po, gond, mi, duin,** and **tawar**.

[42] This is a bit shakier, because in all of the examples we have, the mutation could have been caused by something else, because the verb was the copula. Since a prepositional phrase basically fills the same role as an adverb, it

Hên   laba   bo   'ond.
Child   jumps   on   rock.
A child jumps on a rock.

Prestanneth follows the prepositions, but it's much more complex there, so I will be deferring all of that until you learn the details later on.

3.1.4.1 Exercise

Nouns	Verbs	Prepositional Phrases
Roch	**Padras** It walked	**Bo râd** on a path (from **po**)
horse	**Agarphassen** I	**Hui chên** like a child (from **sui**
Thîr face	spoke	and **hên**)
	Teiliar they play	**Vin gaearon** in the ocean (from **min**)

Translate the following phrases.

1. A horse on a path. _____
2. It walked on a path. _____
3. I spoke like a child. _____
4. A face like a child _____
5. They play in the ocean. _____

3.1.5 Conversation Practice - Describe Someone

This will be a very simple set of phrases, all meaning "_ is _."

- **Ni** ... I am...
- **Me**... We, but not you, are...
- **Gwe**... We all are...
- **De/Le/Ci**... You are...
- **Te**... He/she/it is...
- **Ti**... They are...
- **Se**... This is...
- **Si**... These are...

---

wouldn't be surprising if they were mutated in the same pattern as adverbs are—but, I could be wrong.

- **Sa...** That is...
- **Sai...** Those are...

There are three Sindarin words that we would translate as "you" in English, and the distinction between them is very important.

1. **Ci** is for the singular "you" that is a close friend or family member in an intimate conversation. If you use this word for strangers or people you aren't extremely close to, it's very rude.
2. **Le** is for the singular "you" that is a stranger or someone you aren't close to. It's often referred to as "polite" or "reverential." If you use **le** when you should be using **ci**, it would signal to the person you're talking with that you are rejecting them, treating them like a stranger.
3. **De** is the plural "you"— that is, a group of people you're addressing.

Use lenited adjectives to fill in the blank. Don't forget that you need the plural form of the adjective for talking about more than one person.

English	Adjective	Lenited Adjective	Lenited Plural Adjective
tall	tond	dond	dynd
short	thent	thent	thint
big	beleg	veleg	velig
small	tithen	dithen	dithin
slender	fim	fim	fim
fat	tûg	dûg	duig
frail	mîw	vîw	vîw
strong	belt	velt	vilt
male	anu	anu	eny
female	inu	inu	iny
red-haired	ross	ross	ryss
blond	baen	vaen	vaen
brunet	*merifin	*verifin	*verifin
dark skinned	donn	dhonn	dhynn

red-faced	crann	grann	grainn
pale skinned	maidh	vaidh	vîdh
beautiful	bain	vain	vîn
hideous	uanui	uanui	uanui
good	maer	vaer	vaer
bad	faeg	faeg	faeg

Here are some words for people you can use. When you place them in the phrase, they will be lenited. Remember to use plural nouns with plural adjectives!

English	Sin-darin	Lenited	Lenited Plural	Plural "the" + Plural
woman	dî	nî	nî	i ndî
man	dîr	nîr	nîr	i ndîr
mother	naneth	naneth	nenith	i nenith
father	adar	adar	edair	in edair
wife	bess	vess	viss	i miss
husband	benn	venn	vinn	i minn
girl/ daughter	iell	iell	ill	in ill
boy/son	iôn	iôn	ŷn	in ŷn
sister	muinthel	vuinthel	vuintheli	i muinteli
brother	muindor	vuindor	vuindyr	i muindyr
sworn sister	gwathel	'wathel	'wetheli	iñ gwetheli
sworn brother	gwador	'wador	'wedyr	iñ gwedyr
family	noss	noss	nyss	i nyss
baby	laes	laes	laes	i laes
child[43]	hên	chên	chîn	i chîn
relative	gwanur	'wanur	'wenuir	iñ gwenuir
enemy	coth	goth	gyth	i chyth
friend	mellon	vellon	vellyn	i mellyn

---

[43] In *Morgoth's Ring*, page 228. Tolkien wrote, "Though no Elf would speak of possessing children; he would say: 'three children have been added unto me', or 'are with me', or 'are in my house'."

Here are possessive pronouns and demonstrative/interrogative adjectives. You'll learn about these in greater detail in chapter 7.

English	Adjectives	Lenited
my/mine	nîn	nîn
our/ours (excluding you)	mîn	vîn
our/ours (including you)	gwîn	'wîn
your/yours (informal)	cîn	gîn
your/yours (polite)	lîn	lîn
your/yours (plural)	dîn	dhîn
his/her/hers/its/their /theirs	tîn	dîn
this	sen	hen
these	sin	hin
that	san	han
those	sain	hain
which	man	van

Here are some adverbs that can modify adjectives.

English	Adverb	Lenited Adverb
daily	ilaurui	ilaurui
enough	far	far
especially	edregol	edregol
for a long time	anand	anand
long ago	io	io
now	sí	hí
only	îr	îr
still	eno	eno
very	dae	dhae

3.2 Genitives, Possessives, the Copula, and Conjunctions

Now we are reaching the more difficult parts of Sindarin. Here you will learn how to use "of" and its special qualities, how possessives and "of" tie together, the mysterious verb "to be," and how to use conjunctions in Sindarin.

3.2.1 Genitives

When speaking of "of," I'm talking about the possessive "of," not "from," "about," or "concerning."

In Sindarin, there's no word that means just "of." Instead, this is conveyed by word order. We actually do something similar in English sometimes. When we take "of" out of a phrase in English, we switch the order of the nouns.

> a <u>cushion</u> of a chair → a chair <u>cushion</u>

In Sindarin, the word order doesn't switch. The second word isn't lenited.[44]

> **ivor hîr** - a <u>crystal</u> of a lord (lenited, it'd be **chîr**)

Tolkien had a few different ideas about how Sindarin ended up this way. One was that there was a suffix that marked the second word, but that suffix was lost. He changed his mind on what that suffix used to be a few times, going through everything from **-a** to **-ion**. Another idea he played with was a preposition, **na** or **an** that eventually was lost. We're not sure which he chose (if he did), since **na** and **an** already have other roles in Sindarin grammar.

---

[44] Tolkien had this to say on the subject of Sindarin genitives in *The Road Goes Ever On*, a collection of his poetry with sheet music by Donald Swann, on page 65: "In S[indarin] the simple genitive was usually expressed by placing the genitive noun in adjectival position (in S[indarin] *after* the primary noun)." That makes this section one of the least controversial, most concrete pieces of Neo-Sindarin grammar.

3.2.1.1 Exercise

English	Sindarin	Sindarin w/Mutation
book	parf	barf
books	pairf	i phairf
foliage	golas	ʻolas
scribe	tegilbor	degilbor
new	gwain	ʻwain
forest	tawar	dawar

Translate these phrases.

1. The book of foliage _____
2. The new book of a scribe _____
3. The new foliage of a forest _____
4. A scribe of a forest _____
5. The forest of books_____

3.2.2 Possessives

In many languages, the genitive and the possessive are the same thing. Sindarin falls in this category as well. English is different. In English, we add an **'s** to whomever is possessing something, so you'll need to get used to thinking of possessives as "of" phrases.

A <u>friend's</u> laugh - the laugh <u>of a friend</u> - **i lalaith <u>mellon</u>**

Sindarin has three ways to achieve the possessive meaning. One you already know: the possessive pronoun. The second we just covered above, the Sindarin "of." The third is the preposition **nan** "with/including."[45]

---

[45] This preposition is described in *Parma Eldalamberon #17* page 147.

3.2.2.1 Preposition nan

Use **nan** like a preposition rather than just a possessive. This preposition implies that the possessive relationship between the objects or persons is visible to the speaker in some way.

> **Aran <u>nan</u> ivor** "A king <u>with</u> a crystal" [that he's wearing or holding]

Nan is also used when describing the physical features of something.

Aran <u>na</u> finnel garan	*a king with red hair*
Orod <u>nan</u> eryn	*a mountain with trees*

The **-n** of **nan** sometimes does a disappearing act before a consonant. That is part of *nasal mutation*, which you will learn more about in Chapter 5.

3.2.2.1.1 Exercise

English	Sindarin	With "nan"
cloak	coll	na choll
flowers	lyth	na lyth
maiden	gwend	nañ gwend
garden	sant	na sant

Translate the following phrases.

1. A maiden with a cloak _____
2. A cloak with flowers _____
3. A garden with flowers _____
4. A garden with a maiden _____
5. A maiden with flowers_____

Nan is also as close to an instrumental preposition that we have in Neo-Sindarin. It's used in sentences like "I cut the grass **with** a scythe" or "I painted the wall **with** red paint." This is how we communicate that we were using something to help complete the task. In Sindarin, we can use **nan** to say that you did a task with something on your person or as a feature of yourself.

> **Enengin in yrch na magol nîn.**
> *I slew the orcs <u>with</u> my sword (in my hand).*

We don't know if Tolkien intended **nan** to be used this way, but it's how we Neo-Sindarin translators filled this gap in Sindarin's grammar.

3.2.2.2 "Of The"[46]

When dealing with "the" and "of"-phrases or possessives, take into account what "the" is pointing to. Let's look at two phrases, "The king's crystal" and "Reinor's crystal." At first glance, you might think that "the" isn't needed or that it is modifying "king's," but think about how the possessive is constructed in Sindarin. Turn it into an "of"-phrase.

I ivor en-aran	*The crystal of the king*
I ivor Reinor	*The crystal of Reinor*

You'll notice an odd word meaning "of the" in that example. This special little preposition is used only in "of the"-phrases, when **en** goes between the two nouns it is linking. The plural of **en** is **in**, the exact same as plural "the," and it also uses nasal mutation. **En** uses a completely different sort of Prestanneth called "mixed mutation"[47] and is often distinguished from similar prepositions by a dash between it and the following word, or sometimes dashes on either side to show the way it links the nouns together.

I barth-<u>in</u>-Erais	*The Field <u>of the</u> Dee*r (plural)
I chabad garan <u>eñ</u>-gwend	*The maiden<u>'s</u> red shoe*

---

[46] Helge Fauskanger's description of **en** is an excellent, if you'd like to go into more detail. It's in his article "Sindarin, the Noble Tongue" - The Articles - The genitive articles viewable here: http://folk.uib.no/hnohf/sindarin.htm#Heading9

[47] This is what we Neo-Sindarin translators call it - we don't know if Tolkien had a name for it.

3.2.2.2.1 Exercise

English	Lented Sindarin	Singular, with singular "of the"	Plural, with plural "of the"
butterfly	'wilwileth	eñ-gwilwileth	iñ-gwilwilith
house	mâr	e-mbâr	i-mbair
wolf	dhraug	en-draug	in-droeg
forest	dawar	e-dawar	i-thewair

Translate the following phrases.

1. The house of the butterflies _____
2. The butterfly of the forest _____
3. The forest of the wolves _____
4. The house of the wolf _____
5. The forest of the butterflies _____

3.2.3 The Copula[48]

"To be" is often the most difficult verb to use in languages you are not familiar with. However, in Sindarin, it's slightly easier, because as a verb, you almost never have to use it at all.

3.2.3.1 The Hidden Copula

"To be" and all its forms (am, is, are, was, were, been, being) are left out of Sindarin sentences most of the time.

---

[48] Trying to find the Sindarin copula is like searching for a ghost. Most of this section on the copula is conjecture. We have very very, very little information to go on. We have only a few sentences that it is known to appear in. You can read about this in Thorsten Renk's article, "The verb 'to be' in Tolkien's Elvish languages" http://www.science-and-fiction.org/elvish/to_be.html We do have the addition of "mae govannen" to the list of known "to be" phrases since he posted this article, which unfortunately doesn't add any clarity to the problem of whether or not mutation would happen since it is supposed to be a phrase worn down by time.

As an example, I'll use one of the most common errors in the use of Sindarin, the attempt to translate "my friend"[49] while forgetting the crucial long vowel:

Mellon nin. *A friend [is] me.*

When saying something that follows the pattern: noun [to be] adjective the adjective doesn't undergo any Prestanneth, because it isn't part of the noun-phrase. It's called a *predicate adjective*. It has almost become a sort of verb. It still must be plural to match the noun or nouns that it is describing, but you don't need to lenite it. Look at the example below to see how two phrases with the same word order have different meanings.

I 'wend bain. *The maiden [is] beautiful.*

versus

I 'wend vain *The beautiful maiden*

When a noun is the object of the sentence, it follows this pattern: noun [to be] noun, and unlike adjectives, the second noun is lenited. Prestanneth or lack of it is how we differentiate an "of" phrase from a "to be" sentence.

I ethir geredir. *The spy [is] a craftsman.*

versus

I ethir ceredir *The craftsman's spy*

To restate simply:

Copula+Adjective=No lenition.

Copula+Noun=Lenition.

Even though it is hardly ever used, the verb "to be" still exists as the imperative **No!** "May it be so!" and the exclamation ***Naw!** "It is so!"

---

[49] **Mellon nîn**. Though often, I'd say that you want a diminutive form instead, making it **Melloneg**.

Keep this in mind when we start learning how to conjugate verbs in Sindarin.

3.2.3.1.1 Exercise

English	Sindarin	Mutated Sindarin
frog	cabor	gabor
child	hên	chên
fish	hâl	châl
green	calen	galen
little	tithen	dithen

Translate the following phrases into English. Beware - not all of them will include the copula!

1. **I gabor calen.** _____
2. **I chên dithen cabor.** _____
3. **I gabor chên.** _____
4. **Hâl galen chên cabor.** _____
5. **I châl dithen galen.** _____

3.2.3.2 The Uncertain and Negative Copulas[50]

These two words are helping verbs in their normal function. But since the Sindarin copula usually does a vanishing act, these two words stand on their own.

These two words are:

1. ***law** "not"
2. ***ce** "might/may"

To use them, put them between the two words connected by the copula, and mutate the word following ***law/*ce**. Unlike the English copula, you don't conjugate these words at all. That's because they are just going before the invisible "to be," fulfilling their helping-verb duties.

---

[50] This section is entirely fan-invention. We do know that something like these words probably exists in Sindarin, but we don't know where or what it looks like. This is our best guess based on Quenya grammar, and it's all we have while we try desperately to find ways to communicate in this language.

That means that the adjectives would still become plural to match the noun that they are describing.

I ethir *ce geredir. *The spy might [be] a craftsman.*
Ci *law vain. *You [are] not beautiful.*
Iñ gwind *ce vîn. *The maidens may [be] beautiful.*

For more information read 7.3.5.

3.2.3.2.1 Exercise

English	Sindarin	Lenited Sindarin
dragon	lhûg	thlûg
fish	lim	lim
human	adan	adan
dead	fern	fern
green	calen	galen

Translate the following phrases.

1. A dragon is not a fish. _____
2. The human might be dead. _____
3. The dragon is not dead._____
4. The fish might be green. _____
5. The dragon is not green._____

3.2.4 Conjunctions

In English, we have many conjunctions: *for, and, nor, but, or, yet, so.* In Sindarin, we know of only three: "and" **ah/adh/ar**, "or" **egor**, and "but" **ach**. In a list, the conjunction is only used between the last two items of the list.

3.2.4.1 "And"

"For," "and," and "so" can be translated with **a** (before consonants) and **ar/ah/adh**(before vowels). The following word is lenited. The

Númenorean and Exilic dialects would use **ar** if showing Quenya influences in their speech. If you use **ar** before a consonant, use Liquid Mutation.

Tolkien made **adh** and **ah** for "and" around the same time. They both appear in *Parma Eldalamberon* #17. It isn't clear which he decided to go with, so you are free to use either.[51] For what it's worth, Tolkien did many more translations with **ar** than either **adh** or **ah**, and between the two non-Exilic "and"s, we only have **ah** appearing in another text, *"Athrabeth Finrod ah Andreth."*[52]

3.2.4.2 "But"

"But" and "yet" can be translated with **ach**.[53] It makes the following word undergo Lenition. Its existance was only recently made public, so many people don't know of it yet. Instead, most people still use the reconstruction *****dan**, which makes the following word undergo Nasal Mutation. A few people still use another word that was borrowed from Quenya, *****mal**. Liquid mutation would go with it.

3.2.4.3 "Or"

"Or" and "nor" can be translated with **egor**.[54] It makes the following word undergo Liquid Mutation. Don't worry, I shall provide mutated words for you until you can do mutation yourself.

> **Lunt, roch, ah aran** A boat, a horse, and a king
> **Le melin, ach avon.** I like you, but I refuse.
> *****Law ídhron nâr egor gaur.** I long for neither a rat nor a werewolf.

---

[51] Thorsten Renk wrote a helpful article on the subject, "A brief history of 'and' in Elvish." Read the article here: http://www.science-and-fiction.org/elvish/history_of_and.html

[52] *Morgoth's Ring*, "Part Four - Athrabeth Finrod ah Andreth"

[53] "The 'Túrin Wrapper' by J.R.R. Tolkien" *Vinyar Tengwar* issue 50 March 2013 pages 3-25.

[54] This conjunction can be found in "The King's Letter," a set of texts that were ultimately abandoned and not included in *The Return of the King*. They can be found in *Sauron Defeated*, page 129.

3.2.5 Conversation Practice: Describe Your Origins

Talk about where your homeland is and find out where your friends are from. We'll start with the questions:

- **Ma i eneth-e-mbardor lîn?** What is the name of your homeland? (polite)
- **Ma i eneth-e-mbardor dhîn?** What is the name of (plural) your homeland?
- **Ma in enith-i-mberdyr dhîn?** What are the names of (plural) your homelands?
- **Mivan dorthol?** Where did you live? (polite)
- **Mivan dorthodh?** Where did (plural) you live?
- **Oman trevennil?** From where did you travel? (polite)
- **Oman trevennidh?** From where did (plural) you travel?

Here are a few phrases for answering the questions.

- **... i eneth-e-mbardor nîn.** ... is the name of my homeland.
- **... i eneth-e-mbardor vîn.** ... is the name of our homeland.
- **Dorthon vi ...** I live in ... (Use this only if you know what the mutated form is for the place-name. The type of mutation you will need is Vocalic Mutation)
- **Dorthof vi ...** We live in ... (Use this only if you know what the mutated form is for the place-name. The type of mutation you will need is Vocalic Mutation)
- **Trevennin o ...** I travelled from ... (Use this only if you know what the mutated form is for the place-name. The type of mutation you will need is Vocalic Mutation.)
- **Trevennif o ...** We travelled from ... (Use this only if you know what the mutated form is for the place-name. The type of mutation you will need is Vocalic Mutation.)

Here are a few Sindarin words for generic places, with prepositions and their mutated forms included.

English	Sindarin	With "in" or "in the"	With "from" or "from the"
West	Dûn	mi Nûn	o nDûn
East	Rhûn	mi Thrûn	o Thrûn
North	Forod	mi Forod	oph Forod
South	Harad	mi Charad	o Charad
ocean	gaearon	min gaearon	uin gaearon
mountains	eryd	min eryd	uin eryd
wilderness	rhaw	min 'raw	uin 'raw
forest	tawar	min dawar	uin dawar
city	caras	min garas	uin garas
valley	nand	min nand	uin nand
town	gobel	min gobel	uin gobel

3.3 Basic Sentence Syntax

In the past, people have tried to apply contemporary syntactic analysis to Sindarin and have found that it just doesn't work.[55] Tolkien was using models for syntax that didn't even use syntax trees, making Sindarin syntax slightly contradictory at points and overall odd.

For this lesson, you will need to learn some new grammatical vocabulary to deal with verbs, because if I recall the English-grammar classes from high school correctly, they didn't delve very deeply into these concepts.

We need to learn some new terms for the roles nouns take in a sentence, as these will come up frequently throughout the rest of this book.

- **Nominative** - for describing who is doing the verb, or the **subject** of the verb.
- **Accusative** - for describing what is being acted upon, or the **direct object** of the verb.
- **Dative** - for describing who is affected by the action, but not directly as the Accusative is. This is also called the **indirect object** of the verb. In English, the dative noun is often marked with "to" or "for."

Now that we are armed with grammatical terms, we can finally learn some grammar. Don't worry, with some practice, using these terms will became easier. We are, in a sense, learning the language for describing language as we learn a language.

---

[55] The people I refer to are Aaron Shaw and Rachel Shallit, who wrote an article called "Concerning Syntax," which despite coming out before several important and ground-breaking publications of Tolkien's notes, remains one of the best analyses of Sindarin syntax. I draw heavily from their article, available here: http://www.tolkiendil.com/langues/english/i-lam_arth/concerning_syntax

3.3.1 Sentences with Transitive Verbs

Transitive verbs have two nouns attached to them: the one performing the verb (the subject) and the one the verb is acting on (the direct object). I've underlined the subject and italicized the direct object for the examples.

> <u>The boy</u> punched *his friend.*
> <u>They</u> cut down *the tree.*
> <u>The elf</u> killed *the orc.*

3.3.1.1 Transitive Verbs with Nouns

There is a linguistic abbreviation for showing the basic word order of a sentence. In Sindarin, it's SVO, or Subject-Verb-Object. First the subject, then the verb, then the direct object, which undergoes lenition.

> **<u>Hadhod</u>** **avant** ***lim.***
> <u>dwarf</u>   ate   *fish*
> *A dwarf ate fish.*

> **<u>Îg</u>**   **nastar** *i*   **thail** *lîn*
> <u>Thorns</u> stab   *the*   feet   *your*
> *Thorns stab your feet.*

If the direct object is an adjective, mutate it just like you would a noun.

> **<u>I</u>   'wend** ***ôl**   ***chall.***
> The maiden becomes *tall.*
> The maiden is becoming tall.

> **<u>Reinor</u> thia**   ***nimp.***
> Reinor   seems *pale.*
> *Reinor seems pale.*

3.3.1.1.1 Exercise

Lenited Nouns	Verbs
river **hîr** (from **sîr**)	crossed **athrant**
frog **gabor** (from **cabor**)	jumped **labant**

| stick 'olf (from golf) | caught ant |

Using the words provided, translate these sentences into Sindarin.

1. Lothuial crossed the river._____
2. The frog jumped the stick._____
3. Lothuial caught a frog. _____
4. The river caught a stick. _____
5. The frog caught the stick._____

3.3.1.2 Transitive Verbs with Pronouns

In Sindarin, nouns and pronouns have different sets of rules.

You may have noticed by now that nominative pronouns seem to do a disappearing act most of the time.[56] Well, they aren't disappearing; they are reduced to suffixes on the verbs.

Lastannef   *ial.*
heard-we   *yell*
<u>We</u> *heard a yell.*

Iuithanne<u>dh</u>   **nam**   *hadhod.*
used-<u>you</u>   hammer   *dwarf*
You used a dwarf's hammer.

The accusative pronoun is placed before the verb, and makes the verb undergo nasal mutation because the accusative pronoun ends in an N[57]. The accusative pronoun also undergoes lenition. Because of this, if it's an all-pronoun sentence, it'll end up with the word order reversed compared to sentences with regular nouns in them.

---

[56] see 3.1.5 and 3.2.3 for examples of when you do need nominative pronouns.

[57] This is a pet hypothesis of mine. Nominative pronouns end in vowels, and accusative pronouns end in -N, but the pronoun **le** appeared to break that pattern. I think that the -N vanishes due to Nasal Mutation, meaning that **le** isn't an exception. It's not a widely-accepted theory though, due to there just being so little evidence about the forms and functions of Sindarin pronouns.

Here's a quick chart of the accusative pronouns all mutated for you. Note that in most cases, the -N will be lost before a consonant as part of nasal mutation. We'll go into the usage and meaning of pronouns in greater detail in chapter 7.

ni(n) "me"	**ve(n)** "us (excluding you)"
'we(n) "us (including you)"	
gi(n) "you (informal)"	
le(n) "you (polite)"	**dhe(n)** "you (plural)"
de(n) "him/her/it"	**di(n)** "them"
ha(n) "that"	**hai(n)** "those"
he(n) "this"	**hi(n)** "these"
ma(n) "who/what"	

I roch *ni* **lâf.**
the horse   me   licks
The horse licks me.

Gin **enengin.**
you   killed-I
I killed you.

3.3.1.2.1 Exercise

Verbs
They abandoned **awarthanner**
You (informal) praise **egleriog**
We (exclusive) raise **orthof**

Translate the following sentences into Sindarin.

1. They abandoned me._____
2. You (informal) praise us. _____
3. We (exclusive) raise them. _____
4. You (informal) praise me. _____
5. They abandoned us (exclusive). _____

3.3.1.3 Ditransitive Verbs & Verbs with Indirect Objects

A ditransitive verb is one that needs two objects: a direct object and an indirect object. An indirect object is a noun that the action indirectly affects. In English, this is marked with a "to" or a "for," or, we just put the indirect object before the direct object. To tell which is which, a handy method is to try switching the order and adding "to" and "for" to the second noun-phrase. If the meaning is unchanged, then you know which is the direct object and which is the indirect object.

> The dog fetched *the ball for me.*
> The dog fetched *me the ball.*
> The choir gave *an encore performance to the crowd.*
> The choir gave *the crowd an encore performance.*

The number of ditransitive verbs is pretty small in comparison to other classes of verbs. Be careful - "to" is also a directional preposition. "Take the money to the store" isn't ditransitive, since "to the store" is talking about where the action is heading, not who or what will also be affected.

In Sindarin, the indirect object is marked with the preposition **an** "to/for" and **anin** "to/for the;" and it usually goes after the verb and direct object. As long as it is marked with **an** you can put it anywhere in the sentence, except between a verb and its direct object. Putting it at the beginning of the sentence puts emphasis on it, drawing attention to who the action is to or for.

> **Amathon   aun   *gorf   gelebren   añ Glaewen**
> Amathon   gave   ring   silver   to Glaewen
> *Amathon gave a silver ring to Glaewen.*[58]

---

[58] This is a reference to elven courtship rituals. Giving a silver ring to someone is roughly equivalent to proposing to them. More about this can be found in Tolkien's essay "The Laws and Customs of the Eldar," which is in the 10th volume of *The History of Middle-earth - Morgoth's Ring.*

Añ Glaewen Amathon   aun   *gorf   gelebren.
to Glaewen   Amathon   gave   ring   silver
To Glaewen Amathon gave a silver ring.

Amathon añ Glaewen   aun   *gorf   gelebren.
Amathon   to Glaewen   gave   ring   silver
Amathon gave a silver ring to Glaewen.

Dative pronouns can be deceptive. The preposition **an** is prefixed onto the pronoun, making it look like another word. Here is a brief list of all the dative pronouns.

annin "to/for me"	**ammen** "to/for us (excluding you)"
angwen "to/for us (including you)"	
angin "to/for you (informal)"	
anlen "to/for you (polite)"	**anden** "to/for you (plural)"
anden "to/for him/her/it"	**andin** "to/for them"
anhan "to/for that"	**anhain** "to/for those"
anhen "to/for this"	**anhin** "to/for these"
amman "to/for who/what"	

De   cherir   ammen.
it   do-they   to-us
They do it to us.

Ammen   de   cherir.
to-us   it   do-they
They do it to us.

You can leave **an** out of the *indirect object* (as long as it isn't a pronoun, and only if the verb is actually ditransitive) but if you do, you must place it after the verb and *direct object*.[59] In English we switch the word order, so be careful of this.

Amathon aun   *gorf   gelebren Glaewen.
Amathon   gave   ring   silver   Glaewen
Amathon gave Glaewen a silver ring.

---

[59] We know this because of Gilraen's Linnod: **Ónen i Estel Edain, ú-chebin Estel anim.** - "I gave the Hope [to] Humanity, I can't keep Hope for myself."

3.3.1.3.1 Exercise

Verbs	Lenited Nouns
[he/she/it] gave **aun**	idea **inc**
I gave **ónen**	book **barf** (from **parf**)
[they] confirm **tangadar**	waybread **graim** (from **cram**)

Translate the following sentences into Sindarin using the words above. I chose names that wouldn't change their spellings when mutated by **an**. Some questions have more than one right answer. See how many you can do!

1. Glaewen gave waybread to Lothuial. _____
    _____
2. I gave a book to Glaewen._____
3. They confirm the idea for us._____
4. She gave it to us._____
5. I gave it to Lothuial. _____

3.3.1.4 Helping Verbs

We don't have any helping verbs attested in Sindarin that we know of.[60] But, we extrapolate a few that should exist outside of our current knowledge of Sindarin. They are *law "no/not/don't" [61] and *ce "may/might."[62] Our ideas on where these would go is based on Quenya.

The trick to figuring out where these go is figuring out what the predicate is, because these two helping verbs go directly *before the predicate*. The verb, its direct object, indirect object, prepositional phrases, adverbs, and all of the affixes that modify the verb are what make up the predicate. The subject is not included in the predicate, unless it is a pronoun-suffix on a verb.

---

[60] **Aen** might be one, or it could be an adverb. We don't know.
[61] Read up on *law's creation and use in chapter 6.1.1.2
[62] Read up on *ce's creation and use in chapter 7.3.5

Lenition follows the helping verbs, but only if the following word isn't already lenited. You can't double-mutate a word.

>*Law *gin*   enengi<u>n.</u>
>not   you   killed-<u>I</u>
>*I didn't kill you.*

>*Ce   *gi*   ndegi<u>n.</u>
>might you kill-<u>I</u>
>*I might kill you.*

><u>Îg</u>   *ce   nastar   *i*   *thail*   *lîn.*
><u>thorns</u> may   stab   *the* *feet*   *your*
>*<u>Thorns</u> may stab your feet.*

When you move an adverb or prepositional phrase (including the indirect object) to the beginning of the sentence, that is called "topicalizing," meaning that it has become the topic of the sentence. Such sentences are called Topic-Comment sentences, and are common in languages like Korean. When you make something the topic, it goes in front of everything else in the sentence, even the helping verbs.

>**A<u>ñ Glaewen</u>** **<u>Amathon</u>** *ce   anna   *gorf   gelebren.
>*<u>to Glaewen</u>*   <u>Amathon</u>   might give   *ring*   *silver*
>*<u>To Glaewen</u> <u>Amathon</u> might give a silver ring.*

>**Sîr,**   *law   *bostassen.
>Today   not   rested-I
>*Today, I didn't rest.*

3.3.1.4.1 Exercise

Mutated Verbs	Mutated Nouns
enchants **luitha**	ball **goron** (from **coron**)
it spits *****buia** (from *****puia**)	gem **vîr** (from **mîr**)
threw **achant**	jewel-smith **vírdan** (from **mírdan**)
	magician **ñollor** (from **gollor**)
	on the ground **erin gae** (from **cae**)

Translate these sentences.

1. It might spit on the ground. _____

2. The jewel-smith didn't throw the ball to me. _____
_____

3. The magician may enchant the gem._____
_____

4. The magician didn't throw it. _____
5. The jewel-smith doesn't spit._____

3.3.2 Intransitive Verbs

An intransitive verb isn't being done to anything; it only has a do-er. In other words, it does not use a direct object.

> The dog walked.
> The flowers wilted.
> The hammer fell.

Therefore, these sentences have the laxest sentence structure in Sindarin. The subject can precede or follow the verb. Like-wise for the indirect object. It can go before or after the verb, because it is marked with the preposition **an**.

> **Tôl torog.**
> comes troll
> *A troll* comes!

> **Lothuial padra.**
> Lothuial walks
> *Lothuial* walks.

> **Linnant Gwaeren ani chîn.**
> sang Gwaeren for-the children
> *Gwaeren* sang for the children.

> **An Edain eriasseb.**
> For Humans arose-we
> *We arose for humans.*

3.3.2.0.1 Exercise

Verbs	Nouns	Adverbs
survive **bronar**	mountains **eryd**	for a long time **anand**
I am alive **cuinon**	the dogs **i chui**	still **eno**
breathe **thuiar**	light **calad**	
fades **thinna**	stories **nern**	
die (mutated) **'wannar**		

Translate these sentences. There may be more than one correct answer.

1. The mountains survive for a long time. _____
   _____
2. I am still alive. _____
3. The dogs still breathe. _____
4. Light may fade. _____
5. Stories don't die. _____

3.3.2.1 Intransitive Verbs with Dative Pronouns

When the intransitive verb's indirect object is a pronoun, something interesting can happen. It can be treated like an accusative pronoun, placed directly before the verb, causing Nasal Mutation with its -N. When this happens, it even loses **an** and is indistinguishable from an accusative pronoun.

> **Ivreth cân _angin._**
> Ivreth calls _to-you_
> _Ivreth calls to you._

> **Ivreth _gi_ chân.**
> Ivreth _you_ calls
> _Ivreth calls to you._

> **_Gi_ chân.**
> _you_ calls
> _He/She/It calls to you._

The reason that this happens is that the Common Eldarin word order put the indirect object before the verb - but this feature has been mostly lost in the Elven tongues. The pronouns are showing parts of an older sentence syntax.[63]

3.3.2.1.1 Exercise

Mutated Verbs	Lenited Pronouns
we sang **linnassef**	you (before L) **gi**
tried **rithas**	you (before R) **gidh**

Translate each sentence two different ways.

1. We sang for you(informal)._____

    _____

2. Ivreth tried for you(informal). _____

    _____

3.3.3 Verbs as Direct Objects

When another verb or subordinate clause is a direct object, a very special verb is in play. In Sindarin, such verbs are usually conjugated as intransitive verbs. They can be broken into four categories, but we'll be covering only two[64] of them now: compound predicates and quotations.

For all of these cases, the verb-phrase acting as the direct object is NOT lenited.

3.3.3.1 Compound Predicates

For this type, there are two things to take into account.

---

[63] *Parma Eldalamberon* issue 22, "Quendian & Common Eldarin Verbal Structure," pages 92-95. This part was written in the Late Noldorin timeperiod, but since it reflects grammar that we see in Sindarin sentences, we can guess that this idea carried over.

[64] The other two types we will study in chapter 7.3.

1. The second verb of the compound is the direct object. It will
   be in a noun-like state, called a gerund, and it can't hold any
   information about when the action is happening or who is doing the action. That information is found only on the first part
   of the compound predicate.

> **Aníron**   *linnad.*
> want-I   *singing*
> *I want to sing.*

If the second half of the compound predicate has a subject, that
subject is dative and marked with **an**. [65]

> **Aníron**   **añ Gwaeren**   **linnad.**
> want-I   *for Gwaeren*   singing
> *I want Gwaeren to sing.*

> **Aníron**   **linnad**   **añ Gwaeren.**
> want-I   singing   *for Gwaeren*
> *I want Gwaeren to sing.*

> **Añ Gwaeren**   **aníron**   **linnad.**
> for Gwaeren   want-I   singing
> *It is Gwaeren I want to sing.*

If the indirect object is a dative pronoun, you can treat it like
it's an accusative pronoun, just the same as you would with an
intransitive verb.

> **Aníron**   *anlen*   **linnad.**
> want-I   *for-you*   singing
> *I want you to sing.*

---

[65] We have a handful of examples of the verbs in a compound predicate sentence sharing their subject, but we don't have any examples of the verbs with
different subjects. That the subject of the second verb would become the indirect object is just a fan invention to fill that gap in the grammar. By my esti-
mation, it isn't a risky invention though. In Quenya compound predicates, the
subject of the second verb is dative, so we can guess that something similar
happens in Sindarin.

Len aníron linnad.
you want-I singing
It is you who I want to sing.

2. The direct object and indirect object of the second verb act the same as they would normally.

I-aran aníra maded lembas.
the king wants eating lembas
The king wants to eat lembas.

Nidhin gi ndaged.
intend-I you killing
I intend to kill you.

Den aníron gi ndaged.
him want-I you killing
It is he who I want to kill you.

Aníron añ Gwaeren linnad ani chîn.
want-I for Gwaeren singing for-the children
I want Gwaeren to sing for the children.

Añ Gwaeren aníron linnad ani chîn.
for Gwaeren want-I singing for-the children
It is Gwaeren who I want to sing for the children.

3.3.3.1.1 Exercise

Verbs	Gerunds	Noun
dared **berthas**	to watch **tired**	humans **edain**
[they] want	to examine (mutated)	
anírar	*chethed**	
refuse **ava**	to survive **bronad**	
	to give knowledge *istaned**	

Translate these sentences.

1. Amathon dared to watch 'Laewen.

_____

2.   Humans want them to survive.

   _____

3.   They want Amathon to examine us (exclusive).

   _____

4.   He refuses to give knowledge to them.

   _____

5.   Glaewen doesn't refuse to survive.

   _____

3.3.3.2 Quotations[66]

A quotation goes at the end of the sentence, with some sort of pause before it.

> **Amathon ebent: Le melin.**
> Amathon said: you love-I
> *Amathon said, 'I love you.'*

Who the quotation is said *to* is the indirect object and marked with **an**.

> **Amathon ebent añ Glaewen: Le melin.**
> Amathon said to Glaewen: you love-I
> *Amathon said to Glaewen, 'I love you.'*

> **Amathon ebent anden: Le melin.**
> Amathon said to-her: you love-I
> *Amathon said to her, 'I love you.'*

Since the quotation acts as the *direct object*, the first verb can behave like an intransitive verb. If it has a <u>dative</u> pronoun, it can be treated like an *accusative* pronoun, and put before the verb.

> **Amathon den ebent: Le melin.**
> Amathon her said: you love-I
> *Amathon said to her, 'I love you.'*

_____

[66] This syntax is slightly more theoretical because I base it off of Tolkien's earlier version of Doriathrin, but it has a pattern that I think I see echoed in later translations.

3.3.3.2.1 Exercise

All of the words have been mutated or not mutated as you will need them.

Verb/Adjective	Nouns
ebennin I said	**nana** Mommy
ebent she/he/it said	**dâl** foot (from **tâl**)
harn hurt	

Translate these sentences. If it has more than one possible translation, do all that you can think of.

1. Nimphiel said to Mommy, "My foot is hurt." _____
   _____

2. I said to Mommy, "My foot is hurt." _____
   _____

3. I said to her, "My foot is hurt." _____
   _____

3.3.4 Conversation Practice: Likes and Dislikes

Here are some useful questions for discovering what your friends like or like to do.

- **Ma maer angin?**[67] "What/who do you like?"
- **Ma maer anlen?** "What/who do you like?"
- **Ma maer anden?** "What/who do (plural) you like?"
- **I dass van maer angin?**[68] "What do you like to do?"
- **I dass van maer anlen?** "What do you like to do?"
- **I dass van maer anden?** "What do (plural) you like to do?"

---

[67] Literally, "What is good to you?" this idiom is based off of the Quenya idiom for indicating that you like something, **nas mara nin** - "I like it" from *Vinyar Tengwar* issue 49, page 30.

[68] Literally, "Which task is good for you?"

- **... maer angin?**[69] "Do you like...?"
- **... maer anlen?** "Do you like...?"
- **... maer anden?** "Do (plural) you like...?"

Here are some useful phrases for answering the question:

- **...maer annin** "I like ..." (... is good for me)
- **Fuion...** "I hate..."
- **... *law vaer annin** ... "I don't like..." (... isn't good for me.)
- ***Law fuion...** "I don't hate..."

Here are some words to fill in the blanks. If the lenited form is different, it's in parentheses.

Pronouns

To use an accusative pronoun with **fuion**, drop the -N on it. For **maer an-,** use the nominative pronouns you learned back in 3.1.4.

Nouns

***Muig (*vuig)** cats
Aew little birds
Athrabeth conversation
Bydhu (vydhu) large insects
Dîr (nîr) men
Diss (niss) women
Mellyn (vellyn) friends
Pairf (bairf) books
Pin (bin) people

Eryd mountains
Hui (chui) dogs
i 'aearon the ocean
Im myself
Levain animals
Levain dithin small animals
Rych horses
Tawar (dewair) forests

Verbs

Here are some gerunds that you can use to fill in the blank.
***Cestad vîr** to seek treasure
Cuiad to live
Farad to hunt
Gannad to play the harp

---

[69] Literally, "Is ... good for you?"

***Geliad** to learn

Gladhed to laugh

Linnad to sing

Mudad to labor

Nored to run

Padrad to walk

Peded ani mellyn nîn (be Edhellen) to talk to my friends (in Sindarin)

Suilad ethyl to greet strangers

Teiliad to play games

Teithad to write

***Thered** to sew

3.4 Imperative and Passive Voice

In this lesson we shall study the Sindarin Imperative structure, which turns much of the earlier grammar you studied on its ear, and passive voice, which turns the object of the action into the passive subject.

3.4.1 What does Imperative mean?

The term imperative describes an important action that is desired. When we use it to describe grammatical structures in English, we use it for giving orders or suggestions, using spells, and praying. The imperative isn't just a command. We can use it to express something deeper and more intimate... we can express a wish.

As in English, Sindarin imperative grammar is used to order others around. You can also use it to say that you wish something would happen, and not just in prayer directed at the Ainur. The equivalent structure in English is starting a sentence with "may" or "I hope that" or "I wish that."[70]

3.4.2 Imperative Syntax

In an imperative sentence, the verb always comes before the subject,[71] or any pronouns that would otherwise be placed before the verb.[72]

When you are addressing the order to someone, their name can either come at the beginning or end of the sentence, separated from the rest of the sentence with a pause. You can do the same thing to any part of the sentence, as long as the lenition and prepositions are kept with them.[73] As mentioned in 3.3.1.4, this is called "topicalization," which makes it outside the normal structure of the sentence.

----

[70] This, as does much of our knowledge on imperative verbs, comes from Tolkien's Sindarin translation of the Pater Noster, "Ae Adar Nín," which can be found in *Vinyar Tengwar* issue 44, page 21-30.

[71] As found in "Ae Adar Nín," lines 2, 3, and 4.

[72] As found in Sam's version of the Elbereth hymn, line 4. The poem is in book 4, chapter 10 "The Choices of Master Samwise" of *The Lord of the Rings*.

[73] An example of such topicalization can be found in the praise chanted at Frodo and Sam by the people of Gondor. This is in The *Lord of the Rings*, book

One little note: verbs conjugated in the imperative are easy to spot, they always end with **-o**.[74]

3.4.2.1 With Intransitive Verbs

For intransitive verbs in the imperative, the subject of the sentence follows the verb, without prestanneth.

> **Reinor, tolo n' Imladris!**
> Reinor   come to Rivendell!
> *Reinor, come to Rivendell!*

> **Ego, gwarth!**
> begone traitor!
> *Begone, traitor!*

> **Gladho hîn!**
> laugh   children!
> *May children laugh!*

When you have a "to be adjective" structure, the adjective must follow "to be," and it is lenited.

> **No dhínen, muindoreg!**
> be   silent   brother-dear!
> *Be silent, dear brother!*

> **No vain   i   iell   gîn!**
> be   beautiful the daughter your!
> *May your daughter be beautiful!*

6, chapter 4, "The Field of Cormallen," line 4 of the chant. That's why Frodo's Sindarin name, **Taur**, is lenited to **Daur**, even though it is at the beginning of the line.

[74] The only exception is "Don't!" - **baw**, but as its AW comes from the same, ancient long A that is in all of the command-forms, it hardly counts. It's also a particle, not a conjugatable verb.

3.4.2.2 With Transitive Verbs

For transitive verbs in the imperative, most of the examples we have are orders, where the subject of the sentence is "you."

> **Therio i   vôr.**
> dread   the   darkness
> *Dread the darkness.*

> **Tollo i   'olf   i   chû!**
> fetch   the   stick   the dog!
> *May the dog fetch the stick!*

> **Maetho   i   chyth   nîn!**
> fight   the   enemies my!
> *Fight my enemies!*

3.4.2.3 With Indirect Objects

For imperative statements with indirect objects, either the dative or the accusative could come first, because the dative marked by **an** is free to roam around the sentence.[75]

> **Cuio   angwen,   melethrilig!**
> live   for-us   love-dear!
> *Live for us, my love!*

> **Melloneg,   anno   an   adar   gîn   ant.**
> friend-dear,   give   to   father your   gift
> *My friend, give a gift to your father.*

---

[75] This is a little shaky though, since all of our examples of indirect objects in imperative sentences come from one source, and there, they always directly followed the verb, going before the direct object. But, at the same time, they were always marked with **an** as well. The examples are from "Ae Adar Nín," lines 6 and 7.

3.4.2.3.1 Exercise

Imperative Verbs	Nouns	Adjectives
return **dandolo**	people **pin**	ready **fair**
welcome **nathlo**	book **barf** (from	daily **ilaurui**
write **teitho**	**parf**)	
advise **goro**		**Prepositional phrase**
		about this **o sen**

Translate these sentences.

1. Return to us (exclusive)! _____
2. Be ready daily! _____
3. May people welcome you (polite)! _____
   _____
4. Write a book for us (exclusive). _____
   _____
5. Advise me about this. _____

3.4.3 Impersonal Verbs

We have verbs that are labeled as impersonal in Sindarin, but no examples of them being used. There are examples in Quenya and Tolkien's earlier drafts of Elven languages, indicating that his construction for them hadn't changed. Using this syntax is risky, but it's common enough in Neo-Sindarin circles to include it.[76]

An impersonal verb is one that doesn't have a subject, but can have an object. In English, impersonal verbs still have subjects, like "it's raining," and "it's snowing," but these subjects don't have any meaning, they're just placeholders, because our syntax demands that something

---

[76] An article explaining the justification for this is written by Thorsten Renk, and is available on his website, Parma Tyelpelassiva. It's called "Impersonal constructions in Elvish." http://www.science-and-fiction.org/elvish/impersonal.html

be there. Then, what is doing the action? For English, in our modern era, it appears that it's nature doing the action of "raining" or "snowing." In Sindarin, based on Tolkien's world, we can say that it's the Ainur.

Because of the Ainur and the roles that the Elves believe that they hold on their world, things like sudden, apparently uncaused changes in emotion or mood are attributed to the Ainur, as are dreams, visions, and hallucinations. Having an impulse or having a dream aren't things that you do, they are done *to you*.

The syntax of impersonal verbs is quite similar to the syntax of a command. The impersonal verb goes to the beginning of the sentence, and the indirect object follows. These verbs can't have direct objects, only indirect objects, so you can use the long or short dative as you please[77].

> **Pessa   ammen.**
> causes changes to-us.
> *We are being concerned/affected/moved/troubled/changed.*

> **Pessa   ven.**
> causes changes us.
> *We are being concerned/affected/moved/troubled/changed.*

I mark the dative with **an** when the impersonal verb is forming a compound predicate with another verb, to ensure there is less confusion over who is the object of which action.

> **Boe   anlen ni   ndaged.**
> needs to-you me   killing.
> *You need to kill me.*

3.4.3.1 Exercise

It snows *glosta	on the mountains **erin eryd**
It rains **uil**	with you **a lhen** (from **ah+len**)
It gave a dream **ollas**	about you **o lhen** (from **oh+len**)
It gave an impulse **herias**	to/for the crowd **anin choth**
It needs **moe** (from **boe**)	(from **anin+hoth**)

---

[77] As a reminder: long dative is marked with **an**, short dative is marked with word order.

To stay **darthad**	

Translate these sentences:

1. It rains on the mountains. _____
2. I dreamed about you. _____
3. It snows on the mountains._____
4. The crowd had an impulse._____
5. I don't need to stay. _____

3.4.4 Passive Voice

Passive voice in English is built from [to be] + past participle. Some examples are:

> *I* was bitten by <u>ants</u>.
> *The cookies* were eaten by <u>children</u>.
> *The window* was broken.
> *Your favorite vase* was smashed.

It makes the noun that is acted upon into the subject, by describing its state as something that had an action done to it.

3.4.4.1 Transitive Verbs

Passive voice is used in several ways - it hides the doer of the action. This is especially true of Sindarin, which doesn't have a way to add "by someone" to the sentence, at least not that we know of yet. It also brings the emphasis of the sentence onto who or what the action was done to.

In Sindarin, passive voice is made the same way it is in English:

> noun [to be] past participle

The past participle is an adjective, so this syntax should be review for you. A quick overview: "To be" is left out of the sentence, and the past participle isn't mutated. It is, however, made plural or singular to match the subject.[78]

Ada   dangen.
daddy   slain
Daddy was slain.

I   chenneth   *rangen.
the   window   broken
The window was broken.

Ti   berthennin.
They doomed-plural
They are doomed.

3.4.4.2 Intransitive Verbs

We know that you can make intransitive verbs into past participles in Sindarin. They appear several times in Tolkien's writings.[79] But we don't know exactly how they were used. If you take the subject away, there's nothing left.

Instead, you can use the intransitive verbs to make a past perfect tense - describing an action that not only happen in the past, but has had some time pass after the action was completed. The simple past describes an action that could have happened only moments before.

This syntax only works for the intransitive verbs. English used to have a very similar syntax in it, but it was eventually replaced with "have+past participle." In archaic English texts, you can find sentences like "I am gone to the town" instead of "I have gone to the town."[80]

---

[78] This comes from the way Tolkien broke down the phrase that would become **mae govannen** - "Well thou [art] met." *Parma Eldalamberon* issue 17 page 17.

[79] For example, there's **dannen** from *The Lost Road and Other Writings* "The Etymologies" DAT-, DANT- (page 393) and **rithessin** from *Parma Eldalamberon* issue 17 page 167

[80] This is just a guess though. We don't know what Tolkien intended for the intransitive past participles, since none of Tolkien's writings that really break down the tenses of Sindarin have been published.

I	annon	dannen.
The	gate	fallen

The gate has fallen.

I	chên	galassen.
The	child	grown

The child has grown.

3.4.4.3 Ditransitive Verbs

We'll start this section with the mysterious uses of **Esta-**, and end it with a possible way to deal with ditransitive verbs in passive voice.

3.4.4.3.1 The Problem of Esta-

Esta- "To call, name" breaks with our expectations, and contradicts the syntax described above. The frustrating thing is, there are two examples of its use, and both are shrouded with mystery. One is from "The 'Túrin Wrapper',"[81] and it is in Late Noldorin.

I-Veleglind	i	eithro	en	estar	iChîn	Húrin
The-Epic	which	also		is?[82] called	the-Children	Húrin

The Epic which is also called The Children of Húrin

The first example behaves more like we would expect it to, with the *direct object* following **esta-**. The problem is that because the sentence has been turned into a relative clause[83], we don't know where or how "The Epic" would fit into the sentence if it was "'The Epic' is called 'The Children of Húrin.'"

---

[81] *Vinyar Tengwar* issue 50

[82] We don't know what **en** is supposed to mean, or its function here. This translation was never broken down by Tolkien, and in fact, Tolkien didn't translate it into English at all. The translation I share here is what Carl F. Hostetter, the person who wrote the article, came up with, and it represents our best guess.

[83] Basically, it makes a whole sentence subordinate to a noun, being part of the description of it.

The second example is from "The King's Letter,"[84] which is dated as being early Sindarin or Late Noldorin. Everyone takes a stab at the weird sentence it comes from. This is my stab. Be cautious when using this form though, since it's my little theory, and it may or may not be accepted.

> **Perhael (i   sennui Panthael estathar aen)**
> Samwise (who instead Fullwise called   ought to be?[85])
> *Samwise (who instead ought to be called Fullwise)*

Here, unexpectedly, the *direct object* is placed before **esta-**. And, yet again, it's in a relative clause, and we don't know what it would be like if it was a plain passive sentence. This being the later sample, its syntax overrides the earlier syntax.

One fascinating thing about these examples is that they show what may be the Noldorin passive-voice. In Sindarin, thanks to Tolkien's breakdown of **mae g'ovannen**, we know that the Sindarin passive voice was constructed with past participles. Therefore, it is my personal opinion that while obsessing over **en** and **aen** is fun, they are a relic of Noldorin grammar, like much of the letter.[86] I propose a different idiom based on these phrases for Neo-Sindarin translators, using the past participle **estannen**:

> [someone]   [a name]   **estannen**

> **Aranyo Reinor   estannen be Edhellen**
> Aranyo   Reinor   called   according to Sindarin
> *Aranyo is called Reinor in Sindarin.*

---

[84] It can be found in the 9th volume of The History of Middle-earth, *Sauron Defeated.*

[85] What **estathar aen** means exactly, we aren't sure. It's been argued to death and back twice, but we simply don't have enough data to work with. At least for this one Tolkien provided the loose English translation, but yet again - no breakdown by Tolkien to sort through.

[86] This is most clearly demonstrated in the mutations that Tolkien used. We have **mhellyn** instead of **vellyn**, **phain** instead of **bain**, and **Pherhael** instead of **Berhael**.

> **I   chû hen Huan estannen.**
> the   dog   this   Huan   called
> *This dog is called Huan.*

And if you're introducing yourself, I suggest using the reflexive pronoun **im**. You should recognize this phrase from the "introducing yourself" conversation practice.

> **Im Haengil estannen.**
> self Haengil   called
> *I'm called Haengil.*

3.4.4.3.2 Passive Ditransitive Verbs

Out of the quagmire that is the **esta-** phrases, we can come up with a way to deal with passive ditransitive verbs.[87]

First, turn the direct object of the verb into the *topic* of the phrase. Then the indirect object is made into the subject, and the verb is a past participle.

[Subject] [verb] [direct object] [indirect object]   →   [topic] [subject] [past participle]

> **Reinor aun *gorf añ Gwaeren.**   →   ***corf Gwaeren annen**
> Reinor gave   ring   to Gwaeren.   →   ring   Gwaeren given
> *Reinor gave a ring to Gwaeren.*   →   *Gwaeren was given a ring.*

3.4.4.3.2.1 Exercise

Past Participles	Other Words
amputated **osgarnen**	arm **ranc**
lived **guiassen** (from **cuiassen**)	well **mae**
summoned **tollannen**	here **hi** (from **si**)
protected **beriannen**	family **noss**

---

[87] It hardly needs to be mentioned, but this is me going out on a long, possibly rotting limb that could break off of the tree of Neo-Sindarin grammar at any moment.

Translate these sentences.

1. His arm was amputated. _____
2. You (polite) have lived well._____
3. I am called Olodhin. _____
4. You (polite) were summoned here._____
5. Your (polite) family is protected. _____

3.4.5 Conversation Practice: Talk About Your Feelings

Here are a few questions for enquiring about someone's emotions:

- **Thiog...** You look/seem ... (informal)
- **Thiol...** You look/seem ... (polite)
- ***Elig...** You are becoming... (informal)
- ***Elil...** You are becoming... (polite)
- **Ma *felig?** What do you feel? (informal)
- **Ma *felil?** What do you feel? (polite)

Talking about your ***filf**[88] (feelings) in Sindarin is a little different than it is in English. In English, we consider emotions and feelings as states of being, so they are normally described with adjectives. But, the elves don't see emotions that way. They are things that you are doing or things being done to you.

They divide emotions into two categories: ***Rhofelf**[89] (body-feeling) and *****Faefelf**[90] (soul-feeling).

- A ***rhofelf** originates in the **rhaw** (body). This is a word for feelings like hunger, cold, arousal, jumping from a loud noise – things that we often think of as instinctual or base.
- A ***faefelf** originates in the **faer** (soul). This is a word for emotions like hate, anger, fear, pity, love, compassion, delight, and fairness.[91]

---

[88] Singular: *****felf**
[89] **Hroafelmë** in Quenya.
[90] **Fëafelmë** in Quenya.
[91] *Vinyar Tengwar* issue 41 page 13

In addition, elves believe that strong emotions and dreams or visions are being done to them by outside forces, sometimes by powerful spirits, like Maiar and Valar.[92]

When talking about your emotions, first look to verbs for the emotion or for the symptoms of the emotion. Here a few handy verbs for this:

Intransitive Verbs

- *Gellon**. I rejoice. (for triumphant joy)
- **Girin**. I'm trembling. (could be from cold, fear, or excitement)
- **Gledhin** I'm laughing. (This is the non-Exilic word.)
- **Lelin** I'm laughing. (This is the Exilic word, borrowed from Quenya.)
- **Glavron**. I'm babbling, making excited, confused speech that's not understandable.
- **Gor-thuion**. I'm having difficulty breathing.
- **Grogon**. I feel terror.
- **Hwinion**. I'm twirling, I'm so excited that I'm dancing around, I'm giddy.
- *Merin**. I'm happy.
- *Muion**. I'm whining/whimpering/moaning.
- **Limmidon**. I'm moistening. (from sweat or tears or both)
- **Nimmidon**. I'm paling. (from some sort of shock, the kind that makes your face lose its color)
- **Nídhon**. I'm determined.
- *Nínion**. I'm weeping.
- **Ruthron**. I feel rage/I'm angry.

_____

[92] You can read more about this idea in Thorsten Renk's article, "Impersonal constructions in Elvish." http://www.science-and-fiction.org/elvish/impersonal.html I like the idea, so I use it in my translations.

The impersonal verbs all have the long dative pronoun, though you can use the shorter **nin** too. Many of these can also be used as regular transitive verbs when the source of the feeling is known and acting as the subject.

Impersonal Verbs

- **Boe annin.** I have a need/there is something I must do.
- **Gruitha annin.** I am terrified.
- **Heria annin.** I have a sudden, uncontrollable impulse.
- **Hortha annin.** I am compelled/ I feel I have an urgent task.
- **Naegra annin.** I'm in pain/something or someone is hurting me.
- **Pessas annin.** I am transformed/affected/my heart has been moved (this could be to a good or bad emotion - as long as it's a different one.)
- **Trasta annin.** I'm harassed/annoyed/troubled.

Another way to approach it is to use the verb "I feel..." ***Felin....** You can pair it with an adjective or noun. If they have a distinct mutated form, it's in parentheses.

Nouns

- **achas** dread, fear
- **anwar** awe
- **baur (maur)** need
- **del (dhel)** fear, disgust, loathing, horror
- **delos (dhelos)** abhorrence, detestation, loathing
- **erch** prickle (from an insult)
- ***faul** thirst
- **gae ('ae)** dread
- **gell ('ell)** joy, triumph
- **girith ('irith)** shuddering, horror
- **glass ('lass)** joy
- **gorgor (ñorgor)** extreme horror, terror, haunting fear
- **gorn (ñorn)** dread/awe from reverence
- **gorog (ñorog)** horror
- **goroth (ñoroth)** horror
- **gorth (ñorth)** horror

- **gost ('ost)** dread, fear
- **hûr (chûr)** readiness for action, vigor, fiery spirit
- **hwîn (chwîn)** giddiness, faintness
- **mael (vael)** lust
- **muil (vuil)** drear
- **naeg** pain
- **oroth** wrath, rage
- **rûth** anger, rage
- ***saeg (*haeg)** hunger
- **thang** compulsion, duress, need
- **úthaes** inducement to do wrong, temptation

You can also use **Ni...** "I am ..." with the adjectives. If they have a different lenited form, it's in parentheses.

Adjectives

- **apharch** very dry
- **bara (vara)** eager
- **caeleb (gaeleb)** bedridden, sick
- **crann (grann)** red-faced
- **deleb (dheleb)** horrible, abominable, loathsome
- **dem (dhem)** sad, gloomy
- **ereb** isolated, lonely
- **fair** ready
- **faug** thirsty
- **gem ('em)** sickly
- **gortheb (ñortheb)** horrible
- **harn (charn)** wounded, injured
- **helch (chelch)** bitter cold
- **horn (chorn)** impelled, compelled
- **hwiniol (chwiniol)** whirling, giddy, fantastic
- **laug** warm
- **lhaew (thlaew)** sickly, sick, ill
- **lom** weary

- **maelui (vaelui)** lustful
- **meren (veren)** festive, gay, joyous
- **naer** sad, lamentable
- **neithan** deprived, wronged
- **nîd** damp, wet, tearful
- **níniel** tearful
- **norn** twisted, knotted, crabbed, contorted
- **parch (barch)** dry
- ***pell (*bell)** calm, quiet, still
- **raeg** crooked, bent, wrong
- **raen** smiling, gracious, sweet-faced
- **ring** cold
- ***saeb (*haeb)** hungry
- **talt (dalt)** slipping, falling, insecure
- **tarlanc (darlanc)** stiff-necked, obstinate
- **thaw** corrupt, rotten
- **úrui** hot

3.5 Numbers and Dates

Counting in Sindarin is a little different than you are used to. Like English, you break the number into thousands, hundreds, tens, and ones columns, but in Sindarin, this is done backwards. We know this because of how numbers are written. Unfortunately, we know more about writing Sindarin numbers in script than we know about how they would be pronounced. If you need to write a number that we don't know how to say, just write it with numerals, backwards. So, "4100" would be written, "0014."

In Sindarin, there are several competing sets of numbers to choose from, all slightly different, and most of them frustratingly only cover the first 10 or 12 numbers. We know that Elves can in fact count higher than twelve. How they did it in Sindarin is a mystery.[93]

Another mystery is from how the numbers were derived. Tolkien mentions in *The Lord of the Rings*, Appendix D "The Calendars" that "The Eldar preferred to reckon in sixes and twelves as far as possible." But the numbers for 11 and 12 are clearly based off of words for 1 and 2,[94] indicating that they originally had a base-10 counting system.[95] Perhaps Elves could use both? Perhaps, Tolkien meant that Elves preferred to count time in sixes and twelves, but their counting system itself was base-10.

3.5.1 Cardinal Numbers

These are the numbers that one uses when counting. They communicate the amount of something.

---

[93] An excellent article going over everything we know so far about Elven numbers was written by Thorsten Renk, called "Eldarin Numerals." It's available here: http://www.science-and-fiction.org/elvish/numerals.html I'm drawing from it very heavily for this lesson.

[94] Though this could also be 2x6.

[95] This wasn't always the case: the Noldorin number for twelve has its own root, RÁSAT.

3.5.1.1 The Known Numbers

Here are the numbers from one to twelve:

1	**min/er**
2	**tâd**
3	**neledh**
4	**canad**
5	**leben**
6	**eneg**
7	**odog**
8	**tolodh**
9	**neder**
10	**pae**[96]
11	**minib**
12	**ýneg**

Other than that, we have **host** for 144 in the Etymologies, but we find that root still being used later on as a suffix for groups of hated or feared creatures. This probably isn't a number like the others so much as a fixed number for a certain quantity, like "a baker's dozen" or "a gross."

The other number we know is Sindarin is **meneg** for 1000, isolated from **Menegroth** "1000 Caves." But, this could also mean "a myriad." Elves though, with their long lifetimes, would probably be able to count this high, so this probably is an actual number.

3.5.1.2 Derived Numbers

Looking at the numbers for 11 and 12, a pattern starts to emerge. The number 10 appears to have been shortened down to **-kwe** in Common Eldarin.[97] Therefore, we can derive the rest of the teens based on this.

---

[96] Don't forget that the Woodelves would pronounce the AE as an E, making it **pê** on its own or with a short E when it's in a compound.

[97] You can see the lists of these ancient numbers in *Vinyar Tengwar* issue 47 page 10 and issue 48 page 21.

13	*neleb
14	*canab
15	*lebem
16	*enem
17	*odob
18	*tolob
19	*nederph

Making the multiples of ten is a little easier. In the King's Letter[98], from an earlier version of the Sindarin number-system, we have **nelchaen** given for 30. Back then the number 10 was **caen**, so we can guess that multiples of ten were written with the compound versions of them plus 10 put through the proper mutations. That gives us the following numbers:

20	*taphaen
30	*nelphaen
40	*cambaen
50	*lephaen
60	*enebaen
70	*odobaen
80	*tolophaen
90	*nederphaen

For making the numbers in-between, a common approach[99] is to use the word "and" **a/ar/ah/adh** between the numbers, listing the smaller numbers first, then the larger multiples of ten.

Don't forget to include the vocalic mutation that follows **a**.

| 21 | min a *daphaen |
| 22 | tâd a *daphaen |

---

[98] Found in *Sauron Defeated*, pages 128-131.
[99] The first time I saw it mentioned was in "Summary of Sindarin grammar" by Ryszard Derdzinski. The article is available here: http://www.elv-ish.org/gwaith/sindarin_grammar.htm#adjective

23   neledh a *daphaen
24   canad a *daphaen
25   leben a *daphaen
26   eneg a *daphaen
27   odog a *daphaen
28   tolodh a *daphaen
29   neder a *daphaen

And with a number starting with a vowel, don't forget that you'll need the longer form of **ah/adh/ar** "and." For the example, I'll use the Exilic **ar**.

61   min ar *enebaen
62   tâd ar *enebaen
63   neledh ar *enebaen
64   canad ar *enebaen
65   leben ar *enebaen
66   eneg ar *enebaen
67   odog ar *enebaen
68   tolodh ar *enebaen

And that, folks, is as far as we can take Sindarin numbers at the moment—just to 99.

3.5.1.2.1 Exercise

Translate the following numbers.

53   _____
84   _____
19   _____
46   _____
62   _____

Another good way to practice is to write out all of the numbers from 1 to 99.

3.5.2 Ordinal Numbers

Ordinals are the number-adjectives used to put things into a specific numerical order. In Sindarin, these are adjectives. They follow their nouns and are lenited.

3.5.2.1 The Known Numbers

Sadly, only some of the ordinal numbers can be used with no modifications in late Sindarin. Tolkien gave us the cardinal numbers from 1-12, but failed to give us their ordinal counterparts. Therefore, we have to look to the past and choose the ones that are the most likely counterparts. Here are the ones we can use without alteration:

1st	main/minui/erui
2nd	taid/tadui
3rd	nail/nelui
7th	othui
8th	tollui
9th	nedrui
10th	paenui
Last	medui

3.5.2.2 The Derived Numbers

The pattern that these numbers follow is this: in their ancient forms, their second vowel was lost, then we add the adjective-making suffix -ui. Thus **kanat>canthui, leben>levnui, enek>enchui, otos>othui, tolod>tollui**, and **neter>nedrui**. For the ones that needed to be adjusted to fit late Sindarin, I took the ancient form of the number, deleted the second vowel, traced the consonants through their development, and came up with these:

4th   **cannui**[100]
5th   ***lemmui**[101]
6th   **engui**[102]

For the rest of the numbers, since they are made from compounds, we can just add **-ui** onto them.

11th.   ***minibui**
12th.   ***ýnegui**
20th.   ***taphaenui**
30th.   ***nelphaenui**

For 1000th, we can reconstruct ***mengui**.[103]

When you have a more complex number, only add **-ui** to the last part of the number.

25th   **leben a *daphaenui**
92nd   **tâd a *nederphaenui**
66th   **eneg ar *enebaenui**

3.5.2.2.1 Exercise

Translate the following numbers.

77th   _____
16th   _____
23rd   _____
65th   _____
48th   _____

---

[100] I based this on **canthui**, which can still be used for the South Beleriand/Silvan dialect.

[101] Tolkien changed the ancient version of this word into **lepen**. As a result, this word would have a south Beleriand/Woodelven dialect version of ***lemphui**. This is the only one that's reconstructed. The other two are either derived or updated.

[102] I based this on the earlier **enchui**, which can be used as part of the south Beleriand/Woodelven dialect.

[103] With ***menchui** as a south Beleriand/Woodelven equivalent.

3.5.3 Using Numbers

Number usage in Sindarin is pretty close to how it is used in English. You don't need special numbers for counting different things, and they can be split into the same two grammatical categories that they are in English.

3.5.3.1 Cardinal Numbers as Quantitative Determiners

Using cardinal numbers in text is simple. They aren't counted as adjectives and are placed before the noun, taking the place of the word "the."[104]

As far as we know, numbers don't cause lenition to the nouns, but that's because we don't have examples of them being used. We also don't know if the noun and/or number would be lenited when they are the direct object of a verb. We do know that the noun most likely becomes plural if there is more than one of it.

> **Taphaen levain** 20 animals
> **Min lavan** 1 animal

When you need to use an ordinal number as an adjective, lenite it like any other adjective, and place it after its noun. Here is a short, limited list of the mutations you will need to do this.[105]

---

[104] Our examples of cardinal numbers being used comes from compound words in Sindarin, like **Menegroth** "1000 caves" or **tad-dail** "2-feet." Any other examples come from Noldorin, and unfortunately, not late Noldorin. It's on an inscription on Thrór's map in *Tolkien - Artist and Illustrator*. But, in that inscription, the one came before its noun and the other number replaced its noun entirely. Unfortunately, this gives us no insight into what the Sindarin mutation patterns would be.

[105] These are only the mutations that you need for numbers, but realize that there is a lot more to this chart, as you will see in chapter 5.

Letter	→	Result
The first letter of the number is the only one that changes.		
C	→	G
M	→	V
P	→	B
T	→	D

Here are some examples:

> **Aur gannui** Fourth morning
> **Aew veren neledh ar *enebaenui** Sixty third happy bird

3.5.3.1.1 Exercise

Translate the following phrases.

1. 13th **tirn** watcher _____
2. 29th **ruin** footprint _____
3. 88 **moe** hands _____
4. 10th **inc** idea _____
5. 57 **gynd** stones _____

3.5.4 Conversation Practice: Writing Dates

Elves use a different calendar than humans, and humans have used several different calendars over the years.

A year is an **în** or **idhrin**.[106] The word for an Age is **andran**.

Eldarin Calendar

The Elven calendar is based upon seasons instead of months.

---

[106] This is tricky to deal with, since most of the time-telling words in *The Lord of the Rings* are in Quenya, and Tolkien never bothered to provide many of the words in Sindarin. In Quenya, the cognate to **în** is **yén**, which is the word for the 144-year cycle. The words we have are from Noldorin, and back then, **în** and **yén** mean "year," as in one cycle of the earth around the sun. All of the Sindarin words for holidays throughout the year use **în** for one solar-cycle, so that's what I've elected to use here.

- ***Orvinui**[107] First Day - 1 day long
- **Ethuil** Spring - 54 days long
- **Laer** Summer - 72 days long
- **Iavas** Autumn - 54 days long
- **Enedhin** Mid-year - 3 days long
- **Firith** or **Narbeleth** Fading - 54 days long
- **Rhîw** Winter - 72 days long
- **Echuir** Stirring - 54 days long
- **Penninor** Last Day[108] - 1 day long

Leap Year:

- Every 12 years the **Enedhin** are doubled
- The last leap year of a 144-year cycle, the **Enedhin** are not doubled.

The King's Reckoning

This reckoning system begins with the founding of Númenor, and ends in Arnor and Gondor with the line of Kings.

- ***Orvinui** First Day - 1 day long
- **Narwain** January - 30 days long
- **Nínui** February - 30 days long
- **Gwaeron** March - 30 days long
- **Gwirith** April - 30 days long
- **Lothron** May - 30 days long
- **Nórui** June - 31 days long
- **Enedhin** Mid Year's Day - 1 day long
- **Cerveth** July - 31 days long
- **Urui** August - 30 days long

---

[107] Tolkien didn't give us the word in Sindarin. In Quenya, it's **Yestarë**, which means "first day;" this is a simple translation.

[108] Literally "full-year-day." It'd be **Penthinor** in the Woodelven/South Beleriand dialects.

- **Ivanneth** September - 30 days long
- **Narbeleth** October - 30 days long
- **Hithui** November - 30 days long
- **Girithron** December - 30 days long
- **Penninor** Last Day - 1 day long

Leap Year

- Every fourth year, there are two **enedhin** instead of one.
- The last leap year of the century has no days added.

Steward's Reckoning

With the end of Kings a new calendar began, created by Mardil. This lasted until the end of the War of the Ring.

- ***Orvinui** First Day - 1 day long
- **Narwain** January - 30 days long
- **Nínui** February - 30 days long
- **Gwaeron** March - 30 days long
- ***Tuilor**[109] Spring Day - 1 day long
- **Gwirith** April - 30 days long
- **Lothron** May - 30 days long
- **Nórui** June - 30 days long
- **Enedhin** Mid Year's Day - 1 day long
- **Cerveth** July - 30 days long
- **Urui** August - 30 days long
- **Ivanneth** September - 30 days long
- ***Iavor**[110] Harvest Day - 1 day long
- **Narbeleth** October - 30 days long
- **Hithui** November - 30 days long
- **Girithron** December - 30 days long
- **Penninor** Last Day - 1 day long

---

[109] Another word that I had to coin myself - it's just a translation of the Quenya word **Tuilérë** "Spring Day" into Sindarin.

[110] Yet another word that I had to invent to fill the gap. It's just a translation of the Quenya **Yáviérë** "Fruit Day" into Sindarin.

Leap Year

- Every fourth year, there are two **enedhin** instead of one.
- The last leap year of the century has no days added.

The New Reckoning

The beginning of the year was moved to the spring, like the Eldarin calendar. The change started on March 25th of the Steward's Reckoning, to celebrate the fall of Sauron.

- ***Orvinui** First Day - 1 day long
- **Gwirith** April - 30 days long
- **Lothron** May - 30 days long
- **Nórui** June - 30 days long
- **Cerveth** July - 30 days long
- **Urui** August - 30 days long
- **Ivanneth** September - 29 days long
- ***Corvor**[111] Ring Day - 1 day long
- **Enedhin** Mid Year's Day - 3 days long
- **Narbeleth** October - 30 days long
- **Hithui** November - 30 days long
- **Girithron** December - 30 days long
- **Narwain** January - 30 days long
- **Nínui** February - 30 days long
- **Gwaeron** March - 30 days long
- **Penninor** Last Day - 1 day long

Leap Year

- Every fourth year, ***Corvor** is doubled.
- For the last leap year of each century, no day is added.

---

[111] This is the only one that I had to reconstruct. There is no word for "ring" in Sindarin, so the cognate ***corf** was reconstructed by Ryszard Derdzinski in *Tyalië Tyelellieva* issue 14, page 25. Otherwise it's a simple translation, "ring-day."

We only know how to write dates thanks to the King's Letter,[112] meaning that this syntax comes from only one source.

Literal English	Sindarin
on the August 2nd: 2017	erin Urui dadui: 7102
2nd from the August: 2017	tadui uin Urui: 7102
2nd in August: 2017	tadui ned Urui: 7102

When working a date into a sentence, it's used similarily to an adverb, except that you don't mutate the beginning of the date.

For practice, try translating your birthday, using this format:[113]

I *oronnad nîn... "My birthday is..."

When dealing with a holiday or a day that does not belong to a month, present the date as such:

My birthday is on New Year's Day.
I *oronnad nîn erin *Orvinui.

Or

My birthday is New Year's Day.
I *oronnad nîn *Orvinui.

---

[112] Found in *Sauron Defeated*, pages 128-131.

[113] This webpage is a comparative calendar that allows you to find out what a Gregorian calendar date is in one of the Middle-earth calendars: https://realelvish.net/calendar/comparative/ The Elven and Númenorean calendars are in Quenya, because the Quenya terms are the most complete. To translate the month names and the holiday names, this article I wrote givens all of the known Sindarin and Quenya terms for time telling: https://realelvish.net/calendar/of-arda/

To make dates you will need mixed mutation to use on the months and seasons when following **erin** and **uin**. Here is a chart of mixed mutation for your reference.[114]

Letter	→	Result
Only the first letter of the month or season changes.		
C	→	G
P	→	B
RH	→	'R
T	→	D

You will also need stop mutation to use with the month or season following **ned**, which I've done for you. I haven't included the words starting with vowels, since vowels aren't affected by prestanneth.

in summer	ned Laer
in fading	neph Firith
in fading/October	ne Narbeleth
in winter	ne Thrîw
in January	ne Narwain
in February	ne Nínui
in March	ne Gwaeron
in April	ne Gwirith
in May	ned Lothron
in June	ne Nórui
in July	ne Cherveth
in November	ne Chithui
in December	ne Girithron

And you need to lenite the numbers when they follow the months or seasons. Use the lenition chart above. Now you just need to know the names of the months and seasons.

---

[114] Like the lenition chart, there is much, much more to this chart than you can see here. You will learn more about it in chapter 5.

Chapter 4: Plurals

Sindarin plurals are a lot like many English plurals used to be. We still see this in words like "foot-feet," "goose -geese," "mouse-mice." The vowels inside the words are what change.

But that's only the simple plurals! There also are the class plurals, one for all of something, and several for groups of people united by a common trait.

Then there are the relics, bits and pieces of plurals from systems that are no longer used, their forms forgotten except in a handful of words.

Sindarin plurals are more established and well-known than much of Sindarin grammar, because they are connected to the phonology of Sindarin, which we know a lot about. Tolkien also described them on more than one occasion, making this chapter one of the least likely to see a lot of dramatic changes in the future.

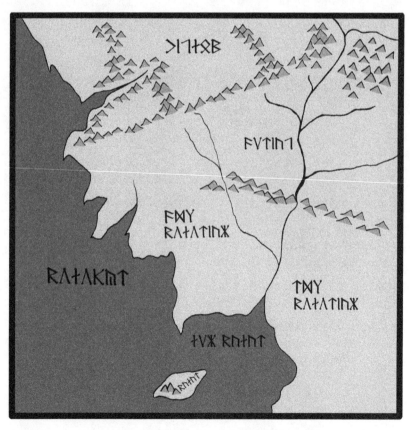

4.1 Simple Plurals

Let's go over what we already know about forming plurals.

4.1.1 What You Already Know

Not all words have distinct plural forms. For such words, you have to look at the context to figure out if they are singular or plural.

1. When a noun is plural, its adjectives are made plural along with it.

   iôn faug thirsty boy → **ŷn foeg** thirsty boys

2. "The" has a singular form, **i**, which causes vocalic mutation in the word it comes before, and a plural form **in**, which causes nasal mutation in the word it comes before. It must match the noun it is attached to.

   i orod the mountain → **in eryd** the mountains
   i goron the globe   → **i cheryn** the globes

3. Verbs must agree with their subjects. So, if a plural noun is the subject, you use the verb with the plural 3rd person pronoun (they) suffix attached, **-r**.

   Padrar. They are walking.
   Iñ gwind padrar. The maidens are walking.

4. If a singular noun is the subject, you use the verb with no pronoun suffixes attached.

   Padra. He, she, or it is walking.
   I 'wend padra. The maiden is walking.

4.1.2 How did the Sindarin plural come to be?[115]

In order to solve this mystery, we're going to go back into Sindarin's past, way back when forming the plural was as simple as adding an **-i** to the end of the word. But then that **-i** started to affect the vowels that came before it. The first change it caused was to the vowel closest to it, if and only if it was a short vowel.

Common Eldarin		Early Old Sindarin
A	→	E
E	→	I
I	→	No Change
O	→	U
U	→	No Change

4.1.2.1 I-Affection

The next set of changes to come are what we refer to as **I-Affection**. You will become very familiar with this set of changes. Again, **I** only affected the short vowels, but it affected all of the short vowels that came in the words before it.

Eldarin		Old Sindarin		Sindarin
A	→	E	→	No Change
E	→	No Change	→	No Change
I	→	No Change	→	No Change
O	→	Œ	→	E
U	→	Y	→	No Change

---

[115] The most thorough analysis of how Sindarin plurals came to be can be found in the article "Vowel Affection in Sindarin and Noldorin" by Bertrand Bellet. The article is available here: http://www.tol-kiendil.com/langues/english/i-lam_arth/vowel_affection_sindarin_noldorin There are a few other germane articles to list: "Noldorin Plurals in the 'Etymologies'" by Bertrand Bellet, available here: http://www.tol-kiendil.com/langues/english/i-lam_arth/noldorin_plurals_etymologies, "Attested Sindarin Plurals" by "Beregond" and Anders Stenström for "Mellonath Daeron," available here: http://www.forodrim.org/daeron/md_plur.html, "Sindarin - the Noble Tongue" by Helge Fauskanger, available here: http://folk.uib.no/hnohf/sindarin.htm#Heading11

This means, that in Sindarin, I-Affection looks like this:

Vowel		With I-Affection
A	→	E
O[116]	→	E
U	→	Y

4.1.2.2 Final Syllables

But the **-i** didn't stop there. Literally. It moved to attach itself to the back-end of the nearest vowel, making the following combinations with vowels that were already affected by I-Affection:

Old Sindarin		Old Sindarin	Sindarin
E	→	EI	EI and later AI
I	→	No Change	No Change
Y	→	YI	Y
Ī	→	No Change	No Change
Ō or O from ancient Ā	→	ŌI or OI	OE
Ū	→	ŪI	UI
EI	→	EĪ	I

Let's take some words through their plural pasts.

Tawar forest: tawari → taweri → teweri → teweir → tewair

Feren beech tree: fereni → ferini → ferin

Pirin winking flower: pirindi → pirind → pirin

Coron globe: coroni → coruni → cœryni → cœryin → cœryn → ceryn

Ulun monster: ulundi → ylyndi → ylyind → ylynd → ylyn

Naur fire: nāri → nóri → noir → noer

Ûn monster: úni → úin → uin

---

[116] Except for Ó or O from an ancient Ā.

Geil star: ŋgiljai → geljai[117] → gelī[118] → geīl → gîl

4.1.2.3 Exceptions and Special Cases

Not all of the vowels behave as you would expect them to. Due to the complications of history, there are some plurals that behave in a way not immediately obvious to us.

4.1.2.3.1 I, E, and Y

Because they are such similar sounds, if you end up with a IY, the I will become part of the Y. This happens with IO, especially. The same happens with IE.

> **iôn** son   → **ŷn** sons
> **iell** daughter → **ill** daughters

4.1.2.3.2 AU and AW

The Ó and O that come from ancient Ā became AU and AW in single-syllable words. Then, even if the AU or AW in a word doesn't come from an ancient /a:/, it is treated as though it does.

> Ancient AU: **taur** forest   → **toer** forests
> Ancient Long A: **naur** fire → **noer** fires

4.1.2.3.3 The Diphthong EI

When EI occurs in the last syllable of a word, it is pluralized as Ī.

When the diphthong EI occurs in the last syllable of a word, in later Sindarin, it becomes AI. This is the only source of AI in Sindarin, so it

---

[117] Why does the i>e? While /i/'s were affecting vowels, other vowels were doing the same thing to the sounds in front of them, like the vowel /a/. This sound shift is called A-Affection, but it's not a productive part of Sindarin grammar (at least, as far as we know).

[118] The vowels at the ends of words were lost at this point. That's why the ī ends up in the first syllable.

will be found only in the last syllable of a word. A final-syllable A changing into EI therefore is marked as archaic speech.

> **geil/gail** star → **gîl** stars
> **celeir/celair** brilliant → **celir** plural brilliant

4.1.2.3.4 A Special W/U

In archaic Sindarin, you'll find many words that end with **-w**, which later on end with a **-u**.[119] These **-w** come from ancient **-we** and **-wa**. The archaic **-w** will not change, but later on, after it's been **-u** for a while, it gets blended in with the other U's and treated the same way.

> Archaic: **malu** pale → **melu** pl. pale
> Later on: **malu** → **mely**

If you're wondering why the A of **malw** was only I-affected, that's because it's not in the final syllable. Archaic Sindarin had a bunch of consonants that could hold up a syllable on their own, without a vowel.[120] They were: W, L, R, and N. This was because of the loss of the vowels that used to follow them, and the reason that Quenya words almost always end in a vowel, but Sindarin words hardly ever do.

4.1.2.3.5 Final A from Ancient G

Only a handful of words fits this pattern. Those words are **fela** "cave," **madha** "mud," **nadha** "fetter," **thala** "stalwart, steady, firm," **thela** "spearpoint," and **tara** "tough, stiff."

---

[119] If the word ends in -DHU because it used to end in /ðβ/, then the U wouldn't be counted as part of this group, though it may be mistaken for it. There's only one word in this group that we know of, **budhu** "large insect." The vowel before the -DHU would be treated like a final vowel and the U would be unchanged, making the plural of **budhu** be **bydhu**.

[120] This is something that occurs in General American English too. You can hear it in words like "litt<u>le</u>," "mount<u>ain</u>," or "runn<u>er</u>."

When the **-i** was moving to the vowel before it, the ancient G had become a /ɣ/, and hadn't yet become the A. When the **-i** moved, it left behind a bit of palatalization on it, making the sound /ʒ/.[121] Then the /ʒ/ became an /i/ instead of an /ɑ/.

This means that the non-final vowel of these words would be treated like the final vowel, and the A at the end becomes an I.

Let's track the one known example of this from its ancient roots to Sindarin.

Plural of **Fela**: /pʰelgi/ → /ɸelɣi/ → /ɸilʒi/ → /ɸilʒ/ → /fili/

4.1.2.3.6 Lost Syllables[122]

Not all multi-syllable words remained multi-syllable words, which leads to some irregular plurals. In good dictionaries, any irregular plurals that we know of will be listed. Such irregular plurals will be reserved for older elves, marking their use as archaic.

This first section is a selection of words that lost their final syllables.

Sindarin	Old Sindarin	Sindarin Plural
ôl (dream)	olo	ely
êl (star)	elen	elin
fêr (beech tree)	feren	ferin
pêl (fenced field)	pele	peli

In this section, just the vowel of the last syllable was deleted, taking with it the **-i** that was attached as well, leaving only the I-Affection on the first vowel. Since I-Affection changes so few sounds, these are much harder to find. We can predict those that we have ancient roots for, but otherwise, we can't be certain.

---

[121] It should be noted that here I'm using ʒ (ezh) in accordance to my linguistic training in IPA, as a voiced palatal fricative. Don't confuse it with the ȝ (yogh) that Tolkien used as a voiced velar fricative, which he picked up from Old English orthography. Many fonts make these two symbols look the same.

[122] A good article on this is "Imparisyllabic nouns in Sindarin" by Bertrand Bellet, available here: http://www.tolkiendil.com/langues/english/i-lam_arth/imparisyllabic_nouns_sindarin

Sindarin	Common Eldarin	Sindarin Plural
fang (beard)	spanga	feng
parf (book)	parma	perf
narn (story)	narna	nern
orch (orc)	urku	erch

4.1.2.4 The Gondorians

Unlike the Elves, among whom there are people alive who remember when O used to be Ā, the Gondorians learn Sindarin almost entirely as a second language. Their version of the plurals is a lot simpler.

- All O's are changed to E's (as long as they aren't in a diphthong), even when they are in the final syllable.[123]
- A's that come from G's are treated like any other A, and the other vowels in those words are treated like the vowels in any other word.
- U is changed to I instead of Y, because Gondorians can't pronounce that vowel.

4.1.3 Plural Charts

Here are some handy plural charts to bookmark and use for quick referencing.

---

[123] This is mentioned in *The Letters of JRR Tolkien*, page 224 (letter #168)

4.1.3.1 Archaic Plural Chart

Non-final syllable (I-Affection)			Last syllable or Single syllable Words		
A	→	E	A/Â	→	EI
E	→	No Change	E/Ê	→	I/Î
I/Í	→	No Change	I/Í/Î	→	No Change
O	→	E	O/Ô	→	Y/Ŷ
O/Ó from Ā	→	No Change	O/Ó	→	OE
U	→	Y	U	→	Y
Ú	→	No Change	Ú/Û	→	UI
Y/Ý	→	No Change	Y/Ý/Ŷ	→	No Change
Diphthongs					
AE	→	No Change	AE	→	No Change
AU	→	No Change	AU	→	OE
AW	→	EW	AW	→	OE
EI	→	No Change	EI	→	Î (1 syllable)
					I (multi-syllable)
OE	→	No Change	OE	→	No Change
UI	→	No Change	UI	→	No Change
Miscellaneous					
			IE/IÊ	→	I/Î
			IO/IÔ	→	Y/Ŷ
			-U/-W	→	No Change
Non-final vowel treated like final vowel			-A from G	→	-I

4.1.3.1.1 Exercise

Make the following words plural, using the archaic plurals chart.

1. **ael** lake_____
2. **aur** day_____
3. **caul** affliction_____

4. **caw** top _____
5. **ceir** ship _____
6. **coth** enemy _____
7. **firion** mortal man_____
8. **firieth** mortal woman _____
9. **lim** fish_____
10. **lhô** marsh_____
11. **nûr** race_____
12. **pen** person _____
13. **rammas** great wall _____
14. **sarn** rock _____
15. **tawar** forest _____
16. **tulus** poplar tree _____
17. **úthaes** temptation _____
18. **elw** blue_____
19. **forgam** right-handed _____
20. **iphant** old _____
21. **narw** red_____
22. **sauthannen** drained _____
23. **tara** tough _____

4.1.3.2 Elven Plural Chart

Non-final syllable (I-Affection)			Last syllable or Single Syllable Words		
A	→	E	A/Â	→	AI
E	→	No Change	E/Ê	→	I/Î
I/Í	→	No Change	I/Í/Î	→	No Change
O	→	E	O/Ô	→	Y/Ŷ
O/Ó from Ā	→	No Change	O/Ó	→	OE
U	→	Y	U	→	Y
Ú	→	No Change	Ú/Û	→	UI
Y/Ý	→	No Change	Y/Ý/Ŷ	→	No Change
Diphthongs					
AE	→	No Change	AE	→	No Change
AU	→	No Change	AU	→	OE
AW	→	EW	AW	→	OE
EI	→	No Change	AI from EI	→	Î (1 syllable)
					I (multi-syllable)
OE	→	No Change	OE	→	No Change
UI	→	No Change	UI	→	No Change
Miscellaneous					
			IE/IÊ	→	I/Î
			IO/IÔ	→	Y/Ŷ
Non-final vowel treated like final vowel			-A from G	→	-I

4.1.3.2.1 Exercise

Make the following words plural, using the Elven plurals chart.

1. **ael** lake_____
2. **aur** day_____
3. **caul** affliction_____
4. **caw** top _____
5. **cair** ship _____

6. **coth** enemy _____

7. **firion** mortal man_____

8. **firieth** mortal woman _____

9. **lim** fish_____

10. **lhô** marsh _____

11. **nûr** race_____

12. **pen** person _____

13. **rammas** great wall _____

14. **sarn** rock _____

15. **tawar** forest _____

16. **tulus** poplar tree _____

17. **úthaes** temptation _____

18. **elu** blue _____

19. **forgam** right-handed _____

20. **iphant** old _____

21. **naru** red _____

22. **sauthannen** drained _____

23. **tara** tough _____

4.1.3.3 Gondorian Plural Chart

Non-final syllable (I-Affec-tion)			Final Syllable or Single-syllable Words		
A	→	E	A/Â	→	AI
E	→	No Change	E/Ê	→	I/Î
I/Í	→	No Change	I/Í/Î	→	No Change
O/Ó	→	E/É	O/Ô	→	E/Ê
U	→	I	U	→	I
Ú	→	No Change	Ú/Û	→	UI
Diphthongs					
AE	→	No Change	AE	→	No Change
AU	→	No Change	AU	→	OE
AW	→	EW	AW	→	OE
EI	→	No Change	AI	→	I/Î
OE	→	No Change	OE	→	No Change
UI	→	No Change	UI	→	No Change
Miscellaneous					
			IE/IÊ	→	I/Î

4.1.3.3.1 Exercise

Make the following words plural, using the Gondorian plurals chart.

1. **ael** lake_____
2. **aur** day_____
3. **caul** affliction_____
4. **caw** top _____
5. **cair** ship _____
6. **coth** enemy _____
7. **fîrion** mortal man_____
8. **fîrieth** mortal woman _____
9. **lim** fish_____
10. **lhô** marsh_____
11. **nûr** race_____
12. **pen** person _____
13. **rammas** great wall _____

14. **sarn** rock _____
15. **tawar** forest _____
16. **tulus** poplar tree _____
17. **úthaes** temptation _____
18. **elu** blue _____
19. **forgam** right-handed _____
20. **iphant** old _____
21. **naru** red _____
22. **sauthannen** drained _____
23. **tara** tough _____

4.1.4 Conversation Practice: Explain "Why"

First, let's ask, "Why?"

- **Am man?** "For what?"
- **O man?** "From what?"
- **Be van?** "In accordance to what?"
- **Man i inn gîn?** "What is your intent?" (informal)
- **Man i inn lîn?** "What is your intent?" (polite)
- **Man i inn dhîn?** "What is (plural) your intent?"

There is no word for "because," but we do have two idioms provided for us by Tolkien. They are:

- **Guren bed enni, ...** "My **gûr** says to me, ..."[124]
- **Inn dha v'im.** "I have/had a good mind to do so." (Literally, "There is/was an **inn** in myself.")[125]

On the surface, **inn** and **gûr** mean almost the same thing. You can translate both as "heart." But there are subtle differences. Your **inn** is your intellect, your will, your mind, where your reason resides. Your **gûr** is your conscience, your inner voice, your intuition. So, when an elf says that their **gûr** is telling them something, that means that they

---

[124] You can find this phrase in *Vinyar Tengwar* issue 41, page 11.
[125] This phrase is listed in *Parma Eldalamberon* issue 22, page 165

were letting their conscience be their guide. If the elf tells you that there was an **inn** in them, that means that it was their resolve to do it.

And a few extra phrases to fill the gaps:

- **Anírassen cared.** "I wanted to do it."
- ***Law anírassen cared.** "I didn't want to do it."
- **Boe.** "Had to." (It is/was necessary.)[126]
- **Boe annin.** "I had to." (It is/was necessary to me.)
- ***Law moe.** "Didn't have to." (It isn't/wasn't necessary.)
- ***Law moe annin.** "I didn't have to." (It isn't/wasn't necessary to me.)

---

[126] **Boe** is an impersonal verb. For more information, review 3.4.3.

4.2 Class Plurals

These plurals are made through suffixes on the words, and they have the interesting property of being able to turn an adjective into a noun.

4.2.1 Vowel Reduction

But first a quick note about vowel length. When a word gets more syllables, its vowels and some diphthongs will shorten. We will call this "Vowel Reduction," and you will see it applied a lot in the future.

There are two types of vowels: those that reduce from circumflex to regular length, and those that reduce to half length (acute accent), which means they can be reduced more than once.

Long Vowel	→	Shortened Vowel
Vowels that Reduce Completely		
AU	→	O
AW	→	O
Â	→	A
Ê	→	E
Í	→	I
Ô	→	O
Ú	→	U
Ý	→	Y
Vowels that Reduce Partially		
AI/EI	→	Í
AI/EI	→	EI
Î	→	Í
Û	→	Ú
Ŷ	→	Ý

west + man: dûn + adan	= Dúnadan "Westman"
thought + all: naw + -ath	= nawath "all thoughts"
thought + group: naw + -rim	= norim "Thought-people"

AW becomes O only at the end of a word, and only if a suffix beginning with a consonant is added.

AI/EI only become Í if the word is a monosyllable whose ancient root vowel was an I. Gondorians would be ignorant of such words, and they'd treat all AI words the same way. For the rest of the AI/EI, they'd stay/become EI. Because the EI→AI change happened only in the final syllable, the conditions for the EI→AI change wouldn't exist anymore.

4.2.2 Becoming Intervocalic

You are going to get a LOT of use out of this list. When I refer to this set of changes in the future, I'll call it "becoming Intervocalic." "Intervocalic" is a linguistic term meaning "between two vowels or diphthongs."

When you add a suffix or another word to the end of a word, one that starts with a vowel, the consonants at the end will change, because sounds between vowels have different histories.

- In single-syllable words, the AI/EI that comes from an ancient I would mean that an -I- would be added to the end of the word before the suffix or word is added. Ignore this rule if the suffix or word starts with an I.
- -A, that comes from an ancient G, becomes an -I-, only if it follows an L or R. For the other two, the A'd be deleted. If the suffix or word being added begins with an I, the -A is simply deleted. There are only a handful of such words and they are: **fela** "cave," **madha** "mud," **nadha** "fetter," **thala** "stalwart, steady, firm," **thela** "spearpoint," and **tara** "tough, stiff."
- -U, that was a -W, goes back to being a -W-.
- -M, -MB, -MM, and -MP become -MM-. For an -M to exist at the end of a word in Sindarin it had to have been long in its past, or it would have become a V or W.
- -NN, -ND, -NT, and -N (that was an -NN, -ND, or -NT) become -NN-. Single Ns that were never long don't change.
- -NC becomes -NG-.
- -S or -SS become -SS-. For an -S to exist at the end of a word in Sindarin it had to have been long in its past, or it would have disappeared completely.
- -LL, -LT, or -L (that was an -LL or -LT) become -LL-. Single Ls that were never long don't change.

- -F becomes -V-. This more has to do with spelling conventions, because -F is pronounced as a V anyways, as you'll recall from the pronunciation lessons.
- -OL or -EL that used to be syllabic Ls would go back to being -L-.[127]
- -OR that used to be a syllabic R would go back to being -R-.

> mortal + female: feir + -eth = firieth
>
> stalwart + male: thala + -on = thalion "Hero"
>
> pale blue + female: elu + -eth = elweth "Blueone"
>
> tongue + my: lam + -en = lammen "my tongue"
>
> hobbit + class plural: perian + -ath = periannath "all hobbits"
>
> jaw + class plural: anc + -ath = angath "all jaws"
>
> hole + class plural: gas + -ath = gassath "all holes"
>
> gold + tree: malt + orn = Mallorn "Goldtree"
>
> branch + long: golf + and = Golvan "Longbranch"
>
> abundant + abstract nominalizer: ovor + -as = ovras "heap, crowd"

4.2.3 -ath, All of the Things

A "class plural," sometimes called a "collective plural" is for **all of** something. "All hobbits," "all stars," "all books," that's what this plural is used for. It's made by adding **-ath** to the end of a word. Use it on nouns only. If an adjective is following a class plural noun, the adjective uses its regular plural form. When you add the class plural suffix to an adjective, it becomes a noun meaning "all of the __ ones/things."

To form the class plural, add **-ath** to the end of the word. This will make the end of the word intervocalic.

---

[127] The syllabic consonants would be unknown to Gondorians.

Use plural "the," plural adjectives, and 3rd person plural verbs with this plural form.

Geil star   → **Giliath** All of the stars in the sky
Bein beautiful   → **Beinath** All of the beautiful ones
Lachen flame-eyed → **Lachennath** All of the flame-eyed ones
Inu feminine   → **Inwath** All of the feminine ones
Thela spearpoint → **Theliath** All of the spearpoints
Aeglos icicle   → **Aeglossath** All of the icicles
Magol sword, from the older word **Magl** → **Maglath** All swords
Adan human   → **Adanath** All humans

4.2.3.1 Exercise

Turn the following nouns and adjectives into **-ath** plurals, and give their meanings in English.

1. **Gwaur** dirty _____
2. **Nawag** Dwarf_____
3. **Bass** bread_____
4. **Naru** red _____
5. **Loth** flower _____

4.2.4 A Group or Tribe of People

There are several of these plurals, all with slightly different meanings. Two of them are grammatically treated like plurals, and the other is more like a common element in compound-words that function as names for groups of people. These plurals are only plurals in a loose sense, since they can't be used for inanimate objects and often end up being the name given or taken by a group.

4.2.4.1 -rim, a Group of People

This is for naming a group of people characterized by whatever you add **-rim** to, whether it's a noun or adjective. When you have a **-rim** noun, its adjective is a normal plural. Use plural "the" with this plural form as well.

If the word ends in any of the following, the suffix and the ends of the words interact differently:

- -A from ancient G deletes.
- -L, then **-lim** is suffixed on instead of **-rim.**
- -LL or -LT, the extra -L or -T are deleted, and **-lim** is suffixed on instead of **-rim.**
- -M, -MM, -MB, or -MP, when **-rim** is added they become -MB-.
- -NN, -ND, -NT, or -N (derived from an -NN, -ND, or -NT), when **-rim** is added they become -ND-.
- -N **not** derived from -NN, -ND, or -NT, when **-rim** is added the -N becomes -DH-.[128]
- -NC, when **-rim** is added it becomes -NG-.
- -S, -SS, or -ST, when **-rim** is added they become -TH-.
- -F, when **-rim** is added -F becomes -V-.[129]
- -W (not in AW), when **-rim** is added, the -W is deleted.

> **Fael** generous → **Faellim** a group of generous people
> **Belt** strong → **Bellim** a group of strong people
> **Randir** wanderer → **Randirrim** A group of wanderers
> **Nost** family → **Nothrim** a group of people from the same family

4.2.4.1.1 Exercise

Turn the following nouns and adjectives into **-rim** plurals, and give their meanings in English.

1. **Gwaur** dirty _____
2. **Nawag** Dwarf_____
3. **Bass** bread_____
4. **Naru** red _____

[128] Except in Doriath. In Doriath, the -N would remain unchanged.
[129] This isn't because the pronunciation changes - this is just to clearly communicate in the orthography what it sounds like.

5. **Loth** flower _____

4.2.4.2 -hoth, The Host of Evil

Used only for military regiments of mistrusted and feared things, it is an old equivalent to **-rim**. For some unknown reason, when dealing with hated or feared creatures the AU diphthong *isn't reduced.*

When it's following a word ending in F/V, PH, DH, TH, S, SS, ST, or CH, only **-oth** is suffixed. Make certain that a single -S at the end of a word is doubled when it has vowels on either side of it. Use plural "the" with this plural form.

> **Gaur** werewolf → **Gaurhoth** a host or regiment of werewolves
> **Dorn** dwarf → **Dornhoth** a host or regiment of dwarves
> **Glam** noisy speech → **Glamhoth** a noisy host
> **Loss** snow → **Lossoth** a host or regiment of snow-people

4.2.4.2.1 Exercise

Turn the following nouns and adjectives into **-hoth** plurals, and give their meanings in English.

1. **Gwaur** dirty _____
2. **Nawag** Dwarf_____
3. **Bass** bread_____
4. **Agarwaen** bloodstained_____
   _____
5. **Îf** cliff_____

4.2.4.3 Gwaith, a Fellowship

A **gwaith** is a group of people, but a more close, more interwoven group of people than is implied by **-rim**. This is what I answer when people ask for a translation of "The Fellowship of the Ring": **I 'Waith-e-*Gorf**. This word can stand on its own easily, but you can also use it as a suffix. Therefore, one could say ***Corvwaith** for "Ring-Fellowship" as well.

The word **gwaith** is singular, therefore the singular "the," singular adjectives, and 3rd person singular verbs should be used with it.

Unlike **-rim** and **-ath**, this is a new compound,[130] so there isn't much in the way of complex mutations to worry about. In new compounds, you just use vocalic mutation on the second element of the compound. According to vocalic mutation, **gwaith** becomes **waith**.

If the word ends in a W, the double-W would reduce to a single W.

In ***Corvwaith**, I changed the spelling of *corf to more closely match the pronunciation, because some people reading the word may not be familiar as you are with the peculiarities of Sindarin Latin orthography.

> **Elu Thingol** → **Eluwaith** followers of Elu Thingol
> **Tawar** forest → **Tawarwaith** Forest Folk
> **Taw** wool → **Tawaith** Wool Folk

4.2.4.3.1 Exercise

Make the following words or names into names for fellowships.

1.   **Glaewen** Salvemaid_____
2.   **Cirion** Sailor_____
3.   **Îf** Cliff_____
4.   **Maeas** Dough_____
5.   **Ael** Lake_____

4.2.5 Lost Plurals

Sindarin has a colorful past with plurals. It's had many of them, and most were discarded and only remembered in a few old words. You won't be tested on these, but it's useful to keep a lookout for these, so you don't end up accidentally making a plural form when there's already an irregular plural of it.

---

[130] This is a compound formed in 2nd and 3rd Age Sindarin.

4.2.5.1 -in Plurals

In a handful of words, you'll find **-in** used as a plural suffix. Tolkien doesn't refer to it as a productive morpheme[131] in Sindarin. It most likely is a carryover from the Doriathrin language, which he abandoned in favor of Sindarin being spoken by the Sindar.

> **Cónin** "princes," plural of **Caun**
> **Drúin** "Woodwoses," plural of **Drû**

4.2.5.2 Noldorin Plural, -ir

It's probably a relative of the plural suffix **-r** in Quenya. We don't know much about it, except that it only appears in *Parma Eldalamberon* issue 17 and that it's a plural form. It may be a remnant of the Early Noldorin plural suffix **-ir**.[132] Most examples that we have of it are in the listing of races, but it also appears combined with several pronoun suffixes. From the lists of races provided, we know that this form is used amongst Exilic-Sindarin speakers because the names of the races are from the Noldor's point of view, modeled off of the Quenya names for them.

> **Egel** Exile, from the older word **Egl** → **Eglir** Exiles
> **Thend** Sindarin Elf → **Thennir** Sindarin Elves

4.2.5.3 Duals, -t and -u

A close relative of the Quenya dual suffixes, these suffixes had fallen out of usage by the time we get to Sindarin. They're only found in old words for pairs of things.

> **Galadhad** "two trees" (from ancient **Galadat**)
> **Hent** "a pair of eyes" (from ancient **Hent**)
> **Lhaw** "a pair of ears" (from ancient **Slasu**)

---

[131] A productive morpheme is one that is being used to make new words and phrases in the language, like the plural suffix -s in English. A non-productive morpheme would be one that isn't used to make new words or phrases anymore, like the plural suffix -en from "children."

[132] *Parma Eldalamberon* issue 13 page 123

4.2.5.4 Using Diminutives for the Singular

This is for denoting one of a word usually considered plural. The diminutive suffixes have taken a variety of forms over the years, and we have examples of **-od, -ig,** and **-og** being used this way.

> **Lhewig** "an ear" from **Lhaw** "a pair of ears"
> **Gwanunig** "a twin" from **Gwanûn** "a pair of twins"
> **Glamog** "an orc" from **Glamhoth** "a noisy horde"
> **Filigod** "a small bird" from **Filig** "Bird" (an ambiguous word that could be singular or plural)

4.2.6 Conversation Practice: Need

We've already covered this partially. You know how to talk about needing to do something:

- **Boe angin?** "Do you need to?" (informal)
- **Boe anlen?** "Do you need to?" (polite)
- **Boe anden?** "Do (plural) you need to?"
- **Boe annin ...** "I need to..." (fill the blank with a gerund)

Here's how to talk about needing a specific object:

- **Sevig maur ...?** "Do you have need of ..." (informal)
- **Sevil maur ...?** "Do you have need of ..." (polite)
- **Sevidh maur ...?** "Do (plural) you have need of ..."
- **Sevin maur ...** "I have need of..."

Here's how to say that something needs to happen, but it isn't known/isn't important who does it.

- **Boe ...** "It is necessary to ..." (use a gerund to fill in the blank)
- **Boe i...** "It is necessary that ..." (fill the blank with a complete sentence)

Chapter 5: Prestanneth

Prestanneth is the Sindarin word for "mutation" because it refers to the ways that words affect each other that make this language beautiful. It comes from the verb **presta**, which means "to change, affect, disturb, or trouble."

There are three types of words, beginning with B, D, and G, that change differently from how you'd expect. In these, the B comes from MB; the D comes from ND; and the G comes from NG. To find out what type of word a B, D, or G word is, you need to look at the ancient root it came from. In the excercises, I'll mark these with a (n) or (m) before the word.

To figure out if a word is one of these, look up words using *The Etymologies*, *Vinyar Tengwar* issues 45 and 46, and *Parma Eldalamberon* issue 17 if you can get them. There isn't a wordlist online or printed for Sindarin that is both up-to-date and includes the etymological roots that Tolkien built the words from, so you need to get used to hunting down these words yourself. Here are the best secondary sources for finding out this information.

- *Parviphith Edhellen*[133] by **Helge Fauskanger** This one is great for Neo-Sindarin translators. It includes the plurals and vocalic and nasal mutations for the words, and it is an English-to-Sindarin dictionary. Unfortunately, it doesn't cite the sources of the words. Also there's a few unmarked reconstructions hiding in there, so use with caution. It hasn't been updated since 2007. Check the words you find in it against other dictionaries.

---

[133] http://www.uib.no/people/hnohf/parviphith.doc

- *Hiswelókë's Sindarin Dictionary[134]* by **Didier Willis** It cites the sources of all of its words, includes suggested Sindarinization of late Noldorin words, but is lacking words from *Parma Eldalamberon* issue #17 or any later 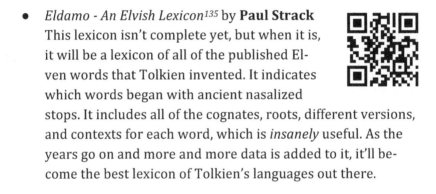 publications and doesn't list the roots. It hasn't been updated since 2008. It remains one of the most thorough Sindarin dictionaries available.

- *Eldamo - An Elvish Lexicon[135]* by **Paul Strack** This lexicon isn't complete yet, but when it is, it will be a lexicon of all of the published Elven words that Tolkien invented. It indicates which words began with ancient nasalized stops. It includes all of the cognates, roots, different versions, and contexts for each word, which is *insanely* useful. As the years go on and more and more data is added to it, it'll become the best lexicon of Tolkien's languages out there.

- *Parf Edhellen[136]* I suggest using a combination of these dictionaries. The Parf Edhellen website is a work in progress that combines all of the best Tolkien-language dictionaries into 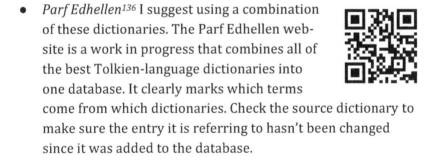 one database. It clearly marks which terms come from which dictionaries. Check the source dictionary to make sure the entry it is referring to hasn't been changed since it was added to the database.

There are many types of mutation to learn because there are many different types of sounds that a word can end in. The etymological history of the word is important when using mutation because it comes from the ancient words being blended together, not the later words. When

---

[134] https://www.jrrvf.com/hisweloke/sindar/online/
[135] http://eldamo.org/
[136] https://www.elfdict.com/

it comes to the rules for Prestanneth in the later Sindarin (as in, after the Sun and Moon are in the sky), they've become arbitrary rules to memorize. A Gondorian noble in the Third Age, therefore, is likely to confuse the Special Cases with the more common forms or ignore one type of mutation to replace it with one they use more often. [137]

5.1 Common Mutations

These are the mutations that you will have to use the most often that I recommend memorizing.

By now you've probably noticed that Prestanneth doesn't affect vowels. Instead, only the beginnings and ends of words are affected. Mutation appearswhen dealing with words that get used a lot in sequence, like prepositions, articles, and conjunctions.

5.1.1 Vowel Reduction with Prefixes

Since we are now tackling prefixes, we should learn about the slightly different vowel reduction used with them first.

Prefixes become part of the word and figure into the stress patterns of the words they are attached to. This sets them apart from prepositions and other words that cause mutation. Because they become part of the word they are attached to, we're adding syllables to the words. With added syllables comes vowel reduction.

As with the simple plural, we will break these changes down to Final and Non-Final vowels/diphthongs.

If a word has more than one syllable, the last syllable will not have a long vowel in it. There are a few exceptions in some compound words,

---

[137] This chapter is largely thanks to the scholarship of those who came before me. Articles to check out are: "Sindarin - the Noble Tongue" by Helge Fauskanger http://folk.uib.no/hnohf/sindarin.htm#mutations and "Mutations in Sindarin" by Thorsten Renk http://www.science-and-fiction.org/elvish/mutations.html Long Mixed, DH, and H Mutations are the only ones different from the other secondary sources. Long Mixed Mutation is an update of Long Nasal Mutation, and DH and H mutations were introduced in *Parma Eldalamberon* issue 17, pages 41, 145, and 147. You can see Tolkien's partial lists of Prestanneth there and in *The War of the Jewels* - The Quendi and Eldar.

which are presumed to have been made after this sound-shift swept through Sindarin.

This means if you have a single-syllable word with a long vowel, that vowel is shortened all the way down, no matter what vowel it was.

The only diphthong that changes is AW/AU. It becomes an O.

If a word has more than one syllable, then the vowels in it have already been reduced. All there would be left is a long I, O, U, or Y. Therefore, there is nothing left for you to reduce!

Ran "to wander" + dîr "man"	= Rand**i**r "wanderer"
Al- "not" + **taw** "woolen"	= Al-d**o** "not woolen"
Pen- "-less" + ta**ur** "king"	= Pen-d**or** "kingless"
Al- "not" + **í**r**ui** "desirable"	= Al-**í**r**ui** "not desirable"

5.1.2 Lenition/Vocalic Mutation

The most often needed type of mutation is called "Soft Mutation" or "Vocalic Mutation." When used for grammatical, not phonetic uses, it is called "Lenition."

These are the grammatical structures that call for Lenition:[138]

1. The direct object of a sentence.
2. An adjective modifying a noun.
3. An adjective being modified by an adverb.
4. An adverb modifying an adjective that is modifying a noun.
5. An adverb modifying a verb.
6. The words of a phrase repeated so often that it has become an idiom.
7. A preposition at the head of a prepositional phrase that is modifying a noun

These words trigger Vocalic Mutation.

---

[138] Of these, 3 and 4 are guesses, but they are educated guesses.

1. The word following singular "the" or "that/who/which," **i**.
2. The word following the conjunction **a** "and."
3. The word following the conjunction **ach** "but."
4. The word following one of the helping verbs, ***ce** or ***law**.
5. The word following a preposition or prefix that ends in a vowel or consonants that don't have a special mutation system of their own.

5.1.2.1 Prepositions

The way prepositions are used in Sindarin is straightforward. They go at the beginning of their phrase. A prepositional phrase can be used to modify verbs as though it was an adverb, or nouns as though it was an adjective.

The following prepositions cause vocalic mutation on the following word.

- **adel** Behind
- ***aden** Until
- **am** Up/Upon
- **be** According to
- **mi** In/between[139]
- **n(a)** To/Towards/At, when referencing motion towards a point in time or space. This preposition loses its vowel if the next word starts with a vowel.
- **nef** On this side of
- **nu** Beneath/under
- **po** On[140]
- **sui** As/like
- **trî** Through/throughout

---

[139] This word has only been attested as **vi**, only found in positions where it would be lenited.

[140] This word has only been attested as **bo**, and found in a position where it would be lenited.

5.1.2.2 Preposition Prefixes

When prepositions are turned into prefixes they go directly onto the noun and they turn the noun into an adjective. On a verb they behave like an adverb prefix.

- **ab-** After
- **ath-** On both sides/across
- **athra-** Across
- **di-** Beneath/under/sub
- **os-** Around/about
- **pen-** Without/-less
- **tre-** Through

5.1.2.3 Adverb Prefixes

These modify the verbs that they are attached to.

- **al-** no/not[141]
- **ath-** Easily
- **(n)dae-** horribly, dreadfully, ghastly
- **dý-** Mistakenly
- **go-** Together
- **oth-** Badly/Improperly
- **ro-** most/-est[142]
- **rhae-** Awkwardly
- **rhu-** Wickedly/Evily
- **thu-** Badly/Incorrectly
- **tre-** Thoroughly
- **ú-** Cannot
- **ui-** Ever/Always

---

[141] For nouns and adjectives only
[142] For adjectives only

5.1.2.4 The Vocalic Mutation Chart

Letter	→	Result	Example
		Voiceless Stops	
C	→	G	**i gerin** the mound
P	→	B	**i berian** the hobbit
T	→	D	**i dalan** the tree-house
		Voiced Stops	
B	→	V	**i vrith** the gravel
D	→	DH	**i dhîn** the silence
G[143]	→	'	**i 'lân** the hem
		Fricatives	
H	→	CH	**i cham** the chair
S	→	H	**i higil** the necklace
		Nasal	
M[144]	→	V	**i virian** the coin
		Voiceless Approximants	
HW	→	CHW	**i chwand** the sponge
LH	→	THL	**i thlewig** the ear
RH	→	THR	**i thross** the whisper
		Ancient Nasal-Stops	
B	→	M	**i mauglir** the tyrant
D	→	N	**i nîr** the man
G	→	Ñ	**i ñolovir** the Silmaril

5.1.2.4.1 Exercise

Mutate the following words with Vocalic Mutation.

1. **Balan** Vala _____
2. **(m)baur** need _____
3. **brethil** birch_____
4. **crist** sword_____

---

[143] The G used to mutate to GH /ɣ/ but this sound was lost.

[144] In archaic speech as well as the dialect spoken in Doriath, M would mutate to MH/Ṽ instead of V.

5. **cugu** dove _____
6. **(n)dôr** land _____
7. **dû** darkness_____
8. **galenas** pipeweed_____
9. **(n)gail** star_____
10. **glad** wood_____
11. **groth** tunnel _____
12. **gwass** stain _____
13. **haru** wound_____
14. **iaeth** neck_____
15. **lhewig** ear _____
16. **minuial** daybreak _____
17. **paur** fist_____
18. **prestad** change_____
19. **rhach** curse _____
20. **solch** root _____
21. **trenarn** story_____
22. **tum** valley_____
23. **bell** strong _____
24. **doll** dark _____
25. **drammen** hewn _____
26. **gael** glimmering _____
27. **gwathui** shadowy _____
28. **hae** distant _____
29. **hwiniol** fantastic _____
30. **taer** straight _____
31. **dadben** downwards _____
32. **mae** well _____
33. **palan** afar _____
34. **mi** in _____
35. **ben** according to the _____

5.1.3 Nasal Mutation

Other than the following prepositions and affixes, Nasal mutation is most commonly used on the verbs following oblique pronouns and the plural "the" - **in**.

5.1.3.1 Prepositions

These prepositions cause Nasal mutation because they end with N.

- **athan** Beyond
- **(n)dan** Against
- **nan** With/Including/Possessing

5.1.3.2 Plural "The" Prepositions

These prepositions combine with the plural "the," and thus use Nasal Mutation. The rest of the prepositions do not combine with "the."

- **anin** To/For the[145]
- **ben** According to the
- **in-** Of the
- **erin** Over/upon the
- **min** In/between the
- **nuin** Under the
- **suin** As/like the
- **uin** From the

5.1.3.3 The Nasal Mutation Chart[146]

Nasal Mutation affects the beginnings AND ends of words. When using this chart, pay attention to the -N and when it vanishes.

---

[145] In Gondor **anin** is said **'nin**. Write it with an apostrophe to distinguish it from the pronoun **nin**.

[146] Tolkien himself described Nasal mutation, at least partially, in *Parma Elda-lamberon* issue 17 page 147.

IN	→	Result	Example
		Voiceless Stops	
IN+C	→	I CH	**i cherin** the mounds
IN+P	→	I PH	**i pheriain** the hobbits
IN+T	→	I TH	**i thelain** the tree-houses
		Voiced Stops	
IN+B	→	I M	**i maid** the paths
IN+D	→	I N	**i naith** the abysses
IN+DR	→	IN DR	**in droeg** the wolves
IN+G	→	I Ñ	**i ñelaidh** the trees
IN+GL	→	IÑ GL	**iñ glain** the hems
IN+GR	→	IÑ GR	**iñ groe** the bears
IN+GW	→	IÑ GW	**iñ gwoen** the geese
		Fricatives	
IN+F	→	I F	**i felais** the shores
IN+H	→	I CH	**i chebaid** the shoes
IN+S	→	I S	**i sigil** the necklaces
IN+TH	→	I TH	**i thaim** the halls
		Nasals	
IN+M	→	I M	**i miriain** the coins
IN+N	→	I N	**i ningloer** the golden water lilies
		Voiceless Approximants	
IN+HW	→	IN 'W	**in 'wand** the sponges
IN+LH	→	ITH L	**ith law** the ears
IN+RH	→	ITH R	**ith ryss** the whispers
		Voiced Approximants	
IN+L	→	I L	**i laiss** the leaves
IN+R[147]	→	IDH R	**idh raef** the nets
		Ancient Nasal-Stops	
IN+B	→	I MB	**i mboeglir** the tyrants
IN+D	→	I ND	**i ndîr** the men
IN+G	→	I ÑG	**i ñgelevir** the Silmarilli

---

[147] Doriathren-Sindarin mutation is different for that particular set. In that dialect, the -N remains unchanged.

Gondorians would likely ignore **N+LH=TH L** and **N+RH=TH R**, leaving them as **N LH** and **N RH** respectively.[148]

5.1.3.3.1 Exercise

Mutate the following words with Nasal Mutation, using the plural "the."

1. **Balan** Vala _____
2. **(m)baur** need _____
3. **brethil** birch_____
4. **crist** sword _____
5. **cugu** dove_____
6. **(n)dôr** land_____
7. **dû** darkness _____
8. **galenas** pipeweed _____
9. **(n)gail** star _____
10. **glad** wood _____
11. **groth** tunnel   _____
12. **gwass** stain _____
13. **haru** wound _____
14. **iaeth** neck _____
15. **lach** flame _____
16. **lhewig** ear _____
17. **minuial** daybreak_____
18. **noss** family _____
19. **paur** fist_____
20. **prestas** change_____
21. **rhach** curse_____
22. **solch** root_____
23. **tham** hall _____
24. **trenarn** story _____
25. **tum** valley

5.1.4 Mixed Mutation

Mixed Mutation is a combination between Nasal and Vocalic Mutation. It's only used with the singular "the" prepositions. Of the "the"-prepositions, only **en** "of the" can lose its -N. The others all keep their -Ns.

- **en-** Of the

---

[148] *Parma Eldalamberon* issue 17, page 147

EN	→	Result	Example
Voiceless Stops			
EN+C	→	E-G	**e-gerin** of the mound
EN+P	→	E-B	**e-berian** of the hobbit
EN+T	→	E-D	**e-dalath** of the tree-house
EN+TR	→	EN-DR	**en-Drann** of the Shire
Voiced Stops			
EN+B	→	E-B	**e-bôr** of the vassal
EN+D	→	E-D	**e-dath** of the abyss
EN+DR	→	EN-DR	**en-draug** of the wolf
EN+G	→	E-G	**e-galadh** of the tree
EN+GL	→	EÑ-GL	**eñ-glân** of the hem
EN+GR	→	EÑ-GR	**eñ-graw** of the bear
EN+GW	→	EÑ-GW	**eñ-gwaun** of the goose
Fricatives			
EN+H	→	E-CH	**e-chabar** of the shoe
EN+S	→	E-H	**e-higil** of the necklace
EN+TH	→	E-TH	**e-tham** of the hall
Nasals			
EN+M	→	E-M	**e-mirian** of the coin
Voiceless Approximants			
EN+HW	→	E-'W	**e-'wand** of the sponge
EN+LH	→	E-'L	**e-'lewig** of the ear
EN+RH	→	E-'R	**e-'ross** of the whisper
Voiced Approximants			
EN+L	→	E-L	**e-lass** of the leaf
EN+R[149]	→	EDH-R	**edh-raef** of the net
Ancient Nasal-Stops			
EN+B	→	E-MB	**e-mbauglir** of the tyrant
EN+D	→	E-ND	**e-ndîr** of the man
EN+G	→	E-ÑG	**e-ñgolovir** of the Silmaril

---

[149] Doriathren-Sindarin mutation is different for this set as well. In that dialect, the -N remains unchanged.

For the other singular "the" prepositions, their -N isn't lost or changed. That means that their Special Cases are also a little different. Mutation with them is otherwise identical to mutation with **en-**.

- **anin** To/For the[150]
- **ben** According to the
- **erin** Over/upon the
- **min** In/between the
- **nuin** Under the
- **suin** As/like the
- **uin** From the

Ancient Nasal-Stops			
ANIN+B	→	ANIN B	**anin bauglir** "to the tyrant"
ANIN+D	→	ANIN D	**anin dîr** "to the man"
ANIN+G	→	ANIN G	**anin golovir** "to the Silmaril"

5.1.4.1 Exercise

Mutate the following words with Mixed Mutation, using **en** "of the."

1. **Balan** – Vala _____
2. **(m)baur** – need _____
3. **brethil** – birch_____
4. **crist** – sword _____
5. **cugu** – dove_____
6. **(n)dôr** – land _____
7. **dû** – darkness _____
8. **galenas** – pipeweed _____
9. **(n)gail** – star _____
10. **glad** – wood _____
11. **groth** – tunnel_____
12. **gwass** – stain _____
13. **haru** – wound _____
14. **iaeth** – neck _____
15. **lach** – flame_____
16. **lhewig** – ear _____

---

[150] In Gondor **anin** is said **'nin**. Write it with an apostrophe at the beginning of the word to distinguish it from the pronoun **nin**.

17. **minuial** – daybreak_____
18. **paur** – fist_____
19. **prestad** – change _____
20. **rhach** – curse_____
21. **solch** – root_____
22. **tham** – hall _____
23. **trenarn** – story_____
24. **tum** – valley _____

5.1.5 Long Mixed Mutation[151]

This type of mutation is almost identical to Mixed Mutation, except that the -Ns on these prepositions and affixes may change to Ñ and M in some cases.

There is only one preposition that uses this type of mutation, and you should be familiar with it by now. It is **an** "to/for," which is used to mark the dative case or the indirect object of a verb.

The rest of the cases where you use long Long Mixed Mutation are adverb-prefixes.

- **an-** Forth/Movement towards somewhere
- **(n)dan-**[152] There isn't a direct English translation for this one, but it means that one is revising a previous action, or undoing it. Three morphemes that come close are: Re-, un-, and back.
- **ein-** Well/Properly
- **palan-** Far and Wide, Afar[153]

---

[151] *Parma Eldalamberon* issue 17 page 147, Tolkien had this to say about this type of mutation: "S *an*, dative chiefly with pronouns or persons. < *ana*, hence vocalic mutation, but takes form *m* before *m, b*. *to, for." This looks more like Mixed Mutation to me, so that's what I built my chart from.

[152] This word has an alternate version, **(n)dad-**.

[153] This is a loan word from Quenya, so it's only for Exilic and Exile-influenced dialects. Everyone else would use the free adverb **hae** "very far away."

AN	→	Result	Example
		Voiceless Stops	
AN+C	→	AÑ G	**añ gerin** "to a mound"
AN+P[154]	→	AM B	**am berian** "for a hobbit"
AN+T	→	AN D	**an dalan** "to a tree-house"
		Voiced Stops	
AN+B	→	AM B	**am bôr** "for a vassal"
AN+G	→	AÑ G	**añ galadh** "for a tree"
		Fricatives	
AN+H	→	AN CH	**an chabar** "to a shoe"
AN+S	→	AN H	**an higil** "for a necklace"
		Nasal	
AN+M	→	AM M	**am mirian** "for a coin"
		Voiceless Approximants	
AN+HW	→	AN 'W	**an 'wand** "for a sponge"
AN+LH	→	AN 'L	**an 'lewig** "for an ear"
AN+RH	→	AN 'R	**an 'ross** "to a whisper"
		Voiced Approximants	
AN+R[155]	→	ADH R	**adh raef** "for a net"
		Ancient Nasal-Stops	
AN+B	→	AM B	**am bauglir** "for a tyrant"
AN+D	→	AN D	**an dîr** "for a man"
AN+G	→	AÑ G	**añ golovir** "for a Silmaril"

5.1.5.1 Exercise

Mutate the following words with Mixed Mutation, using **an** "to/for."

1. **Balan** Vala _____
2. **(m)baur** need _____
3. **brethil** birch _____

_____

[154] We have AN + P- attested as "A PH," but seeing as this was in the "The King's Letter," which has a lot of odd mutations that Tolkien didn't keep, it's hard to tell if it should be considered in later Sindarin. "The King's Letter" can be found in *Sauron Defeated*, pages 128-131

[155] In the Doriathren-Sindarin dialect the -N is left unchanged.

4. **crist** sword_____
5. **cugu** dove _____
6. **galenas** pipeweed_____
7. **(n)gail** star_____
8. **glad** wood_____
9. **groth** tunnel _____
10. **gwass** stain _____
11. **haru** wound_____
12. **iaeth** neck_____
13. **lhewig** ear _____
14. **minuial** daybreak _____
15. **paur** fist_____
16. **prestad** change_____
17. **rhach** curse _____
18. **solch** root _____
19. **trenarn** story _____
20. **tum** valley_____

5.1.6 Super Simplified Mutation List

You may have noticed that certain sounds can only be mutated to a small number of other sounds. So when you're translating something back into English and looking for the right word, you can narrow down your search significantly by taking these lists into account.

Beginning of word → Can become:

- B → V, B, M, MB
- C → G, CH
- D → DH, N, ND, D
- G → apostrophe, NG, G
- H → CH, H
- HW → CHW, 'W, HW
- L → L, LH (super rare)
- LH → THL, 'L
- M → V, M
- P → B, PH
- R → R, RH (super rare)
- RH → THR, 'R
- S → H, S
- T → D, TH

The rest don't change.

Here is the list in reverse:

- apostrophe ← G
- 'L ← GL, LH
- 'R ← GR, RH
- 'W ← GW, HW
- B ← B, P
- CH ← H, C
- CHW ← HW
- D ← D, T
- DH ← D
- G ← G, C, Ñ
- H ← H, S
- HW ← HW
- LH ← LH, L (super rare)
- M ← M, B
- MB ← B
- N ← N, D
- ND ← D
- NG ← G
- Ñ ← G
- PH ← P
- RH ← RH, R (super rare)
- V ← B, M

The following letters only occur at the beginning of a word if that word has been mutated:

Apostrophe, MB, ND, NG, Ñ, CH, DH, PH, and V

5.1.7 Conversation Practice: Comparing Things

In English, you make a superlative adjective with the suffix "-est" or the word "most." For many years we didn't know how to do it in Sindarin other than trying to rip off prefixes from Quenya. Thanks to *Parma Eldalamberon* issue 17, we now have a superlative prefix.[156]

The prefix is **ro-**.[157]

Maer Good   → **Ro-vaer** Best

Iaur Ancient → **Ro-ior** Most Ancient

We don't have anything like English's comparative suffix "-er" or adverb "more" as far as we know in Sindarin. For comparing one thing to another fans have come up with a way around it by using the preposition **athan** for the "greater than", and **nu** for "lesser than."[158]

---

[156] *Parma Eldalamberon* issue 17 page 147

[157] We've only got one example of the prefix in use: **rovaed**.

[158] The first place I came across it was in the Neo-Sindarin textbook written by Thorsten Renk, which can be bought on his website or downloaded for

Sevin i   guru   gannad   athan   edhel.
have-I the skill   playing-the-harp beyond elf
I'm more skilled at playing the harp than an Elf.

Lothuial bain   atha   Churulaer.
Lothuial   pretty beyond Curulaer
Lothuial is prettier than Curulaer.

Lothuial bain   nu   Gurulaer.
Lothuial   pretty beneath Curulaer
Lothuial is less pretty than Curulaer.

For saying that something is "like" something else, use the preposition
sui "as/like." These things could be a noun or a whole sentence.

I varad hen sui oron. *This tower is like a tree.*
Onúren hui aras. *I ran like a deer.*
Linnon hui dhuin glavra. *I sing like a river babbles.*

free: http://www.science-and-fiction.org/elvish/index.html#course_sin-
darin

5.2 Rare Types of Mutation[159]

These are all rarer types of mutation that people like Gondorians wouldn't know. Even many Sindar, if they were young enough, wouldn't know about the last few on this list, replacing them all with Vocalic Mutation.

5.2.1 Liquid Mutation

Of all of the rare types of mutation, this one has the widest use. It's used for prepositions, prefixes, and conjunctions ending in L or R. The -L and -R would remain unchanged.

5.2.1.1 Conjunctions

It's used with two conjunctions:

- **ar** And. only when retaining the R before a consonant.
- **egor** Or

5.2.1.2 Prepositions

- **or** Over/above
- **thar** Across/Athwart/Over

5.2.1.3 Noun Prefixes

- **ar-** Without/outside[160]
- **il-** Every/all
- **per-** Half
- **thar-** Across/athwart/over

---

[159] This section is largely thanks to the scholarship of those who came before me.

[160] This word would be in Exilic and Exilic-affected dialects only.

5.2.1.4 Adverb Prefixes

- ***gal-** Well/blessedly
- **dír-** With difficulty; from physical hardships or lack of trying
- **er-** Alone
- **fer-** Soon/Promptly
- **(n)gor-** With emotional pain, fear, or dread, and therefore difficult to do.
- **per-** Halfway

5.2.1.5 The Liquid Mutation Chart

Letter	→	Result	Example
Voiceless Stops			
C	→	CH	or **cherin** over a mound
P	→	PH	or **pherian** over a hobbit
T	→	TH	or **thalan** over a tree-house
Voiced Stops			
B	→	V	or **vrith** over gravel
D	→	DH	or **dhraug** over a wolf
G	→	'	or **'lân** over a hem
Fricatives			
H	→	CH	or **cham** over a chair
Nasals			
M[161]	→	V	or **virian** over a coin
Voiceless Approximants			
HW	→	CHW	or **chwand** over a sponge
LH	→	'L	or **'ling** over a spiderweb
RH	→	'R	or **'rass** over a precipice

None of the ancient nasalized stops change.

---

[161] In archaic speech as well as the dialect spoken in Doriath, M would mutate to MH/$\tilde{\text{V}}$ instead of V.

5.2.1.5.1 Exercise

Prefix the prefix **il-** "every/all" onto the following nouns.

1. **Balan** Vala _____
2. **brethil** birch_____
3. **crist** sword _____
4. **cugu** dove_____
5. **dû** darkness _____
6. **galenas** pipeweed _____
7. **glad** wood _____
8. **groth** tunnel_____
9. **gwass** stain _____
10. **haru** wound _____
11. **iaeth** neck _____
12. **lhewig** ear _____
13. **minuial** daybreak_____
14. **paur** fist_____
15. **prestad** change _____
16. **rhach** curse_____
17. **trenarn** story _____
18. **tum** valley _____

5.2.2 Stop Mutation

This type of mutation is used for prepositions and prefixes ending in D.

5.2.2.1 Prepositions

- **ed** Out of/forth
- **ned** In/during, referring to time
- **od** From/Of

5.2.2.2 Adverb Prefixes

- **ad-** Re-/Again
- **(n)dad-**[162] There isn't a direct English translation for this one,

---

[162] This prefix has an alternate version, **(n)dan-**.

but it means that one is revising a previous action or undoing it. Three words that come close are: Re-, un-, and back.

5.2.2.3 The Stop Mutation Chart

ED	→	Result	Example
Voiceless Stops			
ED+C	→	E CH	e **cherin** out of a mound
ED+P	→	E PH	e **pherian** out of a hobbit
ED+T	→	E TH	e **thalan** out of a tree-house
Voiced Stops			
ED+B	→	E B	e **brith** out of gravel
ED+D	→	E D	e **dôl** out of a head
ED+G	→	E G	e **galadh** out of a tree
Fricatives			
ED+F	→	EPH F	**eph falas** out of a shore
ED+H	→	E CH	e **chabar** out of a shoe
ED+S	→	ES S	**es sigil** out of necklace
ED+TH	→	ETH TH	**eth tham** out of a hall
Nasals			
ED+M	→	E M	e **mirian** out of a coin
ED+N	→	E N	e **ninglor** out of a golden water lily
Voiceless Approximants			
ED+HW	→	E THW	e **thwand** out of a sponge
ED+LH	→	E THL	e **thlewig** out of an ear
ED+RH	→	E THR	e **thross** out of a whisper
Ancient Nasal-Stops			
ED+B	→	E MB	e **mbauglir** out of a tyrant
ED+D	→	E ND	e **ndîr** out of a man
ED+G	→	E ÑG	e **ñgolovir** out of a Silmaril

5.2.2.3.1 Exercise

Add **od** "from/of" to the following words.

1. **Balan** Vala _____

2. **(m)baur** need _____
3. **brethil** birch_____
4. **crist** sword _____
5. **cugu** dove_____
6. **(n)dôr** land_____
7. **dû** darkness _____
8. **galenas** pipeweed _____
9. **(n)gail** star _____
10. **glad** wood _____
11. **groth** tunnel_____
12. **gwass** stain _____
13. **haru** wound _____
14. **iaeth** neck _____
15. **lhewig** ear _____
16. **minuial** daybreak_____
17. **noss** family _____
18. **paur** fist_____
19. **prestad** change _____
20. **rhach** curse_____
21. **solch** root_____
22. **tham** hall _____
23. **trenarn** story _____
24. **tum** valley _____

5.2.3 H-Mutation

This chart is only for two words which end in a vanishing H.

- **oh** About/around/concerning
- **ah**[163] With/By/Near/Beside/Alongside/And[164]

This type of mutation is so rare that in most non-archaic dialects, Vocalic Mutation is used instead.

The H only appears before vowels.

_____

[163] with Exilic and Númenórean counterpart **ar**
[164] This word could also be **adh**, as you'll recall from Chapter 3.2.4.1

OH	→	Result	Example
OH+C	→	O CH	**o cherin** about a mound
OH+H	→	O CH	**o chabar** about a shoe
OH+HW	→	O CHW	**o chwand** about a sponge
OH+L	→	O LH	**o lhass** about a leaf
OH+P	→	O PH	**o pherian** about a hobbit
OH+R	→	O RH	**o rhaef** about a net
OH+T	→	O TH	**o thalan** about a tree-house

5.2.3.1 Exercise

Add **ah** "and" to the following words.

1. **crist** sword _____
2. **cugu** dove_____
3. **iaeth** neck _____
4. **lach** flame _____
5. **paur** fist_____
6. **prestad** change _____
7. **roch** horse_____
8. **solch** root_____
9. **trenarn** story _____
10. **tum** valley _____

5.2.4 DH-Mutation

This chart is for two words that end in DH.

- **adh**[165] With/By/Near/Beside/Alongside/And[166]
- **nedh-** In/inside/mid-, a preposition prefix

This is such a rare form used that everyone but old Sindar would probably use Vocalic Mutation instead.

Before all of the consonants not on this list, the DH is deleted.

---

[165] with Exilic and Númenórean counterpart **ar**

[166] This word could also be **ah**, as you'll recall from Chapter 3.2.4.1

ADH	→	Result	Example
ADH+C	→	A CH	**a cherin** alongside a mound
ADH+HW	→	ATH W	**ath wand** by a sponge
ADH+L	→	AD L	**ad loth** by a flower
ADH+LH	→	ATH L	**ath lewig** with an ear
ADH+P	→	A PH	**a pherian** with a hobbit
ADH+RH	→	ATH R	**ath rass** alongside a precipice
ADH+T	→	A TH	**a thalan** by a tree-house

5.2.4.1 Exercise

Add **adh** "and" to the following words.

1. **crist** sword _____
2. **cugu** dove_____
3. **iaeth** neck _____
4. **lach** flame _____
5. **lhewig** ear _____
6. **paur** fist_____
7. **prestad** change _____
8. **rhach** curse_____
9. **trenarn** story _____
10. **tum** valley _____

5.2.5 No Mutation

After all of this, it may be hard to recall when *not* to use mutation, so let's go over when you shouldn't.

1. Emphatic Speech - This is when you're putting extra emphasis on a word. When you do this, don't use any mutation on it.
2. Nominative Case - This is the subject of the verb. Unless there's something in front of the noun to make it mutated, the nominative case isn't mutated.
3. Genitive case - the second part of a genitive phrase (the "of ..." part) isn't mutated.
4. An adjective or preposition that is linked to a noun by a copula, as you learned in chapter 3.2.3.

5. Unless there's something that causes it, the verb isn't mutated.

6. An adverb or preposition that has some other words between it and the verb it is modifying.

5.2.6 The All-in-One Prestanneth Chart

Mutation is very hard to remember, so keep this chart close.

	Vocalic	Nasal **in**	Mixed **en**	Long Mixed **an**
Voiceless Stops				
C →	G	I CH	E-G	AÑ G
P →	B	I PH	E-B	AM B
T →	D	I TH	E-D	AN D
TR →	DR	I THR	EN-DR	AN DR
Voiced Stops				
B →	V	I M	E-B	AM B
D →	DH	I N	E-D	AN D
DR →	DHR	IN DR	EN-DR	AN DR
G →	'	I Ñ	E-G	AÑ G
GL →	'L	IÑ GL	EÑ-GL	AÑ GL
GR →	'R	IÑ GR	EÑ-GR	AÑ GR
GW →	'W	IÑ GW	EÑ-GW	AÑ GW
Fricatives				
F →	F	I F	EN-F	AN F
H →	CH	I CH	E-CH	AN CH
S →	H	I S	E-H	AN H
TH →	I TH	I TH	E-TH	AN TH
Nasals				
M →	V	I M	E-M	AM M
N →	N	I N	EN-N	AN N
Voiceless Approximants				
HW →	CHW	IN 'W	E-'W	AN 'W
LH →	THL	ITH L	E-'L	AN 'L
RH →	THR	ITH R	E-'R	AN 'R
Voiced Approximants				
L →	L	I L	E-L	AN L
R →	R	IDH R	EDH-R	ADH R
Ancient Nasal-Stops				
B →	M	I MB	E-MB	AM B
D →	N	I ND	E-ND	AN D
G →	Ñ	I ÑG	E-ÑG	AÑ G

	Liquid	Stop **ed**	DH **adh**	H **oh**
Voiceless Stops				
C →	CH	E CH	A CH	O CH
P →	PH	E PH	A PH	O PH
T →	TH	E TH	A TH	O TH
TR →	THR	E THR	A THR	O THR
Voiced Stops				
B →	V	E B	A B	O B
D →	DH	E D	A D	O D
DR →	DHR	E DR	A DR	O DR
G →	‘	E G	A G	O G
GL →	‘L	E GL	A GL	O GL
GR →	‘R	E GR	A GR	O GR
GW →	‘W	E GW	A GW	O GW
Fricatives				
F →	F	EPH F	A F	O F
H →	CH	E CH	A H	O CH
S →	S	ES S	A S	O S
TH →	TH	ETH TH	A TH	O TH
Nasals				
M →	V	E M	A M	O M
N →	N	E N	A N	O N
Voiceless Approximants				
HW →	‘W	E ‘W	ATH W	O CHW
LH →	‘L	E THL	ATH L	O LH
RH →	‘R	E THR	ATH R	O RH
Voiced Approximants				
L →	L	ED L	AD L	O LH
R →	R	ED R	ADH R	O RH
Ancient Nasal-Stops				
B →	B	E MB	A B	O B
D →	D	E ND	A D	O D
G →	G	E ÑG	A G	O G

Dialect Notes

Archaic/Doriathren

The N doesn't become DH before an R.

The M becomes MH instead of V.

Gondorians

Gondorians can't pronounce CH. It becomes an H before vowels, and a C the rest of the time.

Only the most learned scholars would know more than the 4 most common types of prestanneth. Liquid, Stop, DH and H mutations would be replaced with Vocalic mutation.

In Nasal mutation, they would leave RH and LH unmutated.

5.2.7 Conversation Practice: Giving Directions

Let's start by asking where something is. To do this, just add a preposition to **man** "what," and make a "to be" sentence. Here are a few popular ones that I find myself using often:

- **Mi van...** In where is...
- **Na van...** At where is...
- **Atha man...** Beyond where is...
- **Adel van...** Behind where is...
- **Or van...** Over where is...
- **O man...** From where is...

Here are a few useful verbs for answering this question. They will be in the Imperative form first, and a gerund-like form called a Perfect Participle which means something like "having done..." Use the Perfect participle to put actions in order.

- **Meno** - go; **Míniel** - having gone
- **Tolo** - come; **Túliel** - having come
- **Anglenno** - approach; **Anglenniel** - having approached
- ***Pero im** - turn yourself; ***píriel im** - having turned yourself
- **Dameno** - go back; **Damíniel** - having gone back
- **Dandolo** - come back; **Dandúliel** - having come back
- **Aphado** - follow; **Aphediel** - having followed
- ***Cesto** - search for; ***Híriel** - having found, **Ciniel** - having seen
- ***Mabedo** - ask; ***Mabídiel** - having asked

Some adverbs:

- down - **dad**
- downhill, downwards - **dadbenn**
- here - **si**
- straight - **tîr**
- to the east - **n'amrûn**
- to the left - **na charvo**
- to the north - **na forod**
- to the right - **na forvo**

- to the south - **na charad**
- to the west - **n'annûn**
- up - **am**
- uphill, upwards - **ambenn**
- yonder - **ennas**

Some nouns:

- Bridge - **iant**
- Building - **adab**
- Building - **câr**
- City street - **othrad**
- Enclosed field - **parth**
- Fence - **iâth**
- Fenced field - **pêl**
- Footpath - **pâd**
- Fortified city or town, a fortress - **ost**
- Garden - **sant**
- Gate - **annon**
- Home - **(m)bâr**
- Home - **(m)bardh**
- Outer fence (of a town/city/field) - **ephel**
- Path - **râd**
- Road, way - **mên**
- Sign - **taen**
- Sown field - **rîdh**
- Stair(s) - **dim**
- Stairway - **pendrad**
- Street - **râth**
- Village - **gobel**
- Well - **eithel**

Example

Question:

> **Mi van i mâr Triwath?**
> In   what   the   home Triwath?
> *Where is Triwath's home?*

Answer:

> ***Cesto Ithil-rad.**
> seek   Moon-road
> *Search for Moon-road.*
>
> ***Híriel   i   râd, padro dhadbenn.**
> having-found the   road walk   downhill
> *Having found the road, walk downhill.*
>
> **N'iâth angren, *pero im na charvo,**
> At-gate iron   turn   self to left
> **ar   ennas i   mâr   Triwath.**
> and   yonder the   home Triwath
> *At the iron gate, turn yourself to the left, and yonder is Tri-*
> *wath's home.*
>
> **Taen garan nef   i   mâr   dîn.**
> Sign   red   on-this-side-of the home his/her
> *A red sign is on this side of his/her home.*

Chapter 6: Negation

Negation is another one of those foggy areas in Sindarin. We know what Tolkien intended, more or less, but he changed his mind a lot over the years.

For example, when writing *The Lord of the Rings*, the prefix **ú-** was the general negator in Sindarin. Before that, it had been both **al-**[167] and **ú-**[168], so **al-** appears in a term he'd already made, **alfirin** "immortals," the name of a species of flower. When writing *The Lord of the Rings*, Tolkien decided that **al-** meant "good" or "blessed," and changed the meaning of the word to match, and made a whole host of handy greetings in Quenya.[169]

But later on, he changed his mind again.[170] He decided that **ú-** was too similar to negation in Indo-European languages, and considered removing it altogether, and replacing it with words derived from the ancient root AL/LA.[171] Then he remembered Gilraen's Linnod: **Ónen i Estel Edain, ú-chebin Estel anim.** "I gave the Hope to Men, I don't keep it for myself." He had to keep **ú-** somehow. So he shifted its meaning, making it "cannot"/"impossible." This is a marvelous development for us, giving us whole new shades of meaning and expression! The problem is, Tolkien never got around to telling us what the words derived from AL/LA would be in Sindarin, meaning that all we have is this one word, **alfirin,** to work with.

---

[167] *The Lost Road and Other Writings*, "The Etymologies," LA (page 408)

[168] *The Lost Road and Other Writings*, "The Etymologies," UGU and UMU (page 443)

[169] *Parma Eldalamberon* issue 17, pages 100-101, 143-145, 146

[170] *Parma Eldalamberon* issue 22, page 160

[171] I don't think that we have to outright throw away all of those wonderful **al-** phrases just yet though. From Tolkien's earlier works, there's the ancient root √GALA of the same meaning, which I guess Tolkien forgot about when working on *The Lord of the Rings*. It would result in the same **al(a)-** in Quenya and *****gal-** in Sindarin. We could keep those useful phrases and have a useful adverb-prefix in Sindarin, as well as making some greetings to echo the Quenya ones. We could even say that an influence of Quenya on Sindarin is the dropping of the G- to make phrases more familiar to the Noldor.

Later Tolkien decided to bring back **ú-** and give ALA an entirely differ-ent meaning. [172] Since we don't get any kind of hint of what this would look like in Sindarin and I like the expressive options that the above system allows for, I'm going with ALA as general negation and **ú-** as "can't."

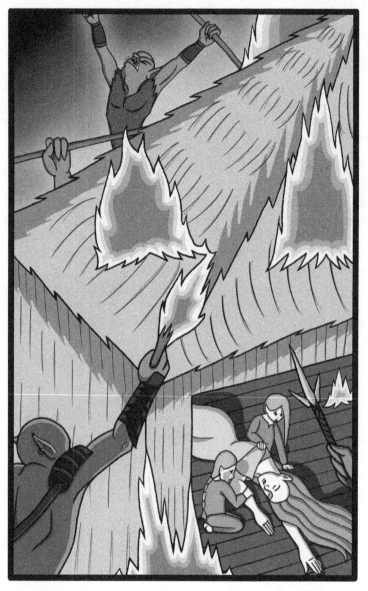

6.1 The four Negation Roots

Sindarin negation is achieved through four root words, AL/LA, ABA, UG, and PEN.

6.1.1 Ancient Root: ALA

For the use of the root ALA in Sindarin we have some grammar and words derived from Quenya's negation, which Tolkien described at length.[173] For Sindarin, we look at how the word ended up in Quenya and hypothesize how the ancient roots were used before the languages split.

The three following negation morphemes tell you that some part of the claim isn't true.

6.1.1.1 Al- for Adjectives and Nouns

We already know that they must have been similar, since they both use **al-** for adjectives. Since the word it's found in, **alfirin**, doesn't have the extra A that shows up in Quenya before consonants, we can guess that it is simply **al-**.

Use this prefix with adjectives or nouns, and use Vocalic Mutation with it, since it lost an -A. You can use it with or without a dash to mark the affix; I'll be using a dash to make the boundaries between it and the other words more visible.

dangen slain	→ **al-nangen** not slain
pen someone, person	→ **al-ben** no one
tolog steady	→ **al-dolog** unsteady
sad somewhere, place	→ **al-had** nowhere

---

[173] Some people prefer to stick to the older usage of **ú-**, or use **av(a)-**, to avoid reconstructing such an important piece of Sindarin grammar. I prefer to stick to my "later is better" motto when dealing with Sindarin, and I find **av(a)-** much too forceful to use as general negation.

6.1.1.1.1 Exercise

Add **al-** to the following adjectives and give their new meanings.

1. **Celeb** silver (the noun, not the adjective)_____
_____
2. **Lagor** swift _____
3. **Nên** water _____
4. **Minai** unique _____
5. **Rend** circular_____

6.1.1.2 *Law for Verbs

This one is based off of the Quenya word **lá**.[174] It is placed before the predicate, meaning that it would go before the verb, any prefixes on the verb, and before any accusative pronouns attached to that verb. The subject of the sentence would go before ***law**, since it isn't in the predicate. Unlike the English verb negation, "do not," ***law** isn't a verb but a particle, and therefore wouldn't take on any conjugation.

I mutate whatever follows ***law** because its predecessors and contemporaries (**ui-** and **avo**) cause mutation. Unlike those two, ***law** goes at the head of the predicate, not the head of the verb. If there is something between ***law** and the verb, that thing is probably already mutating the verb, and you can't mutate something twice. This however, may be completely wrong, since it is speculation.

> **Sîr,   *law   dharthon hi.**
> Today, not   live-I   here
> *Today, I don't live here.*

> ***Law gin   egennin.**
> Not   you   saw-I
> *I didn't see you.*

---

[174] Borrowing Quenya's **lá** actually has a long history of use in Neo-Sindarin, during a time when we had much less data to work with. ***Law** shows up in the Lord of the Rings movies, even. So bringing this out is more like dusting off an old tool you thought you wouldn't need again.

*Law noro o   nin!
Not   run   from me
Don't run from me!

You can also use ***law** as a negative copula. Again, it isn't conjugated for tense or number, and remains ***law**. The word that directly follows ***law** is mutated.

Ni *law vudhu.
I   not   bug
I'm not a bug.

Budhu *law   veleg.
Bug   not   big
A bug is not big.

Budhu *law bo i   nôl lîn.
Bug   not   on the head your
A bug is not on your head.

When negating the imperative copula **no**, treat it like any other verb.

*Law no dhem!
Not   be sad
Don't be sad!

6.1.1.2.1 Exercise

Negate the following sentences.

1. **I 'wend gwain.** The maiden is young. _____
2. **In yrch telir.** The orcs are coming. _____
3. **Te 'warth.** She's a traitor. _____
4. ***Igílen i goll garan.** I chose the red cloak._____
   _____
5. **I barf erin banas.** The book was on the floor._____
   _____

6.1.1.3 *La- for Responses

This is for responses that are shortened, when the verb has been left out. This sort of response is very informal and would be considered slang. Use these in responses to questions only, not in full sentences.

> "Did you run all the way here?"
> "Not me."
> "The leaves are green in Autumn."
> "They aren't." (Not them)

This time, it's conjugated for person (who is doing the subject) and nothing else. The conjugation chart[175] is as follows:[176]

	Singular	Plural
1st	*laen Not me	*laef Not us (excluding you)
1st	*laenc Not you and I	*laeb Not us (including you)
2nd	*laeg Not you (informal)	-
2nd	*lael Not you (polite)	*laedh Not you (pl.)
3rd	*law Not it/him/her	*laer Not them

> **Enengil i adar nîn?** Did you kill my father?
> ***Laen.**

> **Se garan?** Is this red?
> ***Law.**

---

[175] This was invented by looking at the abandoned verb root **gwa-** "to go" which has the present tense conjugation of **gwaen**. There's also the earlier equivalent to ***la-**: **ui-**, which also has the **-i-** as part of the conjugation, between the root and the pronominal suffix. These words themselves may have been abandoned, but how they were conjugated can lend us valuable clues. For the shape of the root itself: in the Quenya version, **la-** was usually left with a short A when it had pronoun suffixes added to it, so I did the same with the Sindarin version.

[176] For the Woodelves and the Southern-Beleriand Sindarin dialects, since the diphthong AE became E, the chart would have these instead: ***lên, *lêf, *lenc, *lêb, *lêg, *lêl, *lêdh, *law,** and ***lêr.**

6.1.1.3.1 Exercise

Answer the following questions "No."

1. ***Ivimminc nuin dobas hen?** Did we kiss under this roof?
   _____

2. **Le i ben i badrast meneg raid?** Are you the person who
   walked a thousand roads?_____

3. ***Teliannedh i dass?** Did (pl.) you finish the task?_____

4. **Lothuial *adhof anin yrch?** Did Lothuial yield to the orcs?
   _____

5. **I chîn Ivreth udúler?** Did Ivreth's children come? _____

6.1.2 Ú- "Cannot/Impossible"

From the description that Tolkien gave us,[177] **ú-** is "near negative" and
means that something is impossible. Thus, prefixed onto a verb, it
takes the meaning "cannot," and when prefixed onto an adjective it
means that whatever it is that it's describing "can't possibly be so." It
is especially used when negating -able adjectives.[178]

Since _Parma Eldalamberon_ issue 22 was published in 2015, at the time
of writing this book, many people still use this prefix as a general negation prefix.

Use Vocalic Mutation following this prefix.

> **Ú-adhóren.** I couldn't halt.
>
> **Ú-thoron i hant.** I can't fence the garden.
>
> **Ú-adhóref ben.** We couldn't halt anyone.
>
> **I hant al-thorannen ú-dhar lavan.** The unfenced garden can't
> stop an animal.
>
> **nodui** "countable → **ú-nodui** uncountable

---

[177] Tolkien wrote that "_ú_ should be from UG 'dislike'" and that in Sindarin, it
had "a meaning intensified to 'impossible' so that it came near to negative."
Parma Eldalamberon issue 22 page 160

[178] _Parma Eldalamberon_ issue 22 page 160

madui "edible" → **ú-vadui** inedible

With this change in meaning, we can expect (if he intended to keep it at all) the interjection **Û** to become "It cannot be so!" or "I don't want it to be so!" rather than "It isn't so!" This expression is made with your lips pursed while shaking your head.[179]

6.1.2.1 Exercise

Add the prefix **ú-** to the following sentences and adjectives.

1. **istadui** knowable _____
2. **Pladon i lass han**. I touch that leaf. _____
3. **pladadui** touchable_____
4. **Na dhû, cenin**. At night, I see._____
5. **cenui** visible_____

6.1.3 Ancient Root: ABA

There is the set of words derived from the ancient verb ABA, "to refuse." This bit of grammar has stayed stable throughout Sindarin's development, and can also be found in Noldorin.[180]

6.1.3.1 Av-, Avo, and Baw! "Don't!"

Av- or **avo-** are used only on the imperative verb. Soft Mutation follows it. Because it is based on the verb **ava-** "to refuse," it has the connotation of "refusing" or "resisting" doing something, so it doesn't replace ***law**, but it does make stronger, more forceful negation.

> **Avo dharo!** Don't halt!
> **Av-edro i fennas!** Don't open the gate!

---

[179] *Parma Eldalamberon* issue 17 page 145
[180] *The Lost Road and Other Writings*, "The Etymologies," AB, ABAR (page 385). *Parma Eldalamberon* issue 17 pages 143-145. *The History of Middle-earth vol. 11 - The War of the Jewels* "The Quendi and the Eldar" pages 370-372

While you can use **avo** on its own as a short "No don't do that!" there is an even shorter expression: **Baw!** According to Tolkien, when you say it, you should jerk your head up.[181]

6.1.3.1.1 Exercise

Use **avo** to negate the following commands.

1. **Noro o nin**! Run from me!_____
2. **Aphado nin**! Follow me! _____
3. **Plado i genedril *ragui**! Touch the fragile mirror!_____
   _____
4. **Gwanno**! Die!_____
5. **Erio**! Stand! (Arise!) _____

6.1.3.2 Ava- "Will Not/To Refuse" for Responses

On the note of "refusing," a stronger way to say, "I won't/wouldn't do it" would be to say **Avon cared** "I refuse to do it." This is often used to answer requests with rejection. If you want to shorten it, just keep the **avon** and drop the other verb.

Here is a full chart of **ava-** conjugated for you. They are organized the same way that the ***la-** chart is.

	Singular	Plural
1st	**avon** I won't	**avof** We (excluding you) won't
1st	**avanc** You and I won't	**avab** We (including you) won't
2nd	**avog** You (informal) won't	-
2nd	**avol** You (polite) won't	**avodh** you (pl.) won't
3rd	**ava** It/He/She won't	**avar** They won't

Note that a gerund follows the main verb, and it isn't lenited as well, since this is a compound predicate like those you studied in chapter 3.3.3.1.

Darathol? Would you please halt?

---

[181] *Parma Eldalamberon* issue 17 page 145

Avon dared! I won't halt!
Avon! I won't!

Darathodh? Would (pl.) you please halt?
Avof dared! We won't halt!
Avof! We won't!

6.1.3.2.1 Exercise

Refuse the following requests/commands with the verb **ava-**.

1. **No dhínen!** Be silent! (the gerund of "to become" is *oled)
   _____

2. **Nin aphadathol?** Would you please follow me? _____
   _____

3. **Pedathodh i cherdir dhîn?** Would (pl.) you please tell (pl.)
   your master? _____
   _____

4. **Ni ñovanatha anin na i annon annui?** Would she please
   meet me at the western gate? _____
   _____

5. **Lastathar i innas nîn?** Would they please hear my will?
   _____

6.1.4 Pen- vs Ar-

In *The Silmarillion*, there is the word **arnœdiad** from **Nírnaeth Arnœdiad** which is translated as "countless lamentations." And in *The Lord of the Rings*, there's **pen-adar** from **Iarwain Ben-adar**, a Sindarin name for Tom Bombadil that means "ancient and young, the fatherless." **Ar-**[182] doesn't appear used that way in Tolkien's later Sindarin, and it appears that he replaced it with **pen-**.[183] He even wrote a few alternative replacements for **arnœdiad,** one of which was **pen-nœdiad.** Neo-Sindarin translators can be found using both, since **ar-** is found in *The Silmarillion*.

---

[182] *The Lost Road and Other Writings*, "The Etymologies" AR²
[183] *Parma Eldalamberon* issue 17 page 144-145, 171, 173.

6.1.4.1 Pen- for "to Lack, Without, -less"

The prefix **pen-** started out as the verb "to lack." It's used as the opposite of **sav-** "to have." You can see how it would have developed quite easily - starting as a phrase, **pên 'lass** "it lacks joy" becomes **pen-'lass** "joyless." Because of this origin as a verb, use vocalic mutation with it, not nasal or mixed mutation as one might guess from its form.

When attached to a noun, it turns that noun into an adjective and it is mutated as an adjective, which is why it appears as **ben-adar** in Tom Bombadil's name. It couldn't be pluralized, however.

As a verb, it's how you would answer "No" to a question starting with "Do(es) _ have...?"

>   **Sevil mass**? Do you have bread?
>
>   **Penin**. I lack.

	Singular	Plural
1st	**Penin** I lack	**Penif** We (excluding you) lack
1st	**Peninc** you and I lack	**Penib** We (including you) lack
2nd	**Penig** you (informal) lack	-
2nd	**Penil** you (polite) lack	**Penidh** you (pl.) lack
3rd	**Pên** he/she/it lacks	**Penir** they lack

6.1.4.1.1 Exercise

Negate the following nouns with the prefix **pen-**.

1. **Cae** earth_____
2. **Gond** stone _____
3. **Thâr** grass _____

Answer the following questions "no" using the verb **pen-**.

1. **Sevil 'lî**? Do you have honey? _____
2. **Sevidh roch**? Do (pl.) you have a horse?_____

6.1.5 Elven Culture: Cosmology

Elves have a very different view of the world than many of us do now. When we look up, we see the endless expanse of space above, stars so far away they have passed away before their light reached us, vast, distant galaxies that look like nothing more than faint specks, and all of it, all of us twirling in a captivating dance in the vacuum of space. But an Elf looking up would see something completely different, or rather, they would see something very close to what many of we humans would have seen hundreds of years ago.

It's important in our play-making of these characters that we try to put ourselves in their shoes, to imagine how they would see the world. There are people in our world right now who still see the world this way, so this is an important exercise in empathy. It also gives added depth to your stories and characterization to know this information.

An Elf looking up would see an ocean of stars. This ocean is called **(n)Gilwen** or **(n)Gilith**.[184] In English it's sometimes called "the waters above" or "the firmament." In that ocean float magical glowing crystals that Elbereth put there. The word for the crystal she used is **Silef**[185] in Sindarin. As you may recall from *The Lord of the Rings*, Galadriel gives Frodo a phial full of captured light. In this world, light is something you can catch and store in various materials, especially transparent materials like water or crystal. That's what Silif are - vessels for light.

Silif aren't stars though, they are the vessels for the stars. The stars go by several names. The first is **êl**, plural **elin**, which is named for the sense of wonder it inspired in the elves. It's no coincidence that the word for "star" is connected to the word for "wow" - **elo!** The next word is connected to the silver light of the stars, **(n)gail**, plural **(n)gîl**. And the last word is **tinu**, which refers to how tiny a light an individual star is. The word also means "spark."

This is also where the sun, **Anor**,[186] is carried across the sky in a boat with the Maia named Arien, and the moon, **Ithil**,[187] is carried by the

---

[184] It's called **Ilmen** in Quenya.
[185] In Quenya, it's **silma**, yes, this is a part of **silmaril**.
[186] The Quenya word is **Anar**.
[187] In Quenya, it's **Isil**.

Maia Tilion. Eärendil is also sailing this sea with a silmaril on his ship (called a **(n)Golodhvir**, or "Noldo-jewel" in Sindarin.)

Beyond Gilwen is **Goe**,[188] the "envelope." It's a sea of air, which envelops the world.

Beyond Goe is **Gast** or **Gaw**, the Void, which is kind of like space, except it's much more empty. It's where Morgoth was imprisoned because he could do no harm there. It's as close as the elves come to having a Hell, but only Morgoth has been imprisoned there. It is also sometimes referred to as **Belegast** or **Belego**[189] meaning the "Vast Void."

Gilwen/Gilith, Goe, and Gast/Gaw/Belegast/Belego can be referred to with a single word, roughly translated as "the heavens" - **Menel**. Below Menel is **Gwelwen**,[190] the "inner air." It's where **gwaew** (wind) and **foen** (clouds) happen, where birds *****gwilir** (fly)... it is where **gwelu** (air) is. When we look for a translation of "sky," Gwelwen is usually the word that we mean.

Below Gwelwen is the "Earth" where we live, **Ceven**.[191] The lands in this creation are called **Gardhon**,[192] the Realm. That is split into two categories. **Avon**,[193] where the Belain[194] and Ódhellim[195] live, the closest thing to Heaven that they have, since it's also where **(m)Bannos**[196] is. This is where the spirits of the dead are collected by Badhron[197] to

---

[188] In Quenya, it's **Vaiya**. This word is originally **Ui** Noldorin, so it needed to be updated to match Sindarin's phonological history. I took the Old Noldorin word, **wōia**, and followed what its phonological development would have been if the word had been introduced in Sindarin, and got **goe**. The route this took was this: **wōia > gwōi > gwoe > goe**

[189] **Cúma** in Quenya.

[190] **Vista** in Quenya.

[191] **Cemen** in Quenya.

[192] This is the updated version of **Ardhon**, from *The Lost Road and Other Writings*, "The Etymologies," ƷAR, because the root of the word was changed to GAR in *War of the Jewels* page 402. The Quenya word is **Arda.**

[193] The Quenya word is **Aman.**

[194] **Valar** in Quenya.

[195] Elves who left Middle-earth for Avon.

[196] **Mandos** in Quenya.

[197] **Námo** in Quenya.

either be reborn or wait for the end of the world. The part of Avon where the Belain live is called **Balannor**.[198] It was "removed from the circles of the world," so it's floating around somewhere in Menel to protect it from Humans who wanted to conquer it, and it's only reachable by "the Straight Way," which is a sea passage set up for the Elves who wish to sail there. The rest of inhabited Gardhon is called **Amar**,[199] "The Settlement," and it's related to the word **(m)bâr** "home." **Ennor**, or Middle-earth, is part of Amar, and it is where Sindarin was born, and most of the history we know from Gardhon was set.

---

[198] **Valinor** in Quenya.
[199] **Ambar** in Quenya.

Chapter 7: Pronouns

Here we enter one of the most hotly and often debated topics in Neo-Sindarin circles: What to do about Pronouns in Sindarin.

The problem is two-fold.

First, Tolkien kept changing his mind. For example, let's look at the "we" suffixes. The inclusive "we" suffix has been **-ch**,[200] **-ngid, -nc, -ngir,**[201] and lastly, **-b.**[202] Exclusive "we" was **-m**[203] for a long time, but he discarded it in favor of **-v/-f**, which we didn't discover until *Parma Eldalamberon* #22.

This leads us to the second problem: we don't have much information on how Sindarin pronouns are used. Even though we have a small mountain of "we"s - they're all for the same two words. Most of the information comes to us scattered across many different eras, and we rarely get anything like a complete picture of what their forms were or how they were used.

The system I use is based off a chart of Common Eldarin pronouns in *Vinyar Tengwar* issue #49.[204] This is because when we got a glimpse of what the late-Sindarin 1st person pronoun suffixes were in *Parma Eldalamberon* issue #22, they showed clear evidence of being related to that chart.

But who knows? There's so little information on Sindarin pronouns that tomorrow some new piece of Tolkien's notes could be published

---

[200] For a long time, **-ch** was believed to mean "you." It was based on an untranslated fragment, "**Arphent Rían Tuorna, man agorech?**" We figured out most of it, "And said Rían to Tuor, what did ___ do?" but didn't know that **-ch** meant "you and I" at the time. This misunderstanding prevailed for such a long time that in the *Lord of the Rings* movies, the suffix **-ch** was used to mean "you!" If you'd like to read a very detailed breakdown of this phrase, I suggest reading *Vinyar Tengwar #50*, pages 20-22.

[201] These three suffixes come from a chart in *Parma Eldalamberon* #17, page 132.

[202] *Parma Eldalamberon* #22, page 167

[203] It's in *Parma Eldalamberon* #17, page 132 & 143; *The War of the Jewels*, page 371; *Vinyar Tengwar #44*, "Ae Adar Nín."

[204] Pages 50-52 and 56-57

that overturns my entire system, and I'll be churning out another edition of this book to keep up with it.

7.1 Basic Pronouns[205]

Sindarin Pronouns are structured in a predictable way. Each pronoun is made from a root that is made up of Consonant+Vowel. When memorizing them, you can just memorize these roots and memorize the case affixes to make any personal pronoun that you need.

7.1.1 Pronoun Charts

Before we get into the Sindarin pronouns themselves, there is a chart I need you to get familiar with. It's a way of organizing pronouns into groups that is very helpful when learning some types of languages. Those of you who have studied Indo-European languages before might recognize it.

	Singular	Plural
First person	I	we
Second person	you	y'all[206]
Inanimate third person	it	-
Masculine third person	he	-
Feminine third person	she	-
Neutral third person	they	
Close demonstrative	this	these
Far demonstrative	that	those
Inanimate interrogative	what	
Animate interrogative	who	

---

[205] Some more articles to view, all of which are outdated at this point, are Thorsten Renk's "Common Eldarin views of the Sindarin Pronominal System" http://www.science-and-fiction.org/elvish/pron_rek.html and Helge Fauskanger's "Sindarin - the Noble Tongue" http://folk.uib.no/hnohf/sindarin.htm#Heading19 I don't use the systems proposed in these articles, but I do build on the theories that they lay down in their articles.

[206] Some dialects of English have a distinct plural 2nd person pronoun. In my dialect, it's "you guys," but I use "y'all" on my website and in this book because "y'all" is a lot more famous, and people outside of my dialect will be familiar with it, even if they don't use it.

This is how you figure out what the technical name for the pronouns are. To do this, list its corresponding row title first, then, if a distinction is made, whether it's singular or plural.

I   = first person singular pronoun

What = inanimate interrogative pronoun

The reason I use such technical language when referring to the pronouns is because Sindarin pronouns have slightly different categories from those used in English. For example, Sindarin has two words that would be translated as "we" in English, and three words that would be translated as "you." This can get awfully confusing, so I use the technical terms to make certain you know exactly what I mean.

7.1.1.1 Exercise

Figure out what the technical names for the following English pronouns are, using the above chart.

1. That _____
2. She_____
3. We _____
4. You _____
5. These_____

7.1.2 Nominative Pronouns

These are pronouns that act as the subject of a sentence. In Sindarin the verbs normally have a nominative suffix, so nominative pronouns aren't needed much of the time. They appear primarily in sentences with copulas.

If you want to make particularly casual speech or a phrase that's repeated so often that the words get contracted together, there is a way to contract the nominative pronouns before vowels (even if it's from a G mutated to nothing). The pronoun loses its vowel. I don't suggest doing this with the demonstrative pronouns, however.

	Singular	Plural
First person exclusive	ni	*me
First person inclusive	*gwe	
Familiar second person	ci	-
Reverential second person	le	de
Doriathren reverential second person	de	
Third person[207]	*te	ti
Close Demonstrative	*se	*si
Far Demonstrative	*sa	*sai
Interrogative	*ma	

First person exclusive/inclusive shows whether "you" (the person addressed) is included or excluded from "we." It's uncertain whether Tolkien wanted the inclusive pronouns to be used in Sindarin or not. In his earlier versions of the language (around the time he wrote *The Lord of the Rings*) he had the inclusive pronouns drop out of use in the language and only be used in the Doriathren dialect as part of its archaic flavor.

The difference between **le** and **ci** relates to degree of familiarity.

Ci is for intimate conversations between people who are very close to each other, like best friends, lovers, and family members. If you use **ci** with someone who isn't in a close relationship with you, you'd be insulting them, treating them like they are lesser than you, or dragging them down to your level. It'd be like cussing at someone in English.

Le is for formal situations and people who are aquaintences or strangers. If you're in a formal situation with others present, use **le** even if you'd use **ci** while alone with the person you're addressing. Use of **le** can be insulting too though. If you're in an intimate situation and should be using **ci** but use **le** instead, it'd be like turning a cold shoulder

---

[207] In Noldorin the 3rd person was a bit different. There were feminine, masculine, and gender-neutral pronouns. Many people use them because of the expressive possibilities, but I prefer the later gender-neutral 3rd person. Here's the chart of these abandoned 3rd person pronouns.

feminine	se	si (pl.)
masculine	so	sy (pl.)
neutral	sa	sai (pl.)

to someone, insinuating that the close relationship between you two is over.

De is used just for addressing a group of people, but that wasn't always the case. The way Tolkien described the usage of **le** and **de** was this: use of **le** dropped out of Old Sindarin, and **de** was used for both the singular and plural. Then the Noldor reintroduced **le** as a polite singular "you." This pronoun spread amongst the other dialects of Sindarin, except the dialect of Doriath.

> **Gwe nethail.** (inclusive)We are guests.
>
> **C'ovannen.** (familiar)You are met.
>
> **Ma tôl?** Who comes?

7.1.2.1 Exercise

Translate the following sentences using the provided vocabulary, into Sindarin.

1. **Galadh** tree "Those are trees."

   _____

2. **(n)Daug** soldier "We (not you) are soldiers."

   _____

3. **Telu** roof "(reverential, singular) You are under a roof."

   _____

4. **Him** cold "I am cold."

   _____

5. **Elleth** elf-woman "She is an elf-woman."

   _____

7.1.3 Oblique Pronouns

These are pronouns that have a variety of duties. In Sindarin they are the direct object of the sentence, and they are used in prepositional phrases. In English we do the exact same thing, actually. That's why these are called "oblique" pronouns and not "accusative" pronouns.

These pronouns are placed before the verb and soft mutation changes the first letter of the pronoun, as it always does to the direct object. The -N causes nasal mutation with the beginning of the verb. Don't forget that intransitive verbs can have indirect objects, and that the

oblique pronoun can be used for the indirect object. This is a good time
to go back to lessons 3.3 and 3.4 to review the sections about verbs
interacting with pronouns.

	Singular	Plural
First person exclusive	nin	men
First person inclusive	*gwen	
Familiar second person	*cin	—
Reverential second person	len	den
Doriathren reverential second person	den	
Third person	ten	*tin
Close demonstrative	*sen	*sin
Far demonstrative	san	sain
Interrogative[208]	man	

> **nu nin** under me
>
> **Gi fuion.** I hate you.
>
> **e thin** out of them
>
> **Dago han!** Kill that!

7.1.3.1 Exercise

> **beria** he's protecting
> **hebin** I'm keeping
> **gostof** (exclusive) we fear
> **aderthathanc** (inclusive) we will reunite
> **eglerianc** (inclusive) we praise

Translate the following sentences.

1. He's protecting me on this side of (reverential, singular) you.

   _____

2. I'm keeping this between (inclusive) us.

   _____

---

[208] This pronoun is often left unmutated because emphasis is being placed on
it. Review this in 5.2.5.

3. (exclusive) We fear (plural) you like those.

    _____

4. (inclusive) We will reunite these with it.

    _____

5. (inclusive) We praise them over that.

    _____

7.1.4 Dative Pronouns

Dative pronouns act as the indirect object of the sentence. They are made by prefixing **an** "to/for" onto the oblique pronouns, just as the indirect object is made.

	Singular	Plural
First person exclusive	annin	ammen
First person inclusive	*angwen	
Familiar second person	*angin	—
Reverential second person	*anlen	*anden
Doriathren reverential second person	*anden	
Third person	*anden	*andin
Close demonstrative	*anhen	*anhin
Far demonstrative	*anhan	*anhain
Interrogative	*amman	

Agóreg thrugar annin. (familiar) You did wrong to me.

Bastathon odog mesgyrn ammen. I will bake seven loaves of bread for (exclusive) us.

Arónef anhan. (exclusive) We wandered to that.

7.1.4.1 Exercise

brother - **muindor**	make come (imperative) - **tollo**
cloak - **coll**	it/he/she gives - **anna**
sister - **muinthel**	(familiar) you walk - **padrog**
	he/she will return - **tôl demened**
	I assisted - **eithannen**

Translate the following sentences.

1. Make (familiar) your brother come to those.

    _____

2. He or she gives cloaks to them.

    _____

3. (familiar) You walk to this.

    _____

4. Reinor will return to (inclusive) us.

    _____

5. I assisted (reverential, singular) your sister for (reverential, singular) you.

    _____

    _____

7.1.5 Possessive, Demonstrative, and Interrogative Adjectives

As you'll recall from chapter 3.1, possessive pronouns, demonstratives, and interrogatives are treated as adjectives. This means that they don't replace the definite articles **i** or **in** (the) as they do in English. This also means that they are mutated with lenition just like adjectives are when they are modifying a noun.

	Singular	Plural
First person exclusive	nîn	mîn
First person inclusive	*gwîn	
Familiar second person	*cîn	—
Reverential second person	lîn	*dîn
Doriathren reverential second person	*dîn	
Third person	tîn	
Close demonstrative	sen	sin
Far demonstrative	*san	*sain
Interrogative	*man	

I mar nîn My house
I vellas dhîn (Doriathren reverential) Your strength
I garab van? Which hat?

7.1.5.1 Exercise

Translate the following phrases into Sindarin.

1. **coll** cloak "these cloaks"

    _____

2. **(m)basgorn** loaf of bread "(inclusive) Our loaf of bread"

    _____

3. **bôr** vassal "(familiar) Your vassal"

    _____

4. **cabor** frog "Its/His/Her/Their frog"

    _____

5. **(n)dîr** man "those men"

    _____

7.1.6 Where the Pronouns Come From

To fill in the gaps in our pronoun charts, we need to gather known Sindarin pronouns.

- **im**[209] "__self" This one's meaning changed a bit over its development. In early Sindarin it appears as an emphatic/reflexive pronoun meaning "myself." Late in its development, Tolkien changed it to being a general Reflexive Indefinite pronoun, making it mean "self." In Quenya he combined **im** with the other pronoun roots to make words like "myself, yourself, himself" but it isn't clear if he wanted this for Sindarin too. This pronoun will be covered in the next lesson, since, like the other indefinite pronouns, it doesn't behave like the pronouns we're studying in this lesson.

- **anim**[210] "to/for __self"

---

[209] *The Lord of the Rings* book II chapter IV; *Parma Eldalamberon* issue 17 pages 41,46; *The Lays of Beleriand* page 421; *Vinyar Tengwar* issue 47 pages 14,37-8

[210] *The Lord of the Rings* A(v); *Parma Eldalamberon* issue 17 pages 117,147

- **ni**[211] "I" - This comes from Old Noldorin, which is an earlier version of Old Sindarin, but from what we can gather looking at Quenya and the Oblique and Dative pronouns, this is a very likely addition. We can't use it as a data point in figuring out Sindarin pronoun cases, but it fits nicely into what we know of Sindarin 1st person Pronouns.

- **nin**[212] "me" - What's interesting about this and other oblique pronouns that end in -N is this trait isn't shared with Quenya. Sindarin and Quenya independent pronouns are otherwise very similar. In Quenya -N marks the dative case, but in Sindarin it appears to mark the Oblique case and a preposition is used to mark the dative case instead.

- **enni**[213]/**annin**[214] "to/for me." - Before we had **annin**, we had an obscure phrase that was meant to be heavily worn down by time, which had **enni** in it. Many people still use **enni**, but I think its use is restricted to that one little phrase.

- **nîn**[215] "my"

- **men**[216] "us" This is exclusive, so it excludes the listener. This pronoun is also deduced as a part of **ammen**.

- **ammen**[217] "to/for us" Like **men**, it is exclusive.

- **mîn**[218] "our" This is also exclusive. From its use in Tolkien's translation of the Patre Nostre, some believe that it's also a word for "us," but I cherry-pick that away to mean just "our."

---

[211] *Parma Eldalamberon* issue 22 pages 98,121

[212] *The Lord of the Rings* book IV chapter X; *Parma Eldalamberon* issue 17 page 95; *The Road Goes Ever On* page 62; *The Letters of J.R.R. Tolkien* letter #211

[213] *Vinyar Tengwar* issue 41 page 11

[214] *Parma Eldalamberon* issue 17 page 147

[215] *Unfinished Tales* pages 40,54; *Vinyar Tengwar* issue 44 pages 21-2

[216] *Vinyar Tengwar* issue 45 page 37

[217] *The Lord of the Rings* book II chapter IV; *Parma Eldalamberon* issue 17 pages 38,45,147; *The Lays of Beleriand* page 421; *Vinyar Tengwar* issue 44 pages 21,27

[218] *Vinyar Tengwar* issue 44 page 21

Most of the time it's found lenited into **vîn**.

- **ech**[219] Earlier, around the time that Tolkien was working on writing the appendix for *Return of the King*, we have an off-hand note about second person and third person pronouns to match **im** for the first person. They weren't defined in the text, and their forms suggest they are made from duplicating their consonant, but we have no mention of them in Tolkien's later Sindarin, so I've decided to not use them.

- **ci**[220] "you" - This is singular, familiar, and nominative. It's reduced to **g'** in **mae g'ovannen**.

- **le/de**[221] "you" These two were listed as roots only, so we're not sure what case these are in. We do know that they are both for formal, and in dialects of Sindarin that gained **le**, **de** was used only for the plural "you" while **le** was used for the singular "you." Before **le** was reintroduced into Sindarin, it only had one formal "you" for both the singular and plural: **de**.

- **le(n)**[222]/**de(n)**[223] "to you" It is my theory that even though it is attested as just **le**, there was an -N on it, but it was lost to nasal mutation. **De**, also shown lenited as **ðe**, is given as an alternate form that would be used in "pure Sindarin." I also think that these are in the oblique form because I think that they can be used in place of a Dative pronoun with an intransitive verb, as I described in Chapter 3.3.2.1.

- **lîn**[224] "your" This is a polite pronoun.

---

[219] *Parma Eldalamberon* issue 17 page 46

[220] *Parma Eldalamberon* issue 17 page 17

[221] *Vinyar Tengwar* issue 49 pages 51,56

[222] *Parma Eldalamberon* issue 17 pages 26,94; *The Lays of Beleriand* page 421; *The Lord of the Rings* book II chapter I, book IV chapter X

[223] *Parma Eldalamberon* issue 17 page 26

[224] *Vinyar Tengwar* issue 44 page 21

- **e**[225]/**est**[226] "he" The guess is that **e** is an earlier form of **est**, which is listed without a definition alongside **im** and **ech**. I consider this pronoun to have been dropped in Tolkien's later Sindarin.

- **ten**[227] "it" This is the oblique pronoun, not a nominative pronoun. This was attested with lenition making it **den**.

- **tîn**[228] "his" This was attested with lenition as **dîn**.

- **ti**[229] "they" This one was complex because it had to be the object of one verb, and because it was being modified by a relative clause, had to be the subject of another. The solution? Have it be in the nominative case, lenite it to **di** like it's a direct object, have it follow the verb like a regular noun, then attach the relative clause.

- **în**[230] "__ own" theorized to be a reflexive indefinite possessive pronoun.

- **sen**[231] "this" as a demonstrative adjective. Also attested lenited as **hen**.

- **sin**[232] "these" as a demonstrative adjective. Also appears lenited as **hin**.

- **san**[233] "that" as an oblique demonstrative pronoun. Also appears lenited as **han**.

---

[225] *Sauron Defeated* pages 129-31

[226] *Parma Eldalamberon* issue 17 page 46

[227] *Vinyar Tengwar* issue 44 page 21

[228] *Sauron Defeated* pages 129-31

[229] *Vinyar Tengwar* issue 44 page 21

[230] *Sauron Defeated* pages 129-31

[231] *Parma Eldalamberon* issue 17 page 44

[232] *The Lord of the Rings* book II chapter IV; *Parma Eldalamberon* issue 17 page 44

[233] *Parma Eldalamberon* issue 17 page 42

- **sain**[234] "those" as an oblique pronoun. Appears lenited as **hain**, and an archaic form, **hein**, is also listed.

- **man**[235] "what" as an oblique interrogative pronoun.

Now we organize them in a nice big chart:

	Nominative	Oblique	Dative	Posses-sive /Adjec-tive
1st person singular		nin	annin	nîn
1st person exclusive plural		men	ammen	mîn
1st person inclusive plural				
2nd person familiar singular	ci			
2nd person reverential singular		le(n)		lîn
2nd person reverential plural		de(n)		
3rd person singular		ten		tîn
3rd person plural	ti			
Close demonstrative singular				sen
Close demonstrative plural				sin
Far demonstrative singular		san		
Far demonstrative plural		sain		
Interrogative		man		

After we spot the patterns we can use them to fill out the rest of the chart.

- Nominative Case: Naked root.
  - We can make more nominative pronouns by finding their root forms. This gets us ***ni, *me, *le, *de, *te, *se, *si, *sa, *sai,** and ***ma.**
- Oblique Case: Root + -N.
  - This gets us the following new pronouns: ***cin, *tin, *sen,** and ***sin.**
- Dative Case: **an** + oblique pronoun

---

[234] *The Lord of the Rings* book II chapter IV; *Parma Eldalamberon* issue 17 page 42

[235] *Vinyar Tengwar* issue 50 page 21

- o This gets us the following new pronouns: ***angin,**
  *anlen, *anden, *anden, *andin, *anhen, *anhin,
  *anhan, *anhain,[236] and ***amman.**
- Adjective: Root + -N
  - o This gets us the following new pronouns: ***san, *sain,**
    and ***man.**
- Possessive: Lengthen vowel of the adjective form and add -N.
  - o This gets us the following new pronouns: ***cîn, *dîn,**
    and ***tîn.**

7.1.6.1 The Making of 1st Person Inclusive Pronouns

The chart is looking almost full now, but we still have an entire row left empty! I didn't make the 1st person inclusive pronouns out of nothing, let me assure you. They are the only ones that are truly reconstructed from Common Eldarin. From a chart of Common Eldarin pronouns,[237] I pulled the ancient inclusive pronoun **we.** In Sindarin, words that started with W added an initial G, making the root ***gwe.** With this root, we can make the rest of the first person inclusive pronouns: ***gwen, *angwen,**[238] and ***gwîn.** The use of this root also nicely matches the corresponding pronominal suffix, which we will study in the next lesson.

7.1.7 Elven Culture: Fingers

This is taken from *Vinyar Tengwar* issues 47-49, which cover an essay by Tolkien called "Eldarin Hands, Fingers & Numerals." I suggest reading it if you'd like to go into this topic in more depth, since I'll be listing

---

[236] Some people believe that in a compound, **an** should assimilate with the prepositions following it to a greater degree. Therefore, many people use ***allen, *assen, *assin, *assan,** and ***assain** instead. Because some people think that **an** would react differently to voiceless stops, some people use ***achin, *athen,** and ***athin,** which allows for greater differentiation between the different pronouns, which I admit would be nice. Until we know more about the use of **an,** it's hard to say which is right.

[237] *Vinyar Tengwar* issue 49 page 52

[238] Another possibility for this pronoun's derivation is ***anwen,** considering that mutation with **an** started out as vocalic mutation.

the way you count on your fingers and the play-names of the fingers only.

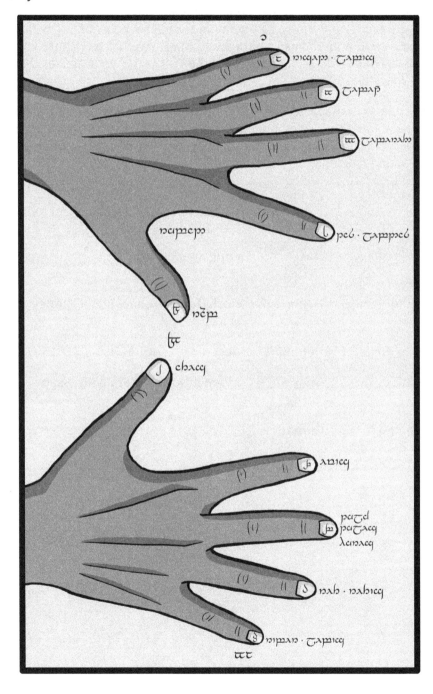

When an Elf counts on their fingers, they count to 12. The hands are laid palms down, with the thumbs close together. You start with either pinkie as 1, and when you've done 5 on your thumb, 6 is the space be-tween your two thumbs, as a stand in for your whole hand. 7 will be your next thumb, and you continue counting on your fingers up to your pinkie, which will be 11. Then count the space after your pinkie as 12, for your other hand.

The names of the fingers are as follows, including the play-names that children call them. One of the ways Elven children play with their fin-gers is they turn each hand into a family, with each finger represented by a family member.

Finger	Name	Play-name
Thumb	**naub**	**atheg** daddy
Index-finger	**tas/ lebdas**	**emig** mommy
Middle-finger	**lebenedh**	**tolch/toleg** prominent one, **honeg** bro
Ring-finger	**lebent**	**neth** sister, **nethig** sis
Pinkie	**niged/ lebig**	**niben** little one, **gwinig** little baby
Thumb & Pointer-finger	**nobad**	--

7.2 Pronominal Suffixes and Indefinite Pronouns

In this lesson I will cover the pronominal suffixes, indefinite pronouns, and some things that are mistaken as pronouns.

7.2.1 Nominative Pronoun Suffixes

As I mentioned in the previous lesson, nominative pronouns are usually suffixes on the verbs. These are the suffixes:[239]

---

[239] Some people prefer to use the slightly older set of suffixes from a chart in *Parma Eldalamberon* issue 17 page 132, because it allows for more nuance, including a set of dual-plural pronominal suffixes. I myself clung to it for a long time because it was the most complete chart of Sindarin verb pronominal suffixes that we've had to this day. There are a few reasons that I only use a small portion of the chart these days.

-**m** as the suffix for "we" no longer makes sense. It assumes a derivation of -**mme**. In *Vinyar Tengwar* issue 49, we get a clear picture of Tolkien's later versions of the Quenya suffixes, and the consonant doubling was moved from the regular plural suffixes to the dual plural suffixes and described as a Quenya-only innovation. Therefore, the ancient suffix would have to have been -**me**, which would make the suffix result in -**(o)f** in Sindarin. This is confirmed in *Parma Eldalamberon* issue 22 page 167. Therefore, I cut all suffixes made from consonant doubling, which included -**ch**, -**st** and -**m**, and I replaced the "we" suffixes with the newer ones.

-**nc** as "you and us" doesn't make sense, since it is clearly derived from **ni** + **ci**, "you and I." This is confirmed in *Parma Eldalamberon* issue 22 page 167. I moved -**nc** to mean "you and I" and included the new suffix -**b** into the chart.

Nowhere else do you find the suffixes -**ir** for plural pronouns and -**id** for dual plural pronouns. They also don't make sense from a historical derivational view, because many of the ancient pronouns ended with E's and not I's. -**mmid** for example would make more sense as *-**mmed**, but that's not what is listed. So, I cut all of those from the list.

In *Vinyar Tengwar* issue 49, Tolkien establishes **ci** as a singular-only "you," **le** as a Quenya loanword for the singular formal "you," and **de** for the formal and plural "you." This cuts from the chart the dual and plural informal "you."

If you're curious, the chart showed the following suffixes:

	Singular	Plural
First person exclusive	-(o)n	-(o)f
First person inclusive[240]	-nc	-b
Familiar second person	-(o)g	—
Reverential second person	-(o)l	-(o)dh
Doriathren reverential second person	-(o)dh	
Third person	No suffix	-r

The suffix is added after the verb has been conjugated. In the exercises, I'll end such verbs in a dash, like this:

> **evíne-** (__ went) + **-nc**   = **evínenc** (you and I went)
> **teli-** (__ come) + **-r**   = **telir** (they come)

There will always be a vowel before the dash. If that vowel is an A and the suffix you're adding has **(o)** before it, change the A into an O.

> **linna-** (__ sing) + **-(o)n**   = **linnon** (I sing)
> **linna-** (__ sing) + **-b**   = **linnab** (you and we sing)

The third person singular is done not with a suffix, but a unique conjugation of the verb, so I won't have you doing those until you reach the verb chapter. The exception is when the verb ends in an A. Those are made by simply not adding a pronominal suffix to the verb.

> **linna**   = he/she/it sings
> **evin**   = he/she/it went
> **tôl**   = he/she/it comes

1st ex.	-(o)n	-m	-mmid	
1st inc.		-nc	-ngid	
	2nd f.	-(o)g	-gir	-ch
	2nd r.	-(o)dh	-dhir	-dhid/-st
	3rd	-	-r	-st

[240] These Inclusive suffixes are the result of pronouns being squished together. In the case of **-nc** the pronouns were "I" ni + "you" ci, and **-b** is from "you" ci + "us" **we** (which became KW, and KW became P, and P became B following a vowel). Thus, you can think of these two pronouns as "you and I" and "we and you."

7.2.1.1 Exercise

Add the pronoun suffixes to these two verbs.

ebenni- said	Singular	Plural
1st exclusive		
1st inclusive		
2nd familiar		■■■■■■■
2nd reverential		
3rd	ebent	

padra- walk	Singular	Plural
1st exclusive		
1st inclusive		
2nd familiar		■■■■■■■
2nd reverential		
3rd		

7.2.2 Possessive Pronoun Suffixes[241]

These are contracted forms, like how you can contract "is" into 's on the end of any noun in English. Therefore, these are more likely to show up in casual speech or in idioms, but not in archaic speech, nor any dialect not affected by the Noldor.

To use these, put them on the noun being possessed, never an adjective. If the noun ends in a vowel, then just put it onto the end of the noun. If the noun ends in a consonant, put an **-e-** between the end of the word and the pronoun suffix and the consonant becomes Intervocalic. Don't forget vowel reduction, as described in 4.2.1. Here are the suffixes:[242]

---

[241] We have two samples of a suffixed possessive pronoun in use, both "my." We can tell there is an influence from Quenya, since the chart of these suffixes provided includes **-nt** for "their," which shows a striking resemblance to the Quenya suffix **-nta** of the same meaning. The rest are based on the verb suffixes, except for the 3rd person singular suffix, which is based on the corresponding independent pronoun.

[242] The original chart of these can be found in *Parma Eldalamberon* issue 17 page 46. The chart I provide is a bit different, seeing as there have been a few

	Singular	Plural
First person exclusive	-n	*-f
First person inclusive	-nc	*-b
Familiar second person	-g	—
Reverential second person	-l	*-dh
Third person	-d	-nt

My book – I barf → I barv**en**
Our thread – I thlê → I thlê**f**
Your jaw – I anc → I ang**eg**
Your prison – I mand → I mann**el**
Y'all's tongues – I laim → I laimm**edh**
His/Her claw – I 'amp → I 'amm**ed**
Their reek – I osp → I osb**ent**

7.2.2.1 Exercise

Add the possessive pronoun suffixes onto these two nouns.

ant gift	Singular	Plural
1st exclusive		
1st inclusive		
2nd familiar		
2nd reverential		
3rd		

lanc throat	Singular	Plural
1st exclusive		
1st inclusive		
2nd familiar		
2nd reverential		
3rd		

---

changes in the 1st person plural pronominal suffixes over the years. I also added the plural 2nd person suffix. The original chart had the suffixes:

1st ex.	-n	-m(ir)
1st inc.		-nc/-ngir
2nd f.	-g	-gir
2nd r.	-l	-l(ir)
3rd	-d	-nt

7.2.3 Indefinite Pronouns

In English, indefinite pronouns begin with "some-," "any-," "every-,"
and "no-."

To fill in a few blanks, I used the prefixes **al-** "no" and **il-** "every" with
the pronouns.

7.2.3.1 Pen

The pronoun for "one/person/somebody/someone" is **pen**. Its opposite, "no one," is *****alben**. "Everyone" is *****ilphen**. Use normal lenition
rules for them; treat them like normal nouns.

> **Cenin ben.** I see someone.
>
> **Alben len gweriant.** No one betrayed you.
>
> **Ilphen istar.** Everyone knows.

7.2.3.2 Nad

The pronoun for "thing/something" is **nad**. Its opposite, "nothing," is
*****alnad**. "Everything" is *****ilnad**. Treat them as normal nouns.

> **Mado nad egor 'wanno!** Eat something or die!
>
> **Ach evennin alnad!** But I ate nothing!
>
> **Ilnad *rangen.** Everything is broken.

7.2.3.3 Sad

The pronoun for "place/someplace/somewhere" is **sad**. Its opposite,
"nowhere," is *****alhad**. "Everywhere" is *****ilhad**. Treat them as normal
nouns.

> **Telithon na had laug.** I will go to somewhere warm.
>
> **Baren alhad.** My home is nowhere.
>
> **Trevennin ilhad.** I've traveled everywhere.

7.2.3.4 Im, Anim, and În

A reflexive pronoun is a pronoun that reflects the subject of the sentence. In English, reflexive pronouns end in "-self." In Sindarin, the reflexive pronouns **im, anim**, and **în** are not marked by person or number, so you can use them to refer to any subject. **Im** could mean "myself, ourselves, yourself, yourselves, itself, herself, himself, themself, themselves" depending on the context its in. **Anim** is just the dative version of **im**. Likewise, **în** could mean "my own, our own, your own, y'all's own, its own, her own, his own, their own."

Im can be used in four different ways.

1. It can be used as the object of a verb. When it's being used this way, put it after the verb, like any other noun, just like the other indefinite pronouns are used.[243]

    Ristannen im.
    cut-I   self
    I cut myself.

    Harnol   im.
    hurt-you   self
    You hurt yourself.

    Amathon   a   Reinor   *law   eglerianner   im.
    Amathon   and   Reinor   no   glorified-they self
    Amathon and Reinor didn't glorify themselves.

2. It can be used with a preposition like any other pronoun or noun.[244]

    Ónen   ant   anim.
    gave-I   gift   to-self
    I gave a gift to myself.

---

[243] We don't have an example of this happening, but we guess that this is how it works.

[244] We have an example of it being used in the dative: **anim** in Gilraen's Linnod.

Peliant laiss oh im.
spread leaves around self
<u>It</u> spread leaves around <u>it</u>self.

3.   It can be used to emphasize the subject of the sentence, when used alongside the subject of the sentence. It's placed directly before the subject.[245] If the subject is a pronominal suffix, then it goes in the place that a noun subject would usually go.

Im   Glaewen   di   nestatha.
self   Glaewen   them heal-will
Glaewen herself will heal them.

Im   degin   yrch.
self   slay-I   orcs
I myself slay orcs.

Im   peniathol i   banas?
self   fix-will-you   the   floor
Would you yourself please fix the floor?

Im   Triwath   peniathol   i banas?
self   Triwath   fix-will-you the floor
Would you Triwath please fix the floor?

4.   It's used to introduce yourself, since it basically means "self." Don't mutate the name, because it is in the vocative case and you want people to know your non-mutated name.

---

[245] We have two examples of this, the first from the inscription on the Gate of Moria, and the other in *Vinyar Tengwar* issue 47 page 38.

Im   Nimmiel.

self   Nimmiel.

I'm Nimmiel.

Treat **în** as any other possessive pronoun. It is especially useful in the 3rd person, since the 3rd person possessive pronoun is the same for the singular and plural.

Ivreth sogant i   nên   în.

Ivreth   drank   the   water own

Ivreth drank her own water.

If you used **tîn** instead, it'd mean, "Ivreth drank his/her/its/their water," implying that she drank someone else's water, instead of her own!

7.2.3.4.1 Exercise

dough - *****maeas**	... kneaded - *****medhianne-**
son - **iôn**	... betrayed - **gwerianne-**
word - **peth**	... plays the harp – **gannada-**
	... wrote - **teithanne-**

Translate the following sentences:

1. I am Barawen.

    _____

2. (exclusive) We kneaded the dough ourselves.

    _____

3. (reverential, singular) You betrayed yourself.

    _____

4. My son plays the harp well himself.

    _____

5. (familiar) You wrote these words for yourself.

    _____

7.2.4 Conversation Practice: Diminutive Suffixes

A diminutive suffix is an affix that belittles, cutesy-fies, or "diminishes" whatever it is attached to. Often it is used as an endearment amongst family members or people in a very close relationship. In English, it takes several forms. Most often you'll see it as "my ___" or "my little ___." Sometimes we use a suffix from French, "-ette" or suffixes from Spanish, "-ina/-ino," or one from our own language, "-y." For example, you can use diminutive suffixes to make cute nicknames for loved ones. You could use the word for how they are related to you, like **benn** "husband" to make **bennig** "hubby." You could use their professional title, like **Tân** "smith" to make something like **Taneg** "little smith," or you can use part of their name, as long as it makes sense and is still meaningful. Take **Lothuial**, "Twilight Flower." You could take the "flower" part, **loth**, and make it **Lotheg**, "little flower." I wouldn't suggest it with a name like **Glaewen**, which means "Salve Maiden."

Other than endearments, these can also be used to insult someone, much the same way that using **ci** when you should be using **le** or **de** would be insulting. It'd be like calling someone a bad name. It's perfectly acceptable among people you're close to, but really rude with strangers or people above you in the hierarchy.

For example, you shouldn't call a Dwarf "**noged**." **Naug**, meaning "short" is already pretty insulting to a Dwarf, but **noged** "little short one" is a good way to get a mouthful of Dwarvish fist.[246] Some other good insults are **hírig** or **brethig** for bossy or proud people, meaning "little lord" or "little queen."

The more common use of the diminutive suffixes, however, is to indicate that there is only one of the things, as we learned in chapter 4.2.5.4 or that this thing is smaller than other things like it. Thus, you could say that there is **limmig** - "just one fish" or **filigod** "only one bird."

The suffixes are: (they all mean the same thing, and are interchangeable).

- **-eg**
- **-og**
- **-ig** This suffix triggers I-affection.

Before adding the suffix, Make the end of the word intervocalic, and reduce the vowels. If the word ends in a -G or -C, the -G in the suffix turns into a -D.

---

[246] Only if you're slow on your feet, **sui noged...**

If you add one of these suffixes onto an adjective, the adjective becomes a noun meaning "little ___ one."

Loth flower	→ **Lotheg** Little flower
Naug short	→ **Noged** Little short one/Petty Dwarf
Glamhoth orc-horde	→ **Glamog** one Orc
Filig little bird	→ **Filigod** Just one little bird
Benn "husband	→ **Bennig** hubby

Tolkien has already provided us with some pre-made diminutive familial terms:

- Daddy: **ada, atheg**
- Mommy: **nana, emig**
- Sis: **nethig**
- Bro: **honeg**
- Baby: **gwinig**

It may be possible to use **nîn** "my" as a diminutive too, like we do in English. It is done in Quenya. We have examples like **meldonya** "my friend" and **tyenya** "my (familiar) you." We might have an example of it in the Sindarin title Tolkien gave to the Pater Noster, **Ae Adar Nín,** which means "Hail My Father," but that is hard to tell since it's a title if it could be counted as a conversational element.

7.3 Relative Clauses and Questions

A subordinate clause is a sentence that can't stand on its own because it starts with a special type of word called a "complementizer," and therefore is part of another sentence. In this section, we will study the complementizers. We'll also be looking at others' reconstructions of these complementizers, because there are a lot of different approaches to them. With the little evidence we have, they all are shaky.

7.3.1 Subordinate Conjunction

This is for the simplest of subordinate clauses, and you will use it the most. Use it for making one sentence the direct object of a verb. In English, this sort of sentence normally goes like this:

"I know that Jimmy fell into the well."

"That Jimmy fell into the well" begins with the complementizer "that," and therefore is a subordinate clause.

Be careful. In English, we often leave "that" out of the sentence, as seen in "I know Jimmy fell into the well." If you can insert a "that" and the meaning is unchanged, then you know that you have a subordinate clause on your hands.

The Sindarin subordinate conjunction is **i**.[247] We don't know if you should mutate the word following it. Sometimes I do, sometimes I don't to distinguish it from the relative pronoun.

---

[247] We don't have any examples of it in action; but because **i** in Quenya is used for both the subordinate conjunction and the relative pronoun, I say that it is safe to use it the same way here. This is, however, an assumption, and you have the option of not building sentences that require subordinate conjunctions. There is a question of whether the **i** can be plural. We know that the relative pronoun can be plural or singular, because the noun it modifies can be plural or singular. In this case, "that" doesn't need to match a noun in number, so I doubt it would become plural to match the subject of the sentence it's complementizing.

Iston i Amathon ananc i orch.
know-I that Amathon slew the orc
I know [that] Amathon slew the orc.

Eru amarthast i adanath firir.
Eru decreed that human-all die-they
Eru decreed that all humans die.

7.3.1.1 Exercise

Subordinate the following sentences to the sentence **Sinnin** "I knew" using the subordinate conjunction.

1. **Udul dess anin fen.** A woman came to the door.
   _____

2. **Ilaurui Anor eria a dhanna**. Daily the sun rises and falls.
   _____

3. **Yrch enengir i adarel**. Orcs killed your father.
   _____

4. **Ni faug.** I am/was hungry.
   _____

5. **Dír-vudassel.** You worked hard.
   _____

7.3.2 Relative Pronouns

A relative clause begins with a complementizer called a Relative Pronoun. A relative clause modifies nouns just as adjectives and prepositional phrases do. In English we often leave this word out, so be careful. The English relative pronouns are "That/Who/Whom/Which."

In Sindarin they take three known shapes. The singular relative pronoun is **i** and its plural is **in** or **ai**.[248] The singular and plural relative pronouns are how a relative clause can become plural to match the noun it's modifying. The word following the relative pronoun is mutated using vocalic mutation for **i** and **ai** and nasal mutation for **in**.

_____

[248] This one is found only in one place, in **Ae Adar Nín.**

Ni	i	'wend	i	dírant	yrch	ú-'onodui.
I	the	girl	who	saw	orcs	un-countable

I am the girl who saw uncountable orcs.

Goston	in yryg	i	phadar	ne	dû.
Goston	in yryg	ai	badar	ne	dû.
fear-I	the monsters	who	walk-they	in	night

I fear the monsters that walk at night.

If a relative pronoun is attached to an accusative pronoun, the pronoun can't go before the verb as it normally does. Instead it follows the verb, with soft mutation still affecting it. Also, whether the pronoun has its Oblique **-n** depends on whether it is the subject or object of the relative clause.

To figure out whether you need an oblique pronoun or a nominative pronoun, look at the relative clause on its own, placing the pronoun back into the clause.

Reinor	mêl	den	i	Faradril	onnant.
Reinor	loves	her	whom	Faradril	begot

Reinor loves her whom Faradril begot.

"Faradril begot **her**" is what the relative clause is on its own. "Her" is the direct object, so you need the oblique pronoun.

Reinor	mêl	de	i	de	nathant.
Reinor	loves	she	who	him	saved

Reinor loves she who saved him.

"**She** saved him" is the relative clause on its own. In this case, the pronoun being modified by the relative clause came from the its subject, therefore it must be the nominative pronoun.

7.3.2.0.1 Exercise

Put together the following sentences, making one sentence a relative clause modifying a noun or pronoun.

1. **Iôn udul.** A boy came. + **Iôn aun 'lî annin.** A boy gave honey to me.

2. **I hell han ruthra.** That girl rages. + **Anno vant anin hell han.** Give food to that girl.

---

3. **I luith galar dhae orchal.** The flowers grow very high. + **Critho i luith.** Reap the flowers.

---

4. **I chui [n]gawar.** The dogs are howling. + **Tirion i chui.** I'm watching the dogs.

---

5. **Gosto i naen.** Fear the corpses. + **I naen cuiar.** The corpses live.

7.3.2.1 "When/While"

The rest of these are highly theoretical but are common fodder amongst Neo-Sindarin translators. Use at your own risk.

"When/while" for beginning relative clauses is **ir**.[249] Mutate the word following it with Liquid mutation.

> **Menathon ir   phenin   vellyn.**
> go-will-I   when lack-I   friends
> *I will go when I have no friends.*

---

[249] It can be found in one place: *The Lays of Beleriand*, in Lúthien's verse, and it was untranslated there. The idea that it means "when" comes from a similar word found in Qenya (an earlier draft of Quenya) that is **irë**. But the use of **ir** as an alternate version of the plural "the" in *Vinyar Tengwar* issue #50, which dates to Late Noldorin, is similar to the writing of Lúthien's verse. On the other hand, in *Parma Eldalamberon* issue 22, on page 147, Tolkien uses **-r** as a way to mark distinguish between "here" and "now," since they can both be translated as **sí**. There, he used **-r** to mark the time-related adverb, so perhaps **ir** is the time-related complementizer? Whether or not this is usable in Neo-Sindarin translation... we don't know. Plenty of people use it, and sometimes I do too.

7.3.2.2 Constructing the Rest of the Relative Pronouns

For the rest of the relative pronouns, there are two different common approaches. One set was designed by Ryszard Derdzinski, based on the Quenya relative pronoun root **ya-** and reconstructed ancient case suffixes.[250] It does make a certain amount of sense, but I disagree on one point. I think that the case endings were lost in Sindarin, and replaced with prepositions, but there really is no evidence either way for now.

The only other way that I can see to give us greater variety with relative pronouns is to use prepositions with the relative pronoun **i**. These would cause mutation to the word that directly follows them, but not to anything else. Below I've included a few examples.

English	Sindarin	Contracted Forms
To/For whom/which	**an i**	*****ani**
In where	**mi i**	*****mî**
From whom/where	**od i**	*****odi**
At where/when	**na i**	*****n'i**
During when	**ned i**	*****nedi**

Iston   ani   den   agóreg.
know-I for-whom it   did-you
I know why you did it.

N'i   genin, tolo   annin.
at-when call-I,   come to-me
When I call, come to me.

Menin n'Ondor   od   i   nidhin   dandoled.
go-I   to-Gondor from where intend-I returning
I will go to Gondor from where I will return.

---

[250] You can see how he derived them here: http://www.elvish.org/gwaith/ce_pronouns.htm#sindarin The list is as follows: "to/for whom" ***iad**, "in where" ***ias**, "from whom/where" ***ial**, and "how" ***ian**.

7.3.2.2.1 Exercise

hado throw (imperative)	**(n)dortha**- live
edra- open	**nôr** it/he/she runs
nella- ring bells	**teli**- come
linnatha- will sing	**ista**- know
medi- eat	**gond** stone
egíne- saw	**annon** gate

Translate the following sentences into English.

1. Hado i 'ond n'i i annon edra._____

    _____

2. Iston an i nellar. _____

3. Linnathof nedi vedil. _____

4. Len egínen vi i northar i vellyn nîn._____

    _____

5. I nîr nôr odi yrch telir. _____

7.3.3 Interrogative Pronouns

You should be able recognize "Interrogative" as an adjective form of "Interrogate." We're learning about Questions! Unfortunately, it is as messy and confusing as the Relative pronouns above.

Yes, this is yet another piece of Sindarin grammar that is almost wholly unknown. All that we have is a little phrase in Doriathrin, one of the languages that was abandoned to make way for Sindarin. The root for "what" in that phrase was **man**, and it appears to have survived to later writings, as we see cognates of it in Quenya in Galadriel's lament in *The Lord of the Rings*. In fact, there is a note in *Parma Eldalamberon* issue #17 about an ancient Elven root, MA, which is the basis for the Quenya **Man(a)** and **Manen**. Many Neo-Sindarin writers simply "Sindarin-ize" the Quenya derivations, but I think a better way would be to use prepositions instead.

We don't know what the word-order would be for the use of the interrogative pronouns, but I have some patterns that I use. If it's with a preposition, I topicalize it and pull the prepositional phrase to the beginning of the sentence. Otherwise I treat it as a pronoun, as you'll recall from 7.1.

In these examples, I've included the answers to the questions so you can see how they'd fit together.

Ma   hen   agor?
who   this   did?
Who did this?

 Yrch hen   agórer.
 orcs   this   did
 Orcs did this.

In   yrch   man   enengir?
the   orcs   whom   killed?
Whom did the orcs kill?

 Enengir   i   naneth   gwanûn.
 killed-they   the   mother   twins
 They killed the mother of twins.

Here are some suggestions for common prepositions to combine with **man**.

English	Sindarin	Contracted Forms
to/for whom/what (why?)	**am man**	*****amman**
in where (where?)	**mi van**	*****mivan**
at/to when/where (where?/when?)	**na van**	*****navan**
from where (whence?)	**o man**	*****oman**
during when (when?)	**ne man**	*****neman**
with[251] what (how?)	**na man**	*****naman**

In the answers, you'd use the same preposition that was used in the question.

Navan   menig?
To-where   go-you?
Where are you going?

---

[251] Review this word's meaning in 3.2.2.1.

Menin   na   mâr   mellon   în.
Go-I   to   house   friend   own.
I'm going to my own friend's house.

Oman   onúreg?
From-what ran-you?
Why did you run?

Onúren o   chin.
Ran-I   from   you.
I ran from you.

Another way to get more interrogatives is to use the interrogative adjective **man**, which basically means "which." Use it just like you use demonstrative adjectives.

English	Sindarin
which place (where?)	sad van
which person (who?)	pen van
which thing (which one?)	nad van
which way/road (how?)	men van

These phrases should be left inside the sentence, not moved to the beginning of the sentence.

Dorthol vi   had van?
Live-you in   place which?
Where do you live?

Dorthon vi   Veleriand.
Live-I   in   Beleriand.
I live in Beleriand.

Udúlel   hí   po   ven van?
Came-you here on   way which?
How did you get here?

Aphadannen i   râd   dholen.
Followed-I   the   road   hidden.
I followed the hidden road.

7.3.3.1 Exercise

Translate the following questions into Sindarin.

it/she/he comes **tôl**
ate **evenni-**
found *ichíre-
it/she/he followed **aphadant**
it/she/he made **echant**

1. Who comes? _____
2. What did you eat? (informal) _____
3. Where did you find it? (formal) _____
4. Which one followed y'all? _____
5. How did she make this? _____

7.3.4 Yes/No Questions

When we write a yes/no question in Sindarin, simply write a normal statement and add a question mark.

Forming an answer for yes/no questions gives a lot of people trouble because catch-all words for "yes" and "no" do not exist in Sindarin, but there are ways to answer such questions. This is a good time to go back and revisit chapter 6.1, and go over negation again.

Let's break Yes/No questions into three categories: Finding out the truth, asking someone to do something, and asking for permission to do something.

7.3.4.1 True or False?

When asking if something is true or not, you phrase it like a statement. Raising your intonation at the end or a question-mark will let the person being asked know that this is a question. When answering, simply repeat the statement with the correct pronouns and negation. There also are a few short words you can use.

For "yes" you can use *Naw! (It is so!), Ma! (Right!/Good!), or Thand! (True!) or if you aren't sure if it's true and want it to be, you can say No! (May it be so!/I hope so!/Make it so!)

For "no" you can use *Law! (It isn't so!), Althand! (Not-true!), or *Lae-, which we studied in 6.1.1.3. If you aren't sure if it's false but you want it to not be, you can say *Law no! (May it not be so!/I hope not!) or Avo no! (Don't make it so!)

I laiss mellin? Are the leaves golden?

> **I laiss mellin.** The leaves are golden.
> **Ma.** Right.
> *****Naw.** It is so.
> **Thand.** True.
> **No.** I hope so.
> **I laiss *law vellin.** The leaves are not golden.
> *****Law.** It is not so.
> **Althand.** Not-true.
> *****Laer.** They aren't.
> *****Law no.** I hope not.
> **Avo no!** Don't make it so!

Enengig i adaren? Did you kill my father?

> **Enengin i adareg.** I killed your father.
> **Agóren.** I did.
> *****Naw.** It is so.
> **Ma.** Right.
> **Thand.** True.
> **No.** I hope so.
> *****Law enengin i adareg.** I didn't kill your father.
> *****Law agóren.** I didn't.
> *****Laen.** Not I.
> *****Law.** It is not so.
> **Althand.** Not-true.
> *****Law no.** I hope not.
> **Avo no!** Don't make it so!

Sevil masgorn? Do you have a loaf of bread?

> **Sevin masgorn.** I have a loaf of bread.
> **Sevin.** I have.
> **Ma.** Right.

*__Naw__. It is so.

__Thand__. True.

__No__. I hope so.

__Penin masgorn__. I lack a loaf of bread.

__Penin__. I lack.

*__Laen__. Not I.

*__Law__. It is not so.

__Althand__. Not-true.

*__Law no__. I hope not.

__Avo no__! Don't make it so!

7.3.4.2 Would you please?

When asking someone to do something, you use the future-tense suffix -__atha__ and otherwise phrase it like a statement. When answering it, repeat the statement with the correct pronouns and negation.

For "yes" you can use __Athon__! (I will!/I'm willing to!/I agree to!/I consent to!) and for "no" you can say __Avon__! (I won't!/I refuse to!)

> __Ni linnathol?__ Would you please sing for me?

>> __Le linnathon__. I will sing for you.
>> __Athon__. I will.
>> __Avon le linnad__. I won't sing for you.
>> __Avon__. I won't.

7.3.4.3 May I?

When asking someone for permission, use the future tense suffix -__atha__ and phrase it like a statement. Or you can use the slightly longer *__devil__/*__devig annin...__ (Do you permit me to...) or you can use the helping verb *__ce__. When answering it, repeat it as a command with the proper pronouns and negation.

For "yes" you can say __Caro__! (Do it!) or __No__! (Make it so!). For "no" you can say, __Baw__! (Don't!) while jerking your head upward or __Avo garo__! (Don't do it!) or the slightly shorter version, __Avo__! (Don't!)

Havathon? Shall I sit?

Devil annin haved? Do you permit me to sit?

Ce chevin? Might I sit?

> **Havo**. Sit.
>
> **Caro**. Do it.
>
> **No**. Make it so.
>
> **Avo chavo**. Don't sit.
>
> ***Law chavo***. Don't sit.
>
> **Avo garo**. Don't do it.
>
> **Avo**. Don't.
>
> **Baw**! Don't!

7.3.4.4 Exercise

Answer the following questions in Sindarin as directed.

1. Q. **Gostol**? Are you afraid?
   A. "Not I."_____

2. Q. **Sevil i 'aud i echennin**? Do you have the machine that I made?
   A. "I hope so." _____

3. Q. **Mudathol hîr**? Would you please work today?
   A. "I will." _____

4. Q. ***Ce gi mibin***? Might I kiss you?
   A. "Don't!"_____

5. Q. ***Devil annin le muiad***? Do you permit me to serve you?
   A. "Make it so."_____

7.3.5 Conditional Phrases

"If" for beginning conditional clauses is ***pi***.[252]

---

[252] I reconstructed *pi from a passage in *Vinyar Tengwar* #49 pages 19-20, 26, 27 and *Parma Eldalamberon* #22 page 158 which named the root KWI meaning "suppose," and a Quenya derivative word, "if" – **qui**. There is another root, EK(E), relating to uncertainty, from which the Quenya terms "may, might, perhaps, if" **ce** and **cé** come from. These, I feel, are better than the previous reconstruction by David Salo, **ae**. It's made from a Quenya term **aiquen**, which comes from *The War of the Jewels*, The Quendi and the Eldar. It appears only

Place it at the beginning of the phrase that it is subordinating. We don't know if it would cause mutation or not, so that is up to you.

Because *ce or *cí also are a modality modifiers for the verb, you can use them for "might" or "may," like in "he might like it" or "I may go to Bree tomorrow." *Cí is a more emphatic version of *ce, and I prefer to use it for interjections "Perhaps" and "maybe." Mutate the word following them.

> ***Pi   le   beren   maethathol.**
> If   you   brave   fight-will-you
> *If you are brave, you will agree to fight.*

> **Ummas   *ce   dôl.**
> Evil   may   come.
> *Evil may come.*

> ***Cí   dolathon   ab   in   yrch dengin.**
> Perhaps   come-will-I after the   orcs slain.
> *Perhaps I will come, after the orcs are slain.*

If you have both ***ce** and ***law** on the same verb, put *law before the verb and ***ce** or ***cí** after it.[253]

> ***Law   hen   anírol   *cí   sîr.**
> No   this   want-you perhaps today.
> *You might not want this today.*

7.3.6 Conversation Practice: "Thank you"

Thanking someone in Sindarin isn't as easy as you may think. There is no verb for "to thank" native to Sindarin. Many people use a loan-word

---

on that word. Because ae appears in the LotR movies, it is the most wide-spread Neo-Sindarin reconstruction for "if." In the more recent *The Hobbit* movies, David Salo seems to prefer using **cí**.

If you don't want to take the chance on these reconstructions, I'd suggest using "when" **ir** instead.

[253] Another guess based on Quenya.

from Quenya, ***hanna-**, but that only works for dialects affected by the Noldor. For everyone else, we need to get creative.

There are a few different ways that I approach this translation. Most importantly, consider what you are thanking someone for. Then give the person a compliment regarding what they did.

- If they gave you something or decided a conflict in your favor, I'd use **Le fael** "You are just/generous."
- If they helped you, you can say **Le athae** "You are helpful."
- If they were kind to you, you can say **Le vilui** "You are kind."
- If you want to be vague, you can say **Le vaer** "You are good."
- If you want to emphasis how happy they've made you, you can say, **Ni 'lassui** "I am happy."

And if you want to use ***hanna-**, it'd be used like this: **Le *channon** "I thank you."

Chapter 8: Verbs

The difficulty and the fun in studying Tolkien's languages is that every once in a while something gets published that completely overturns everything you thought you knew. In most recent memory, that is *Parma Eldalamberon* issues #17 and #22. It's rewritten much of what we thought we knew about verbs and their conjugation, especially when dealing with the past tense. Until then, the system we'd been using was based on Noldorin. It's similar in many respects, especially for the verbs ending in A, but the roots ending in consonants are treated very, very differently. It appears that Tolkien changed his mind a few times on how verbs should be conjugated, and we aren't entirely certain which systems he kept and which systems he discarded. We still lack a complete picture of Sindarin verb tenses and conjugations. If Tolkien ever sat down and described Sindarin verbs in detail, that document has yet to be published.

8.1 Present and Future Tenses

There are two main types of verbs: derived verbs, and root verbs. Both Sindarin and Quenya have them, and they have the same relations. If you go back to Common Eldarin, you'll see the basis of this. These two are:

1. Root verbs are verbs which are a stem with nothing suffixed onto them. In Sindarin these are commonly known as **I-verbs** because in the infinitive they have an **-i** added to them.
2. Derived verbs are a stem plus another element to modify the meaning of the stem slightly. There are several of these additions: **-a**, **-ia**, **-ta**, **-ra**, and **-na**. Because of this, they are often called **A-verbs**.

In this lesson, we will learn the simple present, continuous, and imperative tense conjugations.

When Sindarin verbs are listed in (good!) dictionaries, they are listed by their verb-roots, not as infinitives.

8.1.1 Simple Present Tense[254]

In English, there are two present tenses: the present progressive tense (I am doing) and the simple present tense (I do). Quenya has a way to distinguish them. In Sindarin they are made the same way, or at least that's what we think for now. More on that later.

Present tense for A-verbs is straightforward. It's just the verb root plus the pronominal suffixes. Again, here's the chart of nominative suffixes for quick reference.

---

[254] This is the least controversial and most thoroughly described tense in Sindarin. Here are articles from two different authors on the subject: Helge Fauskanger's "Reconstructing the Sindarin Verb System" http://folk.uib.no/hnohf/sverb-rec.htm and Thorsten Renk's "The Sindarin Verb System" http://www.science-and-fiction.org/elvish/verbs.html These articles are outdated by recent publications when it comes to the other tenses, but they're still good for the Simple present tense.

	Singular	Plural
1st exclusive	-(o)n	-(o)f
1st inclusive	-nc	-b
Familiar 2nd	-(o)g	—
Reverential 2nd	-(o)l	-(o)dh
3rd person	No suffix	-r

Gosta- fear

> **Goston** I fear
>
> **Gosta** It/she/he fears

The present tense for I-verbs is a little more difficult. Because an -i- is inserted between the pronoun suffix and the verb root, I-Affection[255] of the root takes place.

The third person singular is different. If the root of the I-verb is one syllable long, add a circumflex accent to the vowel. If it is more than one syllable long, none of the vowels are lengthened.

If the root ends with an F, then the F becomes a V because an F at the end of a word sounds like a V, as you recall from 2.2.

Laf- lick

> **Levin** I lick
>
> **Lâf** it/she/he licks

Osgar- amputate

> **Esgerin** I amputate
>
> **Osgar** it/she/he amputates

8.1.1.1 Exercise

Conjugate the following verbs into the present tense with the pronominal suffixes attached.

---

[255] Review I-Affection in 4.1.2.1.

thuia- "breathe"	Singular	Plural
1st exclusive		
1st inclusive		
Familiar 2nd		
Reverential 2nd		
3rd person		

haf- "sit"		
1st exclusive		
1st inclusive		
Familiar 2nd		
Reverential 2nd		
3rd person		

*(n)dadhren- "forget"		
1st exclusive		
1st inclusive		
Familiar 2nd		
Reverential 2nd		
3rd person		

8.1.2 Possible Present Progressive

In *Parma Eldalamberon* issue 22, amidst the descriptions of the Sindarin future tenses there was a word introduced to us: **tolen** "I am coming." This contradicts the present tense information that we have. In fact, based on our current present-tense conjugation model, we'd expect it to be **telin**. Is this a new present progressive tense? It's impossible to tell with a data-point of 1. If it is, my prediction is that it would be conjugated like this:

	Singular	Plural
1st Exclusive	Tolen	Tolef
1st Inclusive	Tolenc	Toleb
Familiar 2nd	Toleg	—
Reverential 2nd	Tolel	Toledh
3rd	Tôl	Toler

It's my guess, based on the fact that the vowels at the ends of words were lost in Sindarin, that the 3rd person singular would be the same in both the continuous and simple present tenses, and that A-verbs wouldn't have a distinctive progressive form either.

Keep in mind that this is highly speculative and likely will change. I won't use it in my translations, except with **tol-** in that specific future-tense context for now.

8.1.3 The Imperative

In English, the imperative is made by taking the word "you" out of the subject of the sentence. In Sindarin, the verbs have special forms just for ordering others around. You may recall from 3.4, that this construction can also be used to express hope or longing for an event to take place, like English "may it be so."

The imperative for A-verbs is very easy. Take the A off of the root and add an O in its place.

> **Linna-** sing, chant → **Linno**
>
> **Gosta-** fear   → **Gosto**

It's very easy for I-verbs as well. Take the verb root and suffix an O onto it.

> **Laf-** lick   → **Lavo**
>
> **Tol-** come → **Tolo**

In Sindarin, there is a verb for "to be," **no**, but it only appears in the imperative. When using it, put the mutated adjective right after it, then put in the subject of the sentence.

> **No lagor i roch lîn!** May your horse be swift!
>
> **No dhínen!** Be silent!

8.1.3.1 Exercise

Conjugate the following verbs into the Imperative.

1. **thuia-** breathe_____
2. **haf-** sit _____
3. ***(n)dadhren-** forget_____

4. **iuitha-** use _____
5. **gor-** advise _____

8.1.4 Gerunds

A gerund is a very noun-like verb. It's used in compound predicates, as you learned in 3.3.3.1. A gerund can take on objects and adverbs like a verb, but it can't have a subject. It also can be treated like a noun, though it can't be made plural. In English, gerunds are made by adding -ing to the end of a verb: "(the) singing."

To make a gerund, add **-d** to A-verbs and **-ed** to I-verbs.

> **Linna-** sing → **Linnad** singing
>
> **Dag-** kill   → **Daged** killing

8.1.4.1 Exercise

Make the following verbs into Gerunds.

1. **thuia-** breathe _____
2. **haf-** sit _____
3. ***(n)dadhren-** forget _____
4. **iuitha-** use _____
5. **gor-** advise _____

8.1.5 Future Tense

In English, there are two ways of making the future tense. "I will laugh," and "I'm going to laugh." Sindarin, on the other hand, doesn't have a pure future tense. When saying that something will happen, you use the simple present. So, instead of "It will happen" you'd say "It happens." But there are forms that have future connotations.

This is new information from *Parma Eldalamberon* issue 22. Not everyone will have gotten the new issue, and some websites aren't updated anymore. Therefore, you won't find this information in other places beyond informal blog and forum posts. In order to understand the outdated translations, I'll explain the old system as well.

8.1.5.1 Tol-

The most commonly used is the verb **tol-**, which means "to come." When used with a gerund, it means that the action is approaching in time *and space*.

The examples that have been revealed have a strange conjugation that may be a present progressive, as I described in 8.1.2. For now, we'll use it as part of a formula.

> **Tolen daged yrch**. I'm going to kill orcs.

This would be something that you say while approaching the location where you will do the orc-killing.

> **Telin daged yrch**. I will go to kill orcs.

This would be something you say before you've left.

8.1.5.1.1 Exercise

Conjugate the following verbs into the **tol-** future tense, in 1st person singular.

1. **thuia-** breathe _____
2. **haf-** sit _____
3. ***(n)dadhren-** forget _____
4. **iuitha-** use _____
5. **gor-** advise _____

8.1.5.2 Nidh-

The verb **nidh-** is also commonly used. It means "to intend to." As with **tol-**, the tense and the pronoun suffix go on **nidh-**.

> **Nidhin daged yrch**. I will kill orcs. (I intend to kill orcs.)

8.1.5.2.1 Exercise

Conjugate the following verbs into the **nidh-** future tense, in 1st person singular.

1. **thuia-** breathe_____
2. **haf-** sit _____
3. ***(n)dadhren-** forget_____
4. **iuitha-** use _____
5. **gor-** advise_____

8.1.5.3 -Atha

The suffix **-atha** is used usually in question/answer scenarios, but you can use it to describe an action that the speaker is agreeable towards and will willingly do. It means "to consent to, to agree to, to be willing to." It used to be a verb, but it's become a suffix, **-atha**.

To use it, suffix **-atha** to the root of the verb, then add the pronoun suffix, and treat it like an A-verb.

> **Linnathog**? Are you willing to sing?
>> **Linnathon**. I am willing to sing.
> **Dagathodh yrch**? Do you agree to kill orcs?
>> **Dagathof yrch**. We agree to kill orcs.

8.1.5.3.1 Exercise

Conjugate the following verbs into the **-atha** future tense, in 3rd person singular.

1. **thuia-** breathe_____
2. **haf-** sit _____
3. ***(n)dadhren-** forget_____
4. **iuitha-** use _____
5. **gor-** advise_____

8.1.5.4 Ava-

We covered **Ava-** in 6.1.3 when we learned the various forms of negation, but we'll expand a little on it here. **Ava-** is the semantic opposite of **Atha**. While **Atha** marks consent, **Ava** marks refusal. They both have a future connotation as well. That's why **Avon** is usually translated as "I will not." So, if a question is asked with **Atha** and the speaker doesn't want to do it, they'd respond with **Ava**.

As you should recall, using **Ava-** is just like using **Tol-** and **Nidh-** above.

Linnathog? Are you willing to sing?

Avon linnad. I refuse to sing.

Dagathodh edain? Do you agree to kill humans?

Avof daged edain. We refuse to kill humans.

8.1.5.4.1 Exercise

Conjugate the following verbs into the **ava-** future tense, in 1st person singular.

1. **thuia-** breathe_____
2. **haf-** sit _____
3. ***(n)dadhren-** forget_____
4. **iuitha-** use _____
5. **gor-** advise_____

8.1.5.5 Noldorin Future Tense

In Noldorin, the suffix was **-tha** instead, and we used it with the **-i-**, causing I-affection. Our only sample of it in action was **Le linnathon,** which was translated as "I will sing for you." Therefore, we didn't know its full meaning. Back then we thought that it was a plain future tense like Quenya's **-uva** suffix. But since the publication of *Parma Eldalamberon* issue 22, we discovered that we had it wrong. The older Sindarin grammars and translations will not have this new information and will likely use the suffix **-itha** with I-verbs and use it as a general future tense.

8.1.6 Conversation Practice: Money and Trade

The Elves don't appear to have money, and instead have a barter economy. Here is some useful vocabulary for their negotiations.

- **(m)bach** item for trade
- **(m)banga-** trade
- ***cil-** chose
- ***pil-** steal
- **aníra-** want
- **anna-** give, *irregular gerund*: **aned**

- **farn** enough
- **feira-** suffice
- **gweria-** cheat
- **ídhra-** long for
- **leutha-** pick up/out with your fingers
- **pen-** lack
- **saf-** have

We do know that the Gondorians have money. They have two different coins:

1. **Mirian** – called **castar** in Westron. It's a silver coin.
2. **Canath** – called **tharni** in Westron. It's a fourth of the silver coin, literally chopped into 4 pieces. **Canath**'s resemblance to the number **canad** "four" isn't a coincidence.

This is a good point to go back to 3.5 and brush up on your numbers.

8.2 Past Tense[256]

If you haven't found yourself a copy of *The Lost Road* (the book that has *The Etymologies* in it) get it now. It will be very useful for figuring out the conjugations.

Past tense in Sindarin covers almost all forms of past tense in English. I watched; I have watched; I have been watching – these are all translated the same way.

8.2.1 Weak Past Tense for A-Verbs

This tense is formed by adding a suffix to the verb, so it is referred to as the "weak past tense."[257] Its meaning is exactly the same as the strong past tense, these are just for different classes of verbs.

When conjugating A-verbs, you must take into account whether the verb is intransitive or transitive.

The transitive past tense suffix of the A-verb is -**nt**. (Transitive verbs are verbs that take a direct object.)

Lasta- → **Lastant** it heard
Dolla- → **Dollant** it concealed
Minna- → **Minnant** it entered
Dringa- → **Dringant** it hammered

---

[256] A good article to read is "The Sindarin Past Tense" by Thorsten Renk, found here: http://www.science-and-fiction.org/elvish/sindarin_past_tense.html It's the most updated article, but it's missing new information revealed in *Parma Eldalamberon* issue 22, which I have incorporated here.

[257] This terminology Tolkien took from the study of Anglo-Saxon, which has "strong" and "weak" conjugations of adjectives, verbs, and nouns.

To make the forms for the other pronouns, you add an -e to the end of the past tense verb, which turns the **nt** into **nn,**[258] then add the pronoun suffix. In the case of roots that end in **-nna**, to avoid **-nnanne-** it is simplified down to **-nne-**.

> **Lastant**   → **Lastannen** I heard
> **Dollant**   → **Dollanneg** you concealed
> **Minnant**   → **Minnedh** y'all entered
> **Dringant** → **Dringanner** they hammered

The intransitive/impersonal[259] past tense suffix is **-s** or **-st**. There is no difference in meaning between them; they can be used interchangeably.

> **Lasta-**   → **Lastas** it listened
> **Delia-**   → **Deliast** it hid
> **Muda-**   → **Mudas** it labored
> **Brona-**   → **Bronast** it survived

To make the other pronouns' forms, add an -e, and it will make the -s or -st into an -ss-. Then add the pronoun suffix.

> **Lastas**   → **Lastassef** we, not you, listened
> **Deliast**   → **Deliasseg** you hid
> **Mudas**   → **Mudassedh** y'all labored
> **Bronast**   → **Bronasser** they survived

Notice how the -s(t) suffix can be used to change a verb's meaning slightly? With this, you can make a verb intransitive. So, if you have a word that has a very similar meaning in the transitive like "to hear," you can put it into its intransitive version: "to listen." Keep in mind that there are some verbs that this just won't work on, like "to come." There's no way you can make that transitive.

---

[258] **NT** becomes **NTH** intervocalically in the South Beleriand and Woodelven dialects.
[259] Review 3.3.2 and 3.3.

8.2.1.0.1 Exercise

Conjugate the following verbs into the past tense, in the 3rd person singular and 1st person singular.

1. **Narcha-** rend (transitive) _____
2. **Hwinia-** twirl (intransitive)_____
3. **Groga-** feel terror (intransitive) _____
4. **Critha-** reap (transitive) _____
5. ***Glosta-** snow (impersonal) _____

8.2.1.1 -TA Verbs

Long ago, when the languages were still Common Eldarin, the verb-augmenting suffix -tā was a separate morpheme. It was causative, which means the subject is causing someone/something else to do the action, which is why they often are transitive verbs. In Sindarin, -tā has long since been absorbed into the verbs. The only times that we see evidence of it having been there is in the past tense and (rarely) in gerunds. The -tā will be dropped from the verb root and these words will be treated like I-verbs instead of A-verbs. Therefore, they'll be covered in the I-Verb section.

These verbs are listed with the portion dropped for the past tense in (parentheses). These aren't all of the TA-verbs, just the ones that we have evidence to suggest would lose the TA and act like I-verbs.

> **an(na)-** give *Gerund*: **aned**
>
> ***(n)danan(na)-** give back, return
>
> **dan(na)-** fall
>
> **dol(la)-** hide, conceal (sundóma U)
>
> **edon(na)-** beget
>
> ***istan(na)-** give knowledge, teach, instruct
>
> **men(na)-** send
>
> **on(na)-** beget
>
> **suilan(na)-** give greetings
>
> **tol(la)-** fetch, make come (sundóma U)

8.2.2 Strong Past Tense for I-Verbs

This tense is made by changing the root of the verb instead of adding a morpheme to it, thus it's called the "strong past tense." It's used with the TA-verbs and I-verbs.

For the I-verb, there are three ways that the past tense is made, and these are often combined: adding an extra vowel, lengthening the root's vowel, and a nasal infix.

For I-Verbs, you don't need to worry about transitive/intransitive.

8.2.2.1 Prefixes and I-verbs[260]

If there is a prefix on the verb root, the prefix is added onto the conjugated verb.

> **A-char-** → **Ad-agor** it did __ again
> **Ú-bed-**   → **Ú-ebent** it couldn't say

However, if the prefix was added back in Common Eldarin the vowel is <u>not</u> prefixed onto the main root. These are pretty easy to pick out because the roots have more than one syllable.

> **Govan-** → **Govon**, not **Goavon** "it met"
> **Echad-** → **Echant**, not **Edagant** "it fashioned"

8.2.2.2 I-Verbs Ending in Stops

The nasal suffix -n is for I-verbs that end in stops (B, D, G), but it's not as simple as you would hope. The -n mutates the consonant it is attached to.

---

[260] In *Parma Eldalamberon* issue 17 page 42, Tolkien mentions this specifically with the verb **echad-**, making its past tense **echant**.

Ending	+	Nasaliza-tion	=	Result	Intervocalic
-b	+	n	=	-mp	-mm-[261]
-d	+	n	=	-nt	-nn-
-g	+	n	=	-nc	-ng-

But these aren't the only changes that occur. Take the vowel of the root, called the **sundóma** (plural **sundómar**) and put a copy of it before the root—if the root starts with a consonant. Because of this, the following consonant is put under Soft Mutation.

Heb- → **Echemp** it kept

Mad- → **Avant** it ate

Gad- → **Ant** it caught (the G mutates to nothing, leaving the sundóma at the beginning of the word)

Tog- → **Udunc** it led

Tob- → **Odomp** It covered

As you can see, finding the sundóma isn't always so simple. Some Os will become Us, because in ancient times they *were* Us. To know this, you must go back to the ancient root. **Tog-** is from the ancient word **tuk-**, and **tob-** is from the ancient root **top-**.

To make the other forms, add an **-i** to the end. This will cause I-affection in the vowels preceding it, and it would make the nasalized consonants intervocalic. Finally, add the pronoun suffix onto the **-i**.

Echemp → **Echemmin** I kept

Avant   → **Evennif** we, not you, ate

Udunc   → **Ydyngig** you led

Odomp   → **Edemmir** they covered

---

[261] In the South Beleriand and Woodelven dialects, **MP** becomes **MPH** intervocalically, and **NT** becomes **NTH**, and **NC** becomes **ÑCH**.

8.2.2.2.1 Exercise

Conjugate the following verbs into the past tense, in the 3rd person singular and 1st person singular. I've included the sundóma information that you need so that you won't have to look these up.

1. **Blab-** beat, flap _____
2. **Had-** hurl, throw _____
3. **Nag-** bite _____
4. **Nod-** tie, bind (sundóma U) _____
5. ***Rag-** break_____

8.2.2.3 I-Verbs Ending in Continuants

Verb roots ending in other consonants (**V, DH, N, L, R, TH,** and **W**[262]) don't use any nasal augmentation and instead only lengthens the verb roots' Sundómar.

When making this type of past tense, you duplicate the sundóma at the beginning of the word then "lengthen" the sundóma. That lengthening happened long ago, before long vowels in the last syllable of multi-syllable words were shortened. Here is a chart of the way that the sundómar change.

Sundómar	→	Last Syllable of a Multi-syllable Word	Single Syllable Word
A	→	O	AU
E/I	→	I	Î
O/U	→	U	Û

If you end up with a verb ending in -OW, the W would be lost.

If the sundóma of the Sindarin verb is a Y, it came from an ancient JU or JO, and would become IU in Sindarin.

---

[262] We used to include V, DH, and N in the Stop-group. But because in Sindarin we only have examples of the Stop-I-verbs with nasalization and a couple examples of verbs ending in N with sundóma lengthening and no nasalization, they were moved to the second class of I-Verbs.

If you have a root that starts with G, the G is deleted and you're left with nothing but the lengthened sundóma. Because it wouldn't be two syllables long, it'd keep its length.

Dar-   → **Adhor** it halted

Thel-   → **Ethil** it intended

Anna-   → **Aun** it gave

Tir-   → **Idir** it watched

Gor-   → **Ûr** it advised

Nor-   → **Onur** it ran

Tol-   → **Udul** it came

Yr-   → **Uiur** it ran

Doing the extra forms for these is a little different than the other I-verbs. The length on the sundómar will reappear, because they aren't in the final syllable and wouldn't have lost their length. Here is a chart of what they'd be:

Shortened Sundómar	→	Long Sundómar
AU/O	→	Ó
I	→	Í
U	→	Ú

Then an E is suffixed on, followed by the pronoun suffix. You have no I-Affection to worry about this time.

Adhor → **Adhóren** I halted

Ethil   → **Ethíleb** we, and you, intended

Aun   → **Ónef** we, not you, gave

Idir   → **Idírel** you watched

Ûr   → **Úreg** you advised

Onur   → **Onúredh** y'all ran

Udul   → **Udúlen** You and I came

Uiur   → **Uiúrer** they ran

8.2.2.3.1 Exercise

Conjugate the following verbs into the past tense, in the 3rd person singular and 1st person singular.

1. **Dew**- fail, miss_____
2. *__Ren__- remember _____
3. **Badh**- judge _____
4. **Dolla**- conceal, hide_____
5. **Gir**- shudder_____

8.2.3 The Irregular Verbs

Not all verbs follow the rules. Here are the verbs that won't conjugate as you would expect them to. They'll just have to be memorized.

(m)boe "It is necessary"[263] an impersonal verb[264] that can't be conjugated

caw- "Taste, Select, Choose"
    Past Participle: **caun**

carfa- "Speak, Pronounce"
    Strong Past Tense 3rd Person Singular: **agramp**
    Strong Past Tense with Pronoun Suffixes: **egremmi**-
    Transitive Weak Past Tense 3rd Person Singular: **agarfant**
    Intransitive Weak Past Tense 3rd Person Singular: **agarfas(t)**
    Past Participle: **crammen**

damma- "Hammer"
    Past Tense 3rd Person Singular: **dammint**
    Past Tense with Pronoun Suffixes: **damminni**-

egledhia- "Go into Exile"
    Strong Past Tense 3rd Person Singular: **eglant**
    Strong Past Tense with Pronoun Suffixes: **eglenni**-
    Weak Past Tense 3rd Person Singular: **egledhas(t)**

---

[263] This is an updated Noldorin term. It used to be **bui**.

[264] Review 3.4.3 for how to use them in sentences.

ista- "Have Knowledge, Know"
> Past Tense 3rd Person Singular: **sint**
> Past Tense with Pronoun Suffixes: **sinni-**

limmida- "Moisten"
> Past Tense 3rd Person Singular: **limmint**
> Past Tense with Pronoun Suffixes: **limminni-**

nimmida- "Whiten, Blanche"
> Past Tense 3rd Person Singular: **nimmint**
> Past Tense with Pronoun Suffixes: **nimminni-**

ortha- "Raise, Lift up"
> Past Tense 3rd Person Singular: **oront**
> Past Tense with Pronoun suffixes: **erenni-**

reitha- "Try, Strive"
> Transitive Past Tense 3rd Person Singular: **rithant**
> Intransitive Past Tense 3rd Person Singular: **rithas(t)**

sav- "Have"
> Past Tense 3rd Person Singular: **aw**
> Past Tense with Pronoun Suffixes: **awe-**

uil "It's raining"[265] an impersonal verb that can't be conjugated

8.2.4 Elven Culture: Time of Day

Let's go through the words for the time of day, starting with the early, early morning.

The **arad** (day) starts with **minuial**, the first **uial** (twilight).

Then as the sun **eria** (rises), it's **aur** (day-time).

The sun's name is **Anor**, The Fire, and its light is called **glawar**, a word closely related to the Quenya name Laurelin. Anor **gâl**[266] (shines with radiance).

---

[265] This is an updated Noldorin term. It used to be **œil**.

[266] This is an NG- word.

Then Anor **danna** (falls).

It **thinna** (fades, grows dark, turns grey) as aur becomes **aduial**, the second uial.

When the first stars appear, it becomes **tinnu** (starry twilight).

And when it's **dûr** (dark), it's **dû** (night).

The name of the moon is **Ithil**, The Sheen. **Elenath** (all of the stars in the sky) and Ithil **sílar** (shine with silver light). **Gilgalad**[267] (starlight) and **Calad Ithil** (Ithil's light) are **silivrin**[268] (silver-white).

---

[267] This is an NG- word.

[268] This is the plural of this adjective. The singular is **silivren**.

8.3 Participles

Verbs can become Participles. They're still slightly verb-like, as they can occasionally have direct objects, but they also behave very similarly to adjectives – following nouns, being lenited, and some of them become plural with their nouns.

8.3.1 The Habitual Participle

This type of participle means that whoever the adjective is describing does the action often, regularly, every day, or all of the time. In Sindarin, these adjectives appear to be half-way between adjective and noun. They can often be used to represent a noun with that quality, like **rhúgar** (doing-evil) can be used for "evil deed."

With I-Verbs, use only the verb root with no suffixes.

> **Mel-** love → **Mel** loving (in general), kind

With A-verbs, add a **-d** to the verb. This is identical to the gerund form of the verb. We only have examples of A-verb habitual participles in combination with other affixes.

> **Nedia-** count up + **Pen-** without, less → **pen-nediad** countless, innumerable

8.3.1.1 Exercise

Turn the following verbs into the habitual participles.

1. **Cab-** leap _____
2. **Dew-** fail, miss mark, go wrong _____
3. **Brenia-** endure_____
4. **Echad-** make, fashion, shape _____
5. **Fara-** hunt _____

8.3.2 The Present Participle

This adjective describes something that is being done while people are talking about it. It can't be made plural.

Govónen i   nîr   bedel.
Met-I   the man talking
I met the talking man.

You can also use present participles like a gerund, except that they in-dicate an action that is happening simultaneously with the main action. Both actions must have the same subject.

Pedel   oh   auth padrassen.
Talking about   war   walked-I
(while) Talking about war I walked.

Madel   lembas padrassen.
Eating   lembas   walked-I
(while) Eating lembas I walked.

Padrassen lastol i   veldis nîn i   ebent oh   auth.
Walked-I   hearing the friend my who spoke about war
I walked (while) hearing my friend who spoke about war.

Because present participles end in -ing in English, you must be very careful that you aren't confusing them for gerunds and vice versa.

For the A-verb, take the A off the root and add **-ol**.

glavra- babble → **glavrol** babbling

For the I-verb, add **-el** onto the root.

cab- leap → **cabel** leaping

For I-verbs ending in **-ir**, add **-iel** onto the root.

tir- guard → **tiriel** guarding

In English, we use present participles to make the progressive present tense. This isn't done in Sindarin. If you find yourself translating "[to be] _participle_," you need the present tense verb conjugation.

8.3.2.1 Exercise

Make the following verbs into present participles.

1. **Gir-** shudder_____

2. **Teilia**- play a game _____
3. **Penna**- slide down_____
4. **Nor**- run _____
5. **Haf**- sit _____

8.3.3 The Past Participle

This adjective describes something that was done to its noun.

These participles, like the present participles, are treated like adjectives. They can become plural.[269]

For the A-verb, simply conjugate it in the first person past tense.

> **eitha**- insult → **eithannen** insulted
>
> **cuia**- live   → **cuiassen** lived

For the I-verb, add -**nen** to it. This has a 2-step process.

1. First add the -**n** like you're making the verb into the past tense. The only difference is that verbs ending in continuants aren't excluded. They change as follows:

> -DH → -NN
> -V/F → -MM
> -N   → -NN
> -W   → -WN (If the sundóma is A, then -UN)
> -R   → -RN
> -L   → -LL

2. Then add -**en**, making the end of the verb Intervocalic.

> **gad**- catch → **gannen** caught
> **dag**- slay → **dangen** slain
> **hal**- lift → **hallen** lifted
> **dew**- fail → **dewnen** failed
> **fir**- die   → **firnen** dead
> **laf**- lick → **lammen** licked

---

[269] For more on their uses, review 3.4.4.

In English, we use past participles to make the "past perfect," a past tense that describes an action that was completely finished sometime before being spoken of, and that the effects of the actions' completion are still relevant. Sindarin doesn't appear to have a perfect past tense, except perhaps for intransitive verbs. If you find yourself translating "to have [past participle]" into Sindarin, you need the simple past instead.

> **I 'ond dhannen** The felled stone
>
> **Golf ristannen** A cloven branch
>
> **I ñelaidh bellin** The withered trees

8.3.3.1 Exercise

Make the following verbs into past participles.

1. **Mel-** love _____
2. **Teilia-** play a game _____
3. **Gweria-** cheat/betray _____
4. **Nor-** run _____
5. **Haf-** sit _____

8.3.4 The Perfect Participle

There is no exact equivalent to this form in English, so this will take some explaining. It has several properties:

1. It functions as a gerund – marking dependent clauses, not having its own subject, and having direct objects.
2. It marks an action that had been completed before the action of the main sentence's verb.
3. It can be used alongside verbs of any conjugation: present, future, or past.

The closest we have in English to this grammatical form is "having ___."

Although it is tempting because we only have one Sindarin past tense, it isn't used for the conjugation of the past tense. Instead it shows the order of an event in relationship to the main action of the sentence.

> **Nin   adlígiel,   ni   meria.**
> me   having-released   me   protects
> *Having released me, she/he protects me.*

I   iôn   udul   am   bâr,   tóliel   a   mellyn   în.
the   boy   came   to   home   having-played   with   friends   own

The boy came home, having played with his friends.

8.3.4.1 A-Verbs and TA-Verbs

Remove the A, add **-iel** to the root, and use I-affection on the root vowel.

The only exception is **muda-**, since the U comes from a long O, and long vowels aren't affected by I-affection.

Sindarin	English	→	Perfect Participle
fara-	"hunt"	→	feriel
brona-	"survive"	→	breniel
muda-	"labor"	→	mudiel

8.3.4.1.1 Exercise

Make the following verbs into perfective participles.

1. **Batha**- trample_____
2. **Drega**- flee_____
3. **Rista**- cut _____
4. **Tolla**- bring_____
5. **Luitha**- enchant_____

8.3.4.2 I-Verbs and IA-Verbs

Add **-iel**, or delete the **-ia** and then add **-iel**. For I-verbs and A-verbs ending in **-ia**, the vowels change the same way. To understand which letter changes into which, you must look back to Eldarin. These vowels, like the I-verbs, will lengthen instead of undergo I-Affection.

For the A-verbs ending in **-uia**, remove the A, add **-el**. For **-uia**, there are no vowel changes.

To help you understand this, I've made a chart of the historical changes to these vowels.

Short Sundómar	→	Lengthened Sundómar
A	→ Ó	
E/I	→ Í	
O/U	→ Ú	
Y	→ IÚ	

Because the sundómar of IA-verbs are all I-affected,[270] you need to know what the ancient Eldarin sundóma of the verb was.

Unlike I-verbs, IA-verbs can have a diphthong, EI, in the place of their sundóma. This is usually an alternate version of an E, and you'll find that such verbs usually have both forms, such as **telia-/teilia-** and ***medhia-/*meidhia-**.

Because of the complexity of having to know the ancient sundómar for verbs whose vowels have changed a lot over the years, you can bet that verbs ending in -IA would be given the wrong long vowel by people unaware of the history of the word or not fluent enough to know what form each specific verb should take. In fact, such people may just treat -IA verbs like normal A-verbs. This is another thing to keep in mind when translating.

Sindarin	Sundóma	English	→	Perfect Participle
dag-	A	"slay"	→	dógiel
penia-	A	"fix"	→	póniel
teilia-	A	"play"	→	tóliel
heb-	E	"keep"	→	híbiel
tir-	I	"guard"	→	tíriel
brenia-	O	"endure"	→	brúniel
tog-	U	"lead"	→	túgiel
elia-	U	"pour"	→	úliel
yr-	Y	"run"	→	iúriel

If the verb was made from a compound, only the core root's sundóma is changed.

---

[270] Review this in 4.1.2.1.

Sindarin	Sundóma	English	→	Perfect Participle
echad-	A	"fashion"	→	echódiel
gonedia-	O	"reckon"	→	gonúdiel
govan-	A	"meet"	→	govóniel
neledh-	E	"enter"	→	nelídhiel
nestag-	A	"insert"	→	nestógiel

8.3.4.2.1 Exercise

Make the following verbs into perfective participles.

1. **Buia-** serve _____
2. **Dar-** halt _____
3. **Men-** go _____
4. ***Pil-** steal _____
5. **Nod-** (O sundóma) count _____
6. ***Ostol-** (U sundóma) circumvent_____
7. **Renia-** (A sundóma) wander_____
8. **Feria-** (E sundóma) make ready promptly _____
9. **Dilia-** plug _____
10. **Eria-** (O sundóma) arise_____
11. **Delia-** (U sundóma) hide _____

8.3.4.2.2 Exercise

Translate the following sentences.

Nouns	Verbs
woman **bess**	eat **mad-**
day **aur**	labor **muda-**
field **parth**	slay **(n)dag-**
balrog **balrog**	lead **tog-** (U sundóma)
lady **hiril**	
fortress **ost**	

1. The woman eats well, having labored during the day in the field.

    _____

2. Having slain a balrog, I led the lady to my fortress.

    _____

8.3.5 Conversation Practice: War

This is a set of vocabulary having to do with war, along with some badass things to yell when charging into battle.

First let's recruit people to our cause.

> **Amman maethab?**
> For-what fight-we?
> *What are we fighting for?*

> **Maethab an   acharn!**
> Fight-we   for   vengeance!
> *We fight for vengeance!*

> **Acharo i   mellyn   'wîn!**
> Avenge   the   friends   our!
> *Avenge our friends!*

> **Boe angwen beriad   i   nyss   'wîn!**
> Must for-us   protecting the families our!
> *We must protect our families!*

> **Anírab   bronad!**
> Want-we   surviving!
> *We want to survive!*

> **Nidhib   aderthad i   nôr!**
> Intend-we   reunite   the land!
> *We intend to reunite the land!*

> **Yrch   telir!**
> Orcs   come!
> *Orcs come!*

Ask people to fight with you:

> **Maethathol   i   goth   a   ven?**
> Fight-will-you the   enemy   with us?
> *Would you please fight the enemy with us?*

Sevif   maur   e-guru   lîn   vi   nagor.
Have-we need   of-the-skill your in   battle
We need your skill in battle.

*Pi   maethol   a   ven,   ertherib!
If   fight-you   with us   win-we!
If you fight with us, we will win!

With your army beside you facing the enemy, it's time for some badass battle cries:

Gurth   anin   goth!
Death   to-the enemy!
Death to the enemy!

I   philinn 'wîn   gwathar Anor!
The arrows   our   veil   Sun!
Our arrows will blot out the sun!

I   goth   'wîn drega o   gwen   sui   'wath
The enemy our   flees from us   like   shadow
drega o   glawar!
flees   from sunlight!
Our enemy flees from us like a shadow flees from sunlight!

In   *aich   i-chyth   'wîn thiliar   nu   Anor!
The bones of-the-enemies our   glimmer under sun
The bones of our enemies (will) glimmer under the sun!

And of course, we can't forget the battle cry of the Edain of the North: **Lacho calad! Drego morn!** "May light flare! May darkness flee!"

Calling out the name of a deity or powerful ancestor is a good plan too. That's what Aragorn does, and it seems to work for him pretty well.

Now that the battle has commenced, it's time to give orders to your troops.

You can tell them where/how to move, using the following verbs:

- **Adertha-** reunite
- **Anglenna-** approach

- **Aphada-** follow
- **Athra-** cross to and fro
- **Awartha-** forsake
- **Batha-** trample
- **Breitha-** burst forth
- ***Cesta-** seek, search for (something)
- ***Ceth-** examine (something), search (someplace), interrogate (someone)
- **(n)Dadwen-** return, go back
- **(n)Damen-** return, go back
- **(n)Dandol-** return, come back (U sundóma)
- **Dar-** halt
- **Dartha-** wait, remain, stay, last, endure
- **Delia-** hide (intransitive, U sundóma)
- **Dolla-** conceal, hide (transitive, TA-verb, U sundóma)
- **Drega-** flee
- **Ertha-** unite
- ***Ethog-** lead out
- **Fara-** hunt
- **Gad-** catch
- **Gleina-** bind, enclose, limit
- **Govan-** meet
- ***Hir-** find
- **Men-** go
- **Minna-** enter
- **Mista-** stray
- **Neledh-** enter
- **Nor-** run
- **Northa-** make run, ride
- ***Ostol-** come around,[271] circumvent (U sundóma)
- **Pada-** walk
- **Padra-** walk
- ***Per-** turn
- ***Posta-** rest
- **Rada-** make a way, find a way
- **Ran-** wander
- **Renia-** wander, stray, sail, fly (A sundóma)

---

[271] This doesn't mean "to be convinced." It literally means to come around some obstacle.

- **Tab-** block, stop, close
- **Thora-** fence in, surround
- **Tir-** watch, guard
- **Tog-** lead (U sundóma)
- **Tol-** come (U sundóma)
- **Tollo-** make come, fetch (TA verb, U sundóma)
- **Trevad-** traverse, travel

You'll also need to give instructions about how or when to use weapons. Here are some relevant verbs.

- **Adleg-** loose, release
- **Blab-** beat
- **(n)Dag-** kill, slay
- **(n)Damma-** hammer
- **Dew-** fail, miss mark, go wrong
- **Draf-** hew
- **Eitha-** stab, insult
- **Feria-** make ready promptly (E sundóma)
- **Had-** throw, shoot
- **Hasta-** hack through
- **Maetha-** fight, wield
- **Narcha-** rend, rip
- **Nasta-** prick, stick, thrust
- **Nestag-** insert, stick in
- **Raeda-** catch in a net
- ***Rag-** break
- **Rhib-** scratch
- **Rista-** rip, rend, cut
- **Tortha-** wield, control

Here are some nouns you'll find useful.

People:

- **Callon** – hero (masculine)
- **Caun** – commander
- **Coth** – enemy
- **(n)Dagnir** – bane (masculine)
- ***(n)Dagnis** – bane (feminine)
- **(n)Daug** – soldier

- **(n)Gûd** – foe
- **Hador** – spear/dart thrower
- **Hadron** – male spear/dart thrower
- ***Hedril** – female spear/dart thrower
- **Herth** – troop under the command of a **hîr**
- **Hîr** – lord
- **Maethor** - warrior
- **Magor** – swordsman
- ***Pil** – robber, thief
- **Rochben** – knight, mounted warrior (gender-neutral)
- **Rochir** – knight, mounted warrior (masculine)
- ***Thalieth** – heroine, dauntless woman
- **Thalion** – hero, dauntless man

Battle tactics:

- **(n)Dírnaith** – Men lined up in a wedge-shaped formation for splitting an enemy's ranks.
- **Thangail** – shield-wall. Linking shields together to make an impenetrable wall, like Romans famously did with their large shields.

Weapons:

- **Amath** – shield
- ***Barf** - armor
- **Crist** – cleaver
- **Cû** – bow
- **Hâdh** – cleaver
- **Hadlath** – throwing sling
- **Harn** – helmet
- **Hathol** – broadsword blade, ax blade
- **Lang** – cutlass
- **Magol** – sword
- **Megil** – sword
- **Peng** – bow
- **Tang** – bowstring
- **Thand** – shield
- **Thôl** – helmet

Miscellaneous:

- **Acharn** – vengeance
- **Achared** – vengeance
- **Auth** – war, battle
- **(n)Dagor** – battle
- **Sîdh** - peace

And here's some other fighting-related verbs that you'll find useful:

- **Achar-** avenge, react
- **Beria-** protect (A sundóma)
- **Bertha-** dare
- **Brenia-** endure
- **Brona-** last, survive
- **Buia-** serve, hold allegiance to
- ***Daf-** allow, permit, yield
- **(n)Dagra-** battle
- **Dýgar-** make a mistake
- **Eitha-** ease, assist, help
- **Gonathra-** entangle, enmesh
- **Gruitha-** terrify
- **Gwedh-** bind
- **Gweria-** betray, cheat (A sundóma)
- **Gwesta-** swear an oath
- **Harna-** wound
- **Leithia-** release (E sundóma)
- **Natha-** help
- **Neitha-** wrong, deprive
- **Nesta-** heal
- **Nod-** tie, bind
- **Orthor-** master, conquer (U sundóma)
- ***Pil-** steal, rob, thieve
- **Ref-** ensnare, entangle
- **Taetha-** fasten, tie

Chapter 9: Deriving Words

In this chapter, we will study the most basic and least controversial of the ways to make new words. We'll be making nouns out of adjectives, verbs, and combinations of nouns, verbs, and adjectives. We'll make adjectives out of verbs and nouns. These are the tricks we use to extend the limited vocabulary that Tolkien provided for us.

9.1 Making Adjectives

The most fruitful class of words to turn into adjectives is Verbs, by far. Most of these affixes will be for verbs, though nouns also can be turned.

9.1.1 Suffix -weg

This suffix works in combination with the Habitual participle, and likely can't be made plural.[272]

In meaning, it's very similar to the present participle. It can be used to describe someone who is doing an action right as you describe it, but it has a habitual meaning as well. You can use it to describe someone who does an action regularly.

Say you saw someone that you've seen jogging many times before. In Sindarin, you'd say that the jogger is **norweg**, often running. Or if you saw a jogger, you could say that they are **norweg**, meaning that they are running right now, and they often run.

> **mad-** eat   → **madweg** gluttonous
>
> **trasta-** harass → **trastadweg** annoying

9.1.1.1 Exercise

Make the following verbs into **-weg** adjectives and give a guess at what it would mean in English.

1. **Mel-** love _____
2. **Ped-** speak, talk, say _____
3. **Lal-** laugh _____
4. **Gweria-** cheat, betray _____
5. *****Hanna-** thank _____

---

[272] **-weg** and **-ui** were introduced in *Parma Eldalamberon* issue 17, page 144. We only have examples of them with I-verbs, but we can guess how they'd be used with A-verbs based on the Habitual participle's form.

9.1.2 Suffix -ui

This suffix is added to the habitual participle, and likely can't be made plural.

On a transitive verb this suffix equals the English suffix "-able/-ible" when added to a habitual participle.

On an intransitive verb, this suffix means that whatever you're describing is able to do that action.

> **gonod-** count up → **gonodui** countable
> **brona-** survive   → **bronadui** surviving

When negating these adjectives, instead of using **al-**, use **ú-** as we learned in 6.1.2.

This suffix is also used to turn nouns into adjectives, as I'm sure you've noticed by now. The end of the word becomes Intervocalic[273] and the vowels need to be reduced.[274]

When used with a noun, it means, "having the quality of..., like..., -ful"

> **lith** ash, dust → **lithui** ashen, dusty
> **mael** lust   → **maelui** lustful

9.1.2.1 Exercise

Turn the following verbs and nouns into **-ui** adjectives. Translate the new adjectives into English as well.

1. **Dreg-** flee _____
2. **Egleria-** praise _____
3. *****Ren-** remember _____
4. **Úan** monster _____
5. **Îr** desire _____

---

[273] Review 4.2.2 for more information on making the ends of words Intervocalic.

[274] Review 4.2.1 for more information on reducing vowels.

9.1.3 "Full" -eb and Pant

These are suffixed onto nouns only, and the resulting adjectives can be made plural.

Using **-eb** makes the end of the word intervocalic.

Pant is a little more complex, because you're making a compound word. In the most basic sense, you'll be using vocalic mutation on **pant**, making the "suffix" **-bant**, but that's not always the case. We'll be going into this in more depth in 9.3 when we learn how to make compound words.

- -B, suffix **-ant**.
- -L, -LT, or -LL, delete the extra T or L, and suffix **-phant**.
- -N (not from NN, ND, or NT), use Nasal Mutation.[275]
- -NT, -ND, -NN, or -N that comes NN, ND, or NT, the N becomes M, the extra N, D, or T is deleted, and **-bant** is suffixed.
- -P, delete the -P and add **-bant**.
- -S, SS, or ST, delete the extra S or T, then add **-bant**
- -PH or -F/V, delete them and suffix **-phant**.
- -W, delete and suffix **-bant**.
- For the rest, just use vocalic mutation.

Pant and **-eb** are a word and suffix version of the same word, "full." Added onto a noun, they mean "full of..."

> **aglar** glory → **aglareb** full of glory, glorious
>
> **în** year → **iphant** full of years, old

9.1.3.1 Exercise

Make the following nouns into **-eb** and **pant** adjectives and give their English translations.

1. **Cael** sickness _____
2. **Uir** eternity _____
3. **Nên** water _____

---

[275] For more information on Nasal Mutation, review 5.1.3.

    4. **Ûr** heat, fire _____

    5. **Find** hair _____

9.1.4 Suffix -ren

This is suffixed onto nouns only, and it can be made plural.

When you use **-ren,** its final consonants will change the same way as when you add the plural suffix **-rim.**[276]

This suffix marks the origin of something. It means something like "of, made of" or "from, made from." That's why it's often used for the names of languages.

      Edhel elf   → **Edhellen** of the elves, elvish

      gond stone   → **gondren** made of/from stone

      Harad south → **Haradren** from the South, Southern

9.1.4.1 Exercise

Make the following nouns into **-ren** adjectives and give their English translations.

    1. **Mîr** jewel_____

    2. **Hadhod** dwarf _____

    3. **Madha** mud _____

    4. **Periand** hobbit_____

    5. **Côl** gold (the metal)_____

9.1.5 Elven Culture: Poetry

We know very little about Sindarin poetry forms, but we do know a few of the names for them, and we have theories about what they are.

The shortest form is a **linnod**. We aren't certain about the criteria for a **linnod**, but we have some ideas based on the one example we have,

---

[276] See 4.2.4.1.

"Gilraen's Linnod."[277] The word is a compound of **lind** "song, chant" and the number seven, **odog**.[278] They are as follows:

1. Two lines.
2. Each line is seven syllables long.
3. They have the same stress pattern.
4. They don't need to rhyme.

Here is "Gilraen's Linnod" with the stressed syllables bolded so you can see how they line up.

Ó- nen i **Es**- tel **E**- dain.
Ú- che- bin **Es**- tel **a**- nim.

I gave the Hope to Man.
I can't keep Hope for myself.

Another type of Sindarin poetry is **ann-thennath**, or "all long-shorts." We have very little in the way of information about it, though we know that it's used for long sung epics because Aragorn shares with the Hobbits a translation of a portion of the **Beleglin**[279] "The Lay of Leithian" which apparently was composed in this style.[280]

Ann-thennath is marked by two features.[281]

---

[277] This can be found in *The Lord of the Rings*, Appendix A(v)

[278] The other popular theory is that the -**od** is a diminutive suffix, and **linnod** "little verse." I don't think so, since **lind** doesn't end with a C or G to make the suffix -**od** instead of -**og**.

[279] An epic, a long narrative song or chant.

[280] *The Lord of the Rings*, Book One, chapter XI "A Knife in the Dark."

[281] It's possible that I have this wrong, and this could refer to some sort of quantitative meter instead, but Sindarin phonology doesn't lend itself easily to quantitative meter. A quantitative meter would be something like a Japanese Haiku – a real one, not our poor approximation of them with counted syllables. Real Japanese haiku count morae – how long it takes to say something – not syllables. That's why I think that **ann-thennath** is probably an accentual meter instead.

1. A repeated pattern of stressed and unstressed syllables, giving the verses a rhythmic feel. This most often is iambic[282] or trochee.[283]
2. The lines rhyme.

Let's look at a small segment of the aforementioned Beleglin that Tolkien translated.

Lúthien's Song[284]	Stress[285]		Rhyme
Ir Ithil ammen Eruchín	ᴗ/ᴗ/ᴗ/	iambic	A
menel-vír síla díriel	/ᴗ/ᴗ/ᴗ	trochee	B
si loth a galadh lasto dîn!	ᴗ/ᴗ/ᴗ/	iambic	A
A Hîr Annûn gilthoniel,	ᴗ/ᴗ/ᴗ	iambic	B
le linnon im Tinúviel!	ᴗ/ᴗ/ᴗ	iambic	B

The last type of poetry is the **narn**, a long epic that is spoken, not sung. It's composed in a mode called **minlamad thent/estent**, which means "one short/very short echo." This is marked with one main feature:

1. Uses alliteration, like Old English poetry. The same sounds should be echoed within a line or verse over and over again.
2. Maybe rhymes? Alliteration does mean that rhyming can happen by accident though.

We have no examples of Sindarin verse composed this way, though we do know that **Narn i Chîn Húrin** was composed in this mode.

---

[282] A poetic meter made of an unstressed syllable followed by a stressed syllable, as found in the 1st, 3rd, 4th, and 5th lines of the poem.
[283] A poetic meter made of a stressed syllable followed by an unstressed syllable, as found in the 2nd line of the poem.
[284] This can be found in *The Lays of Beleriand* page 421, lines 99-103. This poem probably isn't in Sindarin, but Doriathrin or Late Noldorin. Either way, it's so close to Sindarin that we can understand most of it easily.
[285] This includes secondary stress, which is found in compound words.

9.2 Making Nouns

We can make nouns out of verbs, adjectives, and other nouns. This process is called "nominalization."

9.2.1 Infinitives

Infinitives are pretty much useless in Sindarin. The only time you will see them is when Tolkien lists words. But they exist and you should know how they are made.

A-verb Infinitives are very easy. They are exactly the same as the A-verb Imperatives.

> **Thora-** fence → **Thoro** to fence

I-verb Infinitives are very easy as well. They are I-verbs in their Present tense conjugation, without any pronoun suffix added.

> **Dar-** halt → **Deri** to halt

This is why dictionaries should never list verbs by their Infinitive forms: when the A, E, and O all are an E in the infinitive, how are you to know how to correctly conjugate it? If you've been using a dictionary that lists Sindarin verbs only by their infinitive forms, then throw it out now.

9.2.2 Gerunds[286]

Gerunds take the place of infinitives in Sindarin grammar. Watch the accusative pronoun carefully. When the gerund acts on an accusative pronoun, the pronoun goes beside it like it was any other verb. It does not go before the active verb.[287]

---

[286] Review how they are made in 8.1.4.
[287] Review compound predicates in 3.3.3.1.

> **In   yrch   anírar gi   ndaged.**
> The orcs   want   you killing
> *The orcs want to kill you.*

When the gerund is used as a noun, it can't be made plural, but otherwise it acts as though it is a normal noun and undergoes mutation.

> **Daro   i   naged.**
> Stop   the   killing
> *Stop the killing.*

9.2.3 The Abstract Nominalizing Suffix -as

This suffix widens the scope of nouns and makes adjectives and verbs into nouns. Oddly enough, it can be pluralized, unlike its cousin the gerund.

The suffix is "-**as**" and it makes the end of the word intervocalic.

9.2.3.1 Adjectives

When adding this suffix to an adjective, it is equivalent to adding -ness to an English adjective.

> **Belt** strong   → **Bellas** strongness, strength
> **Maen** skilled → **Maenas** skilledness, skill

9.2.3.1.1 Exercise

Add the suffix **-as** to these adjectives, and give their English meanings.

1. **Trîw** fine, slender _____
2. **Rhosg** brown _____
3. **Meren** festive _____
4. **Iaur** ancient _____
5. **Brui** noisy _____

9.2.3.2 Nouns

What I meant by "to widen the scope of nouns" is that it makes the noun a word for a group of itself, or it makes a noun stand for something grander, greater, more, but yet still limited. Because this isn't a grammatical concept that occurs in English, it will take some time to get used to the idea. Let's look at a few examples and see how it works.

Pân wooden plank → **Panas** wooden floor

Certh rune → **Certhas** runic alphabet

Sarn a stone → **Sarnas** pile of stones

Send rest → **Sennas** guest house[288]

Tham hall → **Thammas** great hall[289]

Ind heart[290] → **Innas** will

9.2.3.2.1 Exercise

Add the suffix **-as** to these nouns, and give their English meanings.

1. **Ûr** fire _____
2. **Lain** thread _____
3. **Lass** leaf _____
4. **Hâl** fish_____
5. **Nagol** (older **Nagl**) tooth _____

9.2.3.3 Verbs

When added to a verb, it means "the action of..." or "thing that is the result of the action of..."

Toba- to cover → **Tobas** roof

Fara- to hunt → **Faras** hunting

Car- to build → **Caras** city

---

[288] This is a place where a lot of resting takes place.

[289] These are the medieval versions of "hall," rather than the modern usage. A "hall" is a large roofed area. A **thammas** is the huge hall that you see in medieval stories with the Lord and Lady sitting at the head of while they feast.

[290] See 4.1.4 for a more detailed explanation of its meaning.

9.2.3.3.1 Exercise

Add the suffix **-as** to these verbs, and give their English meanings.

1. **Badh-** judge _____
2. **Gor-** advise _____
3. ***Mib-** kiss _____
4. **Northa-** charge _____
5. **Ovra-** abound _____

9.2.4 The Nominalizing Suffix -th for Verbs

This suffix makes a verb into a word for the action itself.

With an A-verb, put it into the past tense as if you were going to add a pronominal suffix to it, but instead add **-th**. This makes the resulting suffix look like **-sseth** or **-nneth**.[291]

> **Presta-** change, affect, mutate → **Prestanneth** mutation, change, effect

With a TA-verb or an I-verb, suffix **-eth**, unless the root ends in **-ir**. Then the suffix is **-ith**.

> **Gir-** shudder → **Girith** shuddering
>
> **Mel-** love   → **Meleth** love

9.2.4.1 Exercise

Use the Nominalizing suffix **-th** on the following verbs, and give their meanings in English.

1. **Tir-** guard, watch _____
2. **Ceth-** examine, interrogate_____
3. **Gohena-** forgive_____
4. **Nídha-** to be determined _____
5. **Osgar-** amputate_____

------

[291] We have only one example of this, and it is with the word **Prestanneth**. Needless to say, if you have a datapoint of one, the conclusion you come up with is pretty iffy. There's a lot of different interpretations of how this works.

9.2.5 Name Making

This is for making new vocabulary as well as naming yourself or your characters. A lot of these techniques can be used for both.

9.2.5.1 The Agentive Suffix -or for Nouns and Verbs

This suffix turns the verb into the someone or something who does the action, like the "-er" suffix in English. It also can be added to nouns and gerunds, referring to the person does the action associated with that noun. This suffix can be combined with name-gender-suffixes.

With an I-Verb, add **-or** to the end of the verb-root. In Archaic Sindarin it's just an **-r**, so it'll behave like a syllabic R.

With an A-verb, replace the A with **-or**. The O in this case is from an ancient long A, so in archaic Sindarin it'd be treated like an O from ancient long A. In later Sindarin, however, because of the association with how it works with the I-verb and attached to nouns, it'll be treated as though the O was inserted before a syllabic R as it is in I-Verbs.

> **Cab-** jump, leap, hop → **Cabor** leaper, frog
>
> **Maetha-** fight   → **Maethor** fighter, warrior
>
> **Bach** ware, item   → **Bachor** merchant
>
> **Dag-** kill   → **Dagor** battle
>
> **Gad-** trap, catch   → **Gador** prison

When adding feminine or masculine suffixes, the O is deleted and **-on** (masculine) or **-il** (feminine) is added. Note that **-il** causes I-Affection. The consonants before the R change as they would with the suffix **-rim**.

If you're making an archaic name/word for the A-verb, the O won't be deleted.

	English	Gender-less	Male	Female
Meleth "love"	lover	*Melethor	Melethron	Melethril
Lasta- "hear"	eavesdropper	*Lastor	Lathron	Lethril
Badh- "judge"	judge	Badhor	Badhron	*Bedhril

9.2.5.1 Exercise

Make the following words into Agentive nouns. Make them genderless, male, and female. Give their English translations too.

1. **Nara**- narrate_____
   _____

2. **Gor**- advise _____
   _____

3. **Lein** thread _____
   _____

9.2.5.2 Agentives from Habitual Participles/Gerunds

You can also form agentives with a Habitual Participle[292] or a Gerund and the words **(n)dîr** for men and **(n)dîs** for women. They cause I-affection unless they result in a consonant cluster directly before them, and that only happens when the word they are attached to ends in a D.

We only have examples of these suffixes with D, N, L, and G, but based on these we can make guesses about how the rest of the suffixes would react to the rest of the I-verb endings.

(based on G) B, TH, DH, V/F: the suffixes become -**nir** and -**nis**.

(based on L and N) R and W: the suffixes stay -**dir** and -**dis**.

Since this is shaky ground, you can use the gerund instead. We do have attested the verb **car-** behaving this way. Below is included all of variety of attested cases of these agentive suffixes with I-verbs and A-verbs.

	English	Male	Female
Fara- "hunt"	hunter	Feredir	*Feredis
Car- "do, make"	crafter	Ceredir	*Ceredis
Dag- "kill"	bane	Dagnir	*Dagnis
Mel- "love"	friend	Meldir	Meldis
Ran- "wander"	wanderer	Randir	*Randis

---

[292] To read up on habitual participles, review 9.1.1.

9.2.5.2.1 Exercise

Make the following verbs into agentive nouns, both male and female. Give their English meanings as well.

1. **Achar-** avenge _____
2. **Cen-** see _____
3. **Critha-** reap _____
4. **Dew-** fail _____
5. **Muda-** labor, toil _____

9.2.6 Name-Making with Suffixes

The easiest way to make an Elven name is to take a noun or adjective and slap a name-suffix onto it. We'll learn about this before we go into the difficult way to make names in the next lesson.

9.2.6.1 Suffixes -ion, -iel, and -ien

These are the suffixes used for the patronymics, the closest thing that an Elf has to a surname. **-ion** means "son of..." while **-iel** and **-ien** mean "daughter of..."

1. These are best used with the entire name, except that these suffixes replace any gender-specific suffixes on the verbs. **Dîr** and **dîs** aren't suffixes, so they wouldn't be deleted.

2. They make the end of the name intervocalic.[293]

3. If the name already has multiple syllables, then you won't have to worry about vowel reduction, but if it's a single-syllable name, do vowel reduction.[294]

    Rîn Queen → **Ríniel** Daughter of the Queen

    Thranduil Vigorous Stream → **Thranduilion** Son of Thranduil

---

[293] Review making the end of the word intervocalic in 4.2.2.

[294] Review vowel reduction in 4.2.1.

9.2.6.1.1 Exercise

Take the following names and add the 3 patronymic name suffixes onto them. Give their English translations.

1. **Talagand** Harper _____

   _____

2. **Redhor** Planter _____

   _____

3. **Candis** Commander_____

   _____

9.2.6.2 Suffixes -on, -eth, -el, and -il

These suffixes just make masculine (**-on**) and feminine (**-eth**, **-el**, and -**il**) names. If you add one of these to an adjective, it means "__ one" On an agentive noun they add gender to the meaning. On any other noun they make names meaning "person who has something to do with__."

They make the end of the word they're attaching to intervocalic. In addition to that, **-il** causes I-affection.

When **-eth** is attached to a word ending in DH or TH, it becomes **-es**.

When **-on** is attached to a word ending in N, it becomes **-or**.

> **Aran** king   → **Aranel** Princess
> **Iaur** ancient → **Ioreth** Ancient One
> **Astor** loyalty → **Astoron** Man who has Loyalty
> **Roch** horse   → **Rochon** Knight, Horseman
> **Thend** grey   → **Thennor** (male) Sindarin Elf

9.2.6.2.1 Exercise

Make names out of the following words, using all four suffixes you just learned. Provide the English translations of the names.

1. **Tân** smith_____

   _____

   _____

2. **Aras** deer _____

_____

_____

3. **Tond** tall _____

_____

_____

9.2.7 Elven Culture: Naming Practices of the Noldor[295]

Elven names are not like modern names. We don't know what our names mean without hefty amounts of research, and our names were chosen from lists of pre-existing, traditional names. Elven names have meaning, and an Elf, upon hearing for the first time the true names of another elf (the first and second names), would know a lot of information about whom they were meeting. They'd know who their father or mother was, and a defining characteristic or interest of the person. When we meet and exchange names, we learn very little about the person we've just met from the name alone. In fact, it's more likely that we'd learn something about the person's parents than the person themselves. This part of Elven culture is very different from our own. If you want your Elven characters to behave truly elf-like, then read up!

9.2.7.1 The First Name

The first name an Elf receives in his/her life is the *ataressë (father-name). It is one of the **anessi** (given-names) that the Elf will receive in their life. It is as close as the Elves get to a surname. It is given soon after birth. It's announced by the father in a ceremony called **essecarmë** (name-making).

The name itself is usually made from one of the parent's names. If the child is a boy, it will be fashioned after one of his father's names; if it's a girl, it will be fashioned after one of her mother's names. It is not unheard of for girls also to have names fashioned after their fathers' or

_____

[295] Most of this information comes from *Morgoth's Ring*, "Laws and Customs of the Eldar" – "Of Names." Since we're dealing with the Noldor, the relevant terms will all be in Quenya, not Sindarin.

boys to have names fashioned after their mothers', or to have a name fashioned after a grandparent's name. This name is sometimes based on someone better known in the family.

The name can be modified later to better fit the personality of its bearer, though it will still be modeled after the parent's name.

There are three ways that this name is formed.

1. Simply using a parent's name. This sort of father name didn't last long, and would be changed to better match the child's personality.
2. A patronymic suffix added to the parent's name. This also often ended up changed as well.
3. The most common way is to use a different name suffix or only part of the parent's name.

This is the first name listed when telling someone their full name. It is considered a public name. Anyone could address the Elf by it.

9.2.7.2 The Second Name

The next name an Elf has could either be their **amilessë** (mother-name) or the **cilmessë** (chosen-name). It's more likely that the amilessë would come first, as often they are given before the elf is old enough to name themself. This name is one of the anessi. There are two types of amilessi.

The most common is the **amilessë tercenyë** (mother-name of insight). "Insight" refers to insight into the child's personality. This sort of name may be given while the child's personality is starting to develop, a few years after the child's birth, which means it could come after the Chosen-Name.

The second type is the **amilessë apacenyë** (mother-name of foresight). This sort of name comes from a vision the mother receives in the hour of birth. This sort of vision isn't all that common, so these names are rare and important gifts.

This name is also considered a public name, and it is listed after the Father-Name when giving one's full title.

The **cilmessë** (chosen-name) is a name that a child chooses for themself, once they have developed their own **lámatyávë**. This basically means that the child is fluent in their mother tongue and knows how to make beautiful sounding names. It also means that the child's personality has developed to the point that the child knows and can name themselves. The age that the child reaches this fluency and understanding is somewhere between 7 and 10 years of age. Since gaining individuality is an important achievement in the child's life, there is a ceremony to go with announcing it, called **essecilmë** (name-choosing).

The name has something to do with the child's personality or talent(s). It can be changed as time passes, as the person's personality and interests change over time, but this is very rare.

This name is a private name. The only ones allowed to address someone by their cilmessë are close family members, one's closest friends, and one's spouse. To address someone you aren't in an intimate relationship with by this name is extremely rude.

It also is one of the names listed when telling someone his/her full name. It can come before or after the amilessë, depending on when they acquired the name.

Adopting the amilessë as the cilmessë is a common practice. In fact, if there was an amilessë, it most likely would be the Elf's cilmessë as well.

Cilmessi are supposed to be unique to the Elf early on in history. As time goes on and more names are taken up, names can be reused.

There is another type of cilmessë, and it doesn't get the fanfare that the previously mentioned one does. It is an alias, and used to conceal one's identity. This sort of cilmessë will be made to look like another type of name, but other than that doesn't have any special characteristics.[296]

9.2.7.3 The Third Name

The last type of name, called the **epessë** (after-name) is one of the anessi. Most of the time it is little more than a nickname, though its making differs quite a bit from our own version of nicknames. It has meaning, and it isn't based off of any of the Elf's other names. It can be

---

[296] *The Peoples of Middle-earth*, "The Shibboleth of Fëanor" – "Note on Mother-names"

a title of admiration or honor, referencing an accomplishment or deed done by the Elf. It also can be descriptive of an odd or out-standing physical or mental trait.

It is a name that can be given by anyone, and sometimes the person being referred to is unaware of this name. Because this sort of name isn't considered one of an Elf's real names, these names could be repeated. More than one elf could be called by the same epessë. That being said, they wouldn't deliberately take another elf's name to use as a nickname for a friend, because the epessë would have a clear meaning connected to who they were naming.

This name can be adopted into the Elf's full title, and when this happens it is listed last.

Due to the nature of the creation of this name, it is public but not considered one of the Elf's actual names until he or she adopts it.

One type of epessë is the name given by lovers to each other. It is the most often adopted epessë, because these names tend to be the most flattering.

Some epessi are names based on the names of places where the events occurred from which an Elf could earn a new name. Take the case of Elrond and Elros. They were abandoned in the woods and found in a cave with a waterfall over its entrance. **Elrond** (Starcave) was found inside the cave, and **Elros** (Starrain) was found playing in the water.[297]

9.2.7.4 General Facts About Elven Names

The first names of the parentless elves – the first elves who woke up on the shores of Cuiviénen – didn't mean anything. Most of them put -**wê** at the end of their names, but the first element would be a random syllable that sounded cool and fit the phonology of their language. Sometimes their name would become a word for something they were well-known for later on.[298]

---

[297] *The Letters of J. R. R. Tolkien*, Letter #211
[298] *The Peoples of Middle-earth*, "The Shibboleth of Fëanor" – "The names of Finwë's descendants"

Elves don't share their Father-Names when they marry. They could gain new Epessi from their spouses, however.

Elves' names change as the language around them changes. This is why Galadriel is known as "Galadriel" in the Third Age. Her name was originally **Alatáriel**. Though the language changed, the name's meaning is still important, so it was translated into Sindarin.

The names are listed in order of acquisition, like this:

> *Ataressë Amilessë/Cilmessë, also called Epessë.

Elves never use the names of Eru, the Valar, or Maiar as their own. It's considered trying to become or impersonate a god. Similarly, they aren't named abstract concepts like "Justice, Mercy, Love, Victory, Life, Death" or the names of countries or natural things like "Star, River, Fire, Earth, Sea." Names referencing these things usually indicate the person's relationship with them, like **Eärendil** (sea-lover) or **Aulendur** (servant of Aulë).

Names about one's ethnicity or homeland are usually indirect references, like **Legolas** (green-leaf), which references his homeland[299] and his ethnicity as a **Legel** (green-elf).

A name referencing something like stars or rivers and so on wouldn't just be "Star" or "River," but would be compound name, showing in what way the character is like the thing, like **Thranduil** (vigorous-stream) who has a river running through his home. The name suggests that he's energetic and strong as this river.

Barring *ataressi, names are usually descriptive of the elf, often just an adjective with a name suffix added or a description of a specific characteristic. So names like **Artanis** (noble woman) or **Glorfindel** (golden-hair) are the most common.[300]

---

[299] Mirkwood is called **Eryn Lasgalen** "forest of green-leaf" in Sindarin, though it uses a different word for "green."

[300] *Parma Eldalamberon* issue 21 pages 83-86

9.2.7.4.1 Example: Fëanor's Names[301]

When he was born, his father, Finwë, named him **Finwion** (Son of Finwë). When his talent for metallurgy started to show, his name was changed to **Curufinwë** (Skill of Finwë).

His mother, who passed away, had insight into his character, and named him **Fëanáro** (Spirit of Fire). He adopted this name as his cilmessë out of love and respect for his mother.

When his father remarried, Fëanor, who was angry with his father, defiantly took his mother's name, **Therindë** (seamstress) as his first name, and started calling himself **Therindion Fëanáro**.

After his death in Beleriand, his name had to be changed into Sindarin for conversing with the Sindar. The pure Sindarin version of his name would be **Faenor**, but his Noldorin followers preserved the sound of his original name slightly, possibly because early on they had difficulty with the Sindarin diphthong AE, making the **Fëanor** that we recognize.

9.2.7.4.2 Example: Galadriel's Names[302]

When she was born, her father, **Arafinwë** (Noble Finwë) gave his daughter the name **Artanis** (Noble Woman).

Her mother gave her an amilessë tercenyë, **Nerwen** (man-maiden) because she grew to be as tall and as fond of sports and hunting as a man. She adopted this as her cilmessë.

The epessë she received from Celeborn was in Telerin, **Alatáriel** (Woman Garlanded with Radiance) in reference to her hair. She adopted this name into her full title, and translated it into Quenya: **Altáriel**. When she came to Middle-earth, she translated it to **Galadriel**, and thus we know her by this name.

---

[301] *The Peoples of Middle-earth*, "The Shibboleth of Fëanor" – "The names of Finwë's descendants"

[302] Unfinished Tales, *Appendix E* – "The Names of Celeborn and Galadriel"

9.3 Compound Words

A compound word is two or more different words put together to make a new word. We've already done this quite a bit by now.

Making compound words is complex in Sindarin.

In the most basic sense, you'll be applying mutation to the combination of the two words. If in doubt, vocalic mutation is the default. But you can also use the other types of mutation, like nasal or long mixed mutation for words ending in N, or stop mutation for words ending in D, or liquid mutation for words ending in L or R. But there's a lot more nuance you'll have to learn. This is Prestanneth, but a hundred times harder. Sometimes you'll have a choice to make.

Say you're combining **thôl** "helm" and **taur** "lord, chieftain." You could use vocalic mutation (**Tholdor**) or liquid mutation (**Tholthor**). Make this choice based on your **lámatyávë**.[303]

9.3.1 Word Order in Sindarin Compounds

The word order within compound words is different from the word order in phrases.

As a general rule, put the person-word at the end of the compound. This usually applies to name-making, because the person-words often have agentive suffixes on them, and those can't be in the middle of a word.

> **Mith** grey + **Randir** male wanderer = **Mithrandir**

Habitual Participles proceed what they modify in the compound.

> **Lal** laughing + **Gwend** maiden = **Lalwen**
> **Eriad** rising + **Dôr** land   = **Eriador**

---

[303] "Linguistic Tastes" in Quenya.

In "pure Sindarin" names, adjectives should follow what they modify, but many names don't follow that pattern. There are several reasons for this. Names designed to sound ancient will put the adjective before its noun. Likewise, names translated from Quenya or influenced by Quenya will do this too. Thus you can choose whichever style you prefer.

9.3.2 How to Combine the Words

This will be reminiscent of the Prestanneth charts from chapter 5, with a slight difference. The rows are for the ends of words, and the columns are for the beginnings of words. If the space is blank, there's not enough information to form a hypothesis, and it's probably best to avoid combining these sounds.

9.3.2.1 Vowels

Let's start with something easy, Vowels. Most of the time, you'll only have to trouble yourself with making ends of words intervocalic[304] and vocalic mutation,[305] but occasionally a word will end in a vowel.

	+A	+E	+I	+O	+U	+Y
AE+	AEA			AEO	AEU	
AW+	AWA	AWE	AWI	Ó	AU	
E+	EA	E	EI	EO	EU	EY
EI+	EIA		Í	EIO	EIU	
I+	IA	IE	I	IO	IU	Y
O+	OA	OE		O		
OE+	OEA	OE		OEO	OEU	OEY
Û/Ú+	ÚA	ÚE	ÚI	ÚO	Ú	
UI+	UIA	UIE	UI	UIO	UIU	
Y+	YA	YE				Y

And here is the chart for adding words starting in diphthongs.

	+AE	+AI	+AU	+EI	+OE	+UI
AE+		AEAI	AEO		AEOE	AEUI
AW+	AWAE	AWAI	Ó	AWEI	OE	
E+	EAE	EAI	EO	EI	EOE	EUI
EI+	EIAE		EIO		EIOE	EIUI
I+	IAE	IAI	IO	IEI	IOE	IUI
O+	OAE	OAI	Ó		OE	
OE+	OEAE	OEAI	OEO			OEUI
Û/Ú+	ÚAE	ÚAI	ÚO	ÚEI	ÚOE	
UI+	UIAE	UIAI	UIO	UIEI	UIOE	
Y+	YAE	YAI		YEI		

9.3.2.2 Consonants

See the following pages.

---

[304] Refer back to 4.2.2 to review this.
[305] Review in 5.1.2

	+P	+PL	+PR	+B	+(M)B
B+	B/PH	BL/PHL	BR/PHR	B	B
D+	DB/PH	PHL	PHR	B/DB/DV	DB
G+	GB			GB/GV	GB
M+	MB/MPH	MBL	MBR	MB	MB
MP+	MB/MPH	MBL	MBR	MB	MB
N+	PH/MB	PHL/MBL	PHR/MBR	M/MB	MB
NN+	MB	MBL	MBR	MB	MB
NT+	MB	MBL	MBR	MB	MB
ND+	MB	MBL	MBR	MB	MB
Ñ+	ÑB	ÑBL	ÑBR	ÑB	ÑB
ÑC+					
PH+	PH	PHL	PHR		
V+	PH	PHL	PHR	V	
TH+	THB			THV	THB
DH+	DHB/PH	PHL	PHR	DHV	B/DHM
S/SS+	SP/SB	SPL/SBL	SPR/SBR	SB	SB
SC+					
SG+					
SP+	SP/SB	SPL/SBL	SPR/SBR	SB	SB
ST+					
CH+	CHB			CHB	CHM/CHB
H[306]+	B/PH	BL/PHL	BR/PHR	B/V	B/M
L+	LPH/LB	LPHL	LPHR	LV/LB	LB
LL+	LPH/LB	LPHL	LPHR	LV/LB	LB
LT+	LPH/LB	LPHL	LPHR	LV/LB	LB
LPH+	LPH	LPHL	LPHR		
LV+	LPH	LPHL	LPHR	LV	
LTH+					
LDH+					
LCH+					
R+	RPH/RB	RPHL	RPHR	RV/RB	RB
RN+	RMB/RPH	RPHL	RPHR	RM/RMB	RMB
RPH+	RPH	RPHL	RPHR		
RV+	RPH	RPHL	RPHR	RV	
RTH+					
RDH+					
RCH+					
W+[307]	B	BL	BR	V	M

---

[306] As in **ah** and **oh**, this is an H that only appears before vowels.

[307] W is deleted before these vowels: U, Y, and O.

	+BL	+BR	+T	+TR	+D	+(N)D
B+	BL	BR	BD		BD	BD
D+	BL	BR	D/TH	DR/THR	D	D
G+			GD		GD	GD
M+	MBL	MBR	MD	MDR	MD	MD
MP+	MBL	MBR	MD	MDR	MD	MD
N+	MBL	MBR	TH/ND	THR/NDR	N/ND	ND
NN+	MBL	MBR	ND	NDR	ND	ND
NT+	MBL	MBR	ND	NDR	ND	ND
ND+	MBL	MBR	ND	NDR	ND	ND
Ñ+	ÑBL	ÑBR	ÑD	ÑDR	ÑD	ÑD
ÑC+						
PH+			PHD		PHD	PHN
V+	VL	VR	VD		VD	VN
TH+			TH	THR	THD	THN
DH+			TH	THR	DH	ND/DHN
S/SS+	SBL	SBR	ST/SD	STR/SDR	SD	SD/SN
SC+						
SG+						
SP+	SBL	SBR				
ST+			ST	STR		
CH+			CHD			CHN
H+	BL/VL	BR/VR	TH/D	THR/DR		N
L+	LVL	LVR	LD/LTH	LTHR	LD/LDH	LD
LL+	LVL	LVR	LD/LTH	LTHR	LD/LDH	LD
LT+	LVL	LVR	LD/LTH	LTHR	LD/LDH	LD
LPH+						
LV+	LVL	LVR				
LTH+			LTH	LTHR		
LDH+			LTH	LTHR	LDH	
LCH+						
R+	RVL	RVR	RTH/RD	RTHR	RD/RDH	RD
RN+			RND/RTH	RTHR	RN/RND	RND
RPH+						
RV+	RVL	RVR				
RTH+			RTH	RTHR		
RDH+			RTH	RTHR	RDH	
RCH+						
W+	VL	VR	WD	DR	WD	WD

	+DR	+C	+CL	+CR	+G	+(Ñ)G
B+		BG			B	BG
D+	DR	DG/CH	CHL		D	DG
G+		G/CH	GL/CHL	GR/CHR	G	G
M+	MDR	MG	MGL	MGR	M	MG
MP+	MDR	MG	MGL	MGR	MM	MG
N+	NDR	CH/ÑG	CHL/ÑGL	CHR/ÑGR	ÑG	ÑG
NN+	NDR	ÑG	ÑGL	ÑGR	ÑG	ÑG
NT+	NDR	ÑG	ÑGL	ÑGR	ÑG	ÑG
ND+	NDR	ÑG	ÑGL	ÑGR	ÑG	ÑG
Ñ+	ÑDR	ÑG	ÑGL	ÑGR	ÑG	ÑG
ÑC+		ÑG	ÑGL	ÑGR	ÑG	ÑG
PH+		PHG			PH	PHG
V+		VG			V	VG
TH+		THG			TH	THG
DH+	DHR	DHG/CH	CHL	CHR	DH	DHG
S/SS+	SDR	SC/SG	SCL/SGL	SCR/SGR	SS	SG*
SC+		SC/SG	SCL/SGL	SCR/SGR	SC	SG
SG+		SG	SGL	SGR	SG	SG
SP+					SP	
ST+					ST	
CH+		CH	CHL	CHR	CH	
H+		CH/G	CHL/GL	CHR/GR	H/G	ÑG
L+	LDHR	LCH/LG	LCHL	LCHR	L	LG
LL+	LDHR	LCH/LG	LCHL	LCHR	L	LG
LT+	LDHR	LCH/LG	LCHL	LCHR	L	LG
LPH+					LPH	
LV+					LV	
LTH+					LTH	
LDH+	LDHR	LCH	LCHL	LCHR	LDH	
LCH+		LCH	LCHL	LCHR	LCH	
R+	RDHR	RCH	RCHL	RCHR	R	
RN+	RNDR	RCH/RÑG	RCHL	RCHR	RÑG	
RPH+					RPH	
RV+					RV	
RTH+					RTH	
RDH+	RDHR				RDH	
RCH+		RCH	RCHL	RCHR	RCH	
W+	DHR	G	GL	GR	W	ÑG

	+GL	+GR	+GW[308]	+M	+N	+F	+TH
B+	BL	BR			BN		PTH
D+	DL	DR	DW	DV	DN	F	TH
G+	GL	GR	GW	GV	GN	GF	CTH
M+	ML	MR		M		MF	MTH
MP+	ML	MR		MM		MF	MTH
N+	ÑGL	ÑGR	NW	M	N	F/NF	TH/NTH
NN+	ÑGL	ÑGR	NW		NN	NF	NTH
NT+	ÑGL	ÑGR	NW		NN	NF	NTH
ND+	ÑGL	ÑGR	NW		NN	NF	NTH
Ñ+	ÑGL	ÑGR	ÑGW			ÑF	ÑTH
ÑC+	ÑGL	ÑGR	ÑGW				
PH+		PHR			PHN	F	
V+		VR		V	VN	F	
TH+		THR	THW		THN		TH
DH+		DHR	DHW		DHN		TH
S/SS+	SGL	THR					
SC+	SGL	SGR					
SG+	SGL	SGR					
SP+		SPR					
ST+		THR					
CH+		CHR	CHW		CHN		
H+	L	R	W	V	N	F	TH
L+	LL	LR	LW	LV	LN	LF	LTH
LL+	LL	LR	LW	LV	LN	LF	LTH
LT+	LL	LR	LW	LV	LN	LF	LTH
LPH+	LPHL	LPHR				LF	
LV+	LVL	LVR		LV		LF	
LTH+	LTHL	LTHR					LTH
LDH+	LDHL	LDHR					LTH
LCH+	LCHL	LCHR					
R+	RL	RR	RW	RV	RN	RF	RTH
RN+			RNW	RM	RN	RF	RTH
RPH+	RPHL	RPHR				RF	
RV+	RVL	RVR		RV		RF	
RTH+	RTHL	RTHR					RTH
RDH+	RDHL	RDHR					RTH
RCH+	RCHL	RCHR					
W+	L	R	W	W	N	F	TH

[308] W is deleted following these vowels: U, Y, and O.

	+S	+H	+L	+LH	+R	+RH	+HW
B+	PS	PCH	BL	BL	BR	BR	
D+	SS	TH	DL	THL	DR	THR	CHW
G+	CH	CH	GL	GL	GR	GR	CHW
M+	MH	MCH	ML	ML	MR	MR	
MP+	MH	MCH	ML	ML	MR	MR	
N+	SS	CH	L	THL	DHR	THR	CHW
NN+	NH	NCH	NDL	NDL	NDR	NDR	NW
NT+	NTH	NCH	NDL	NDL	NDR	NDR	NW
ND+	NH	NCH	NDL	NDL	NDR	NDR	NW
Ñ+	ÑH	ÑCH	ÑGL	ÑGL	ÑGR	ÑGR	ÑGW
ÑC+		ÑCH	ÑGL	ÑGL	ÑGR	ÑGR	ÑGW
PH+	PH	PH	PHL	PHL	PHR	PHR	PHW
V+	V	V	VL	VL	VR	VR	
TH+	TH	TH	THL	THL	THR	THR	THW
DH+	DH	DH	DHL	THL	DHR	THR	DHW
S/SS+	SS	SS	THL	THL	THR	THR	
SC+			SGL		SGR		SGW
SG+			SGL		SGR		SGW
SP+			SBL		SBR		
ST+	SS		THL	THL	THR	THR	
CH+	CH	CH	CHL	CHL	CHR	CHR	CHW
H+	SS	H	THL	THL	THR	THR	CHW
L+	LH	LH	LL	LTHL	LR	LTHR	LW
LL+	LH	LH	LL	LTHL	LR	LTHR	LW
LT+	LH	LH	LL	LTHL	LR	LTHR	LW
LPH+	LPH	LPH	LPHL	LPHL	LPHR	LPHR	
LV+	LV	LV	LVL	LVL	LVR	LVR	
LTH+	LTH	LTH	LTHL	LTHL	LTHR	LTHR	
LDH+	LDH	LDH	LDHL	LTHL	LDHR	LTHR	
LCH+	LCH	LCH	LCHL	LCHL	LCHR	LCHR	LCHW
R+	RH	RCH	RL	RTHL	RR	RTH	RW
RN+	RNH	RCH	RL	RTHL	RDHR	RTHR	RNW
RPH+	RPH	RPH	RPHL	RPHL	RPHR	RPHR	
RV+	RV	RV	RVL	RVL	RVR	RVR	
RTH+	RTH	RTH	RTHL	RTHL	RTHR	RTH	
RDH+	RDH	RDH	RDHL	RTHL	RDHR	RTHR	
RCH+	RCH	RCH	RCHL	RCHL	RCHR	RCHR	RCHW
W+	H	CH	L	THL	R	THR	W

9.3.3 Long Consonants

In archaic compounds these will be retained. For all others, delete the second letter in the following consonant clusters when they occur at the end of a multi-syllable word:

MP, NN, ND, NT, SS, ST, LL, LT

9.3.4 Common Elements in Compound Personal Names

Let's look at some of the most common second elements of personal names and what they mean.

- **Gwend** Maiden
- **(n)Dîs**[309] Woman, Bride
- **Sell**[310] Girl, Daughter
- **(n)Dîr** Man
- **Ser**[311] Lover/Friend of...
- **(n)Dîl** Lover/Friend of...
- **Pen** Person
- **Hîl**[312] Heir/Heiress

9.3.4.1 Exercise

Make the following names, and give their English translations.

1. **Raw** lion + **dîs** _____
2. **Dî** woman + **dîl** _____
3. **Loss** snow + **ser** _____
4. **Sarn** stone + **sell** _____

---

[309] Even though **(n)dîs** means "Bride," in names it appears to be the feminine equivalent to **(n)dîr**. I often also use **(n)dess** "woman" as well.

[310] Tolkien gave **sell** as an alternate to **-iel**.

[311] **Ser** can be given gender with the suffixes **-on** and **-il**.

[312] This is another good one for a patronymic name. Unlike **-ion**, **-ien**, or **-iel**, this word is genderless.

5. **Loth** flower + **gwend** _____
6. **Sîdh** peace + **hîl** _____
7. **Roch** horse + **pen** _____

9.3.5 Common Elements in Compound Place Names

Names for places are usually structured "descriptor/feature + what the place is" but there are a few really common elements that apply to many types of places.

- **Iaun** vast (reduces to **-ion**)
- **Iand**[313] expanse (and plural **iend**)
- **(n)Dôr** land
- **(m)Bâr** home

9.3.5.1 Exercise

Make the following place names, and give their English translations:

1. **Sant** Garden + **iaun** _____
2. **Lhô** marsh + **dôr** _____
3. **Galadh** tree + **iand**_____
4. **Calen** green + **bâr**_____
5. **Lith** sand, ash + **iend** _____

9.3.6 Elven Culture: Naming Practices of the Sindar[314]

Of the naming traditions of the Eldar who lived in Valinor, we know much. However, the naming traditions of the Sindar are largely undocumented. Though Tolkien never explicitly described them, we can guess by looking at their names.

The Elves of Beleriand are the ones most likely to have naming traditions echoing the traditions in Valinor, as they were the closest to Valinor and they had trade and communication with it. Therefore, when Doriath was conquered and the Sindar fled deeper into Middle-earth to live in the lands of other Telerin Elves, they brought these strong

---

[313] In late names it can be reduced to **-an**, like in **Rohan**.

[314] If you haven't yet, read 9.3.7: The Naming Practices of the Noldor. This section won't make very much sense to you without it.

traditions and their language with them. Since the language was adopted, it doesn't seem too strange that the naming traditions would come along too.

But would there be any naming traditions that they didn't already have?

From a linguistic point of view, there is a striking similarity to the Sindarin word **eneth**[315] and the Quenya word anessë, suggesting that the Sindar also have Given-names.

Denethor[316] (Lithe and Lank) is obviously an epessë, given to the hero who saved the Nandor. Another example of an epessë given before the languages had truly split is Elwê's name, **Thindikollo** (Grey Cloak). It refers to his silver hair.

The Parentless Elves[317] all have cilmessi. While the Noldor glorified and enshrined this quite a bit, we don't know to what extent the other cultures developed this. We can guess that they also could choose their own names, like their forefathers did. After all, the person who knows you best is yourself. Also there may be the odd occasion wherein an Elf decides to leave their old names behind and go by an alias, so that type of cilmessë we can't rule out either.

There is little in the way of evidence of amilessi, but it seems unlikely that they wouldn't also exist, as any Elven woman is capable of having insight in the hour of birth into her child's future life and personality. Therefore, I contend that amilessi are also possible.

Finally, the *ataressi. We know that in an earlier version of his Elven language history Tolkien made a way for the Ilkorin Elves[318] to have

---

[315] *Vinyar Tengwar* issue 44, "Ae Adar Nín"

[316] Denethor was originally was a Common Eldarin name, **Denitháró.**

[317] The Elves who first awoke on the shores of Cuiviénen and who therefore have neither parents nor a birth at all.

[318] Uncivilized Elves outside the Elven cities... This idea and their language was scrapped in favor of having all the elves of Beleriand speak dialects of Sindarin.

ataressi. They have a unique patronymic wherein **go-** is prefixed onto a parent's name.[319]

In conclusion, I believe that the naming traditions of the Eldar come from the shores of Cuiviénen, and therefore aren't completely different amongst the sundered Elves. That being said, I believe that the Sindar's names are structured like this:

1.   The first name is an *ataressë, with some portion of the father or mother's name in it, and probably ending a name suffix indicating the relationship between the parent and child.

     There probably would be some sort of ceremony or celebration for the parents to show off their new child, and let everyone know of its existence, wherein they would also tell everyone their new baby's name. This name probably had very little personal significance, and could be used by outsiders.

2.   The second name describes the Elf's personality. It is chosen later in life, when the Elf's personality has taken form.

     For the Sindar, gaining fluency in your native tongue isn't as highly prized as it is for the Noldor, so there probably isn't a Name-Choosing ceremony amongst them. I do think that there can be more than one of these names, possibly one given by the mother, using her unique insight into her child's personality and future. This name probably was much more intimate and personal for the Elf who had it, so using it would require a personal relationship. It would be rude for outsiders to use this name.

3.   The third name is an epessë of some sort, or a professional's title. It can be descriptive of some event the Elf is well known for, the place that such an event took place, or some outstanding physical or mental feature that the Elf is well known for. Other than titles of nobility, Tolkien wrote about two professional titles: **Celebrimbor** for silver smiths and **Tegilbor** for

_____

[319] *The Lost Road and Other Writings* – "The Etymologies" 3Ŏ

scribes.[320] So we can infer that people were sometimes referred to by their occupation instead of their name.

---

[320] *The Peoples of Middle-earth*, "Of Dwarves and Men" – Note #7

Chapter 10: Dialects

In this chapter, you will learn the different dialects of Sindarin, and the history behind them.[321] For the purposes of these lessons, we'll be breaking the dialects into categories. It's good to remember, though, that the categories are much looser than I've defined them.

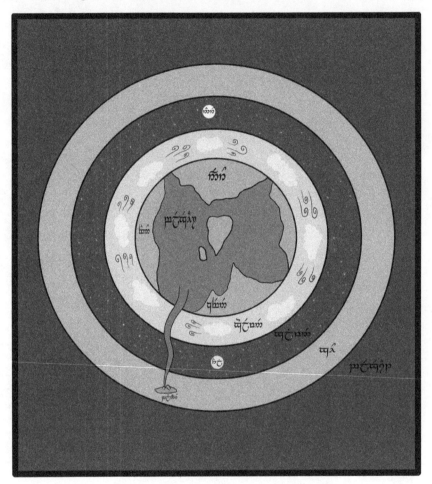

---

[321] Research for this chapter is: *Lord of the Rings*, Appendix F "The Languages and Peoples of the Third Age;" *Parma Eldalamberon 17* pages 127 through 136; *The Silmarillion*: "Of the Sindar," "Of the Return of the Noldor," "Of Beleriand and Its Realms," and "Of the Noldor in Beleriand;" *Unfinished Tales*, "The History of Galadriel and Celeborn" – Appendix A "The Silvan Elves and Their Speech."

10.1 Old versus New

Before we get into dialects, we need to learn one of the key driving forces for the differences between dialects. We'll study the linguistic forces that Tolkien was mimicking, and how these are applied to Sindarin verbs.

10.1.1 Analogy

Just when you thought you had the Sindarin tenses down, it turns out that the people of Middle-earth didn't.

The reason is Analogy. Analogy is a system of logic that can change the structure of a language over time. In cases like this, it happens because the speakers don't quite remember the correct conjugation of a verb, so they make an analogy with another verb and change it in the same way. It is by this theory that many linguists believe English lost much of its complex past tense for the "-ed" suffix, and why nowadays many "-ed" suffixes are replaced with complex past tenses.

Take the English word, "to catch." Its conjugation analogy used to be something like this:

- Snatch, snatched:
- Catch, *catched*.

But it changed to:

- Teach, taught:
- Catch, *caught*.

Fascinating, right? Tolkien probably thought so too. So who would be using these analogous forms? The young elves, the elves who learned Sindarin as a second language, and the humans. Old elves who knew Doriath long before the sun first rose would be using the old conjugations that we learned previously.

Basically, we're learning how those new to the language make mistakes and re-invent the grammar. There is one thing to note – verbs that are used often (to come, to go, to be, to have, to do) will be close to being immune from analogous changes. So don't use analogies to make speech idiosyncrasies for common words as they'd likely just get memorized.

Quick, before we start: This means that the "Special Cases" of the mutation charts are likely to be ignored as well. Past-tense conjugations in particular are affected by this.

10.1.2 I-Verbs Acting Like A-Verbs

There are several different trends to the analogous changes to Sindarin verb-conjugation. We'll focus on I-Verbs being simplified into A-verbs to start off.

This first type of error is likely to be made by those who are familiar with Sindarin, but weren't actually taught it. It's based on the way that I-verbs are conjugated into the present tense and the imperative form.

I-verbs are called such because of the **-i-** used in their conjugations. Because of I-affection, you might not know what the core vowel is when working from the present tense. If you are unfamiliar with Sindarin, you might not know the more complex I-Affection past tense.

When I-verbs play dress-up as A-verbs, they put on the A-verbs' suffixes: **-nt**, and **-s/-st**. This means that you will have to distinguish between transitive and intransitive verbs.

Gwedh- → **Gwedhin** → **Gwedha-** bind
Dag- → **Degin** → **Dega-** slay
Tir- → **Tirin** → **Tira-** guard, watch
Nor- → **Nerin** → **Nera-** run

Next we have the type of errors made by someone who is extremely unfamiliar with Sindarin and who hasn't been schooled in it all, like an Elven child.

In this one it's based off of the imperative conjugation of the verbs. Just take the root, add an -a onto it, and conjugate it like an A-verb.

Gwedho → **Gwedha-** bind
Dago → **Daga-** slay
Tiro → **Tira-** watch
Noro → **Nora-** run

Then, in an attempt to sound more like the older Sindar, a whole new set of mistakes takes place.

10.1.3 A-verbs Acting Like I-verbs

Because I-Verb-like conjugation is difficult, these sorts of errors are made by people who have been schooled in Sindarin, and are trying their best to not sound like the merchants, lower classes, or children.

The people who would use this system are likely to be Noldorin Exiles (they would conjugate much closer to the way that Elves of Doriath would, but are still likely to make a few errors) and the well-schooled Gondorians/Númenóreans who have actually spoken with and learned from Elves.

This set of mistakes occurs when the consonant before the -a is like the consonant at the end of an I-verb. (B, D, G, V, DH, L, R, W, N [not NN]) The -a gets stripped off and the word is conjugated like an I-verb, leading to verb roots like this:

> **Nimmida-** → **Nimmid-** to whiten
>
> **Soga-**   → **Sog-** to drink
>
> **Drava-**   → **Draf-** to hew

And there you have it. Sindarin verbs are a mess.

10.1.4 Shortening Long Consonants at the Ends of Words

You'll notice that in older names like **Beleriand** (balar+iand) that the -ND is intact. And in later names like **Rochan** (roch+iand) the D is missing. You'll also find words with two or three versions of them, like "monster" **ulun**, **ulunn**, and **ulund**. The reason why this happens is that there was a subtle shift in the phonological structure of Sindarin, which, because people had started writing it down, became semi-preserved in the spelling. As English speakers and readers, we are pretty familiar with this concept. To figure out what is going on takes a bit of detective work.[322]

It appears that in the first age, there were words with -NN, -ND, -SS, and -ST, and they were not confused. But then the phonology shifted. -NN and -ND became indistinguishable, and -SS and -ST became indistinguishable.

But there was a problem. Sindarin was being recorded in writing by this time, and they had records and writings with these different endings. Not having dictionaries like we do, they started guessing which words should have -ND versus -NN and which should have -ST versus -SS. Eventually, all one-syllable words with -ND/-NN became -ND, and -SS/-ST were shortened to -S, but something different happened to polysyllabic words.

In words with more than one syllable, -NN/-ND were shortened into -N, and -SS/-ST were shortened into -S.

But our poor writers and readers needed a system to know which -N's and -S's were supposed to be -NN's, -ND's, -SS's and -ST's! They started writing place names that ended with -N's phonetically with an extra D at the end, and just kept guessing with the -S's.

There are a few other long final consonants that were shortened but passed without the confusion above.

- -MM and -MB were shortened to -M.
- -MP, NT, LL, and LT were shortened on polysyllabic words, but kept in monosyllables.

The question remains: how can we tell these apart when translating? You have two options. Research the history of the word, which can take a while, or look up the word's cognate in Quenya. A set of cognates is a group of words that come from the same ancient word. Here are a few examples:

---

[322] There are only two articles about this phenomenon that I know about, and both are by Helge Fauskanger: "The question of nd or n(n)" http://folk.uib.no/hnohf/ndnn.htm "To SS or not to SS – A Gollumish Problem" http://folk.uib.no/hnohf/ss.htm

English	Quenya	Early Sindarin
bread	massa	bass
tongue	lambë	lamb
circular	rinda	rend
nightingale	morilindë	merilind
crested	quinna	penn
chair	hamma	hamm

It should be noted that looking for cognates won't always be the best way to figure out what an earlier form of a word would be. The word may have been lost in Quenya or combined with other morphemes that change the end of the word. Researching words can also lead to dead-ends – as Tolkien didn't draw up histories for every word he ever made. Sometimes he made them up on the spot, and figured out histories for the words later, if he remembered to.

10.1.5 EI versus AI

As you should recall,[323] I wrote about the change from EI to AI in some Sindarin words. Here's a refresher.

If the diphthong EI occurs in the last syllable of a word, in later Sindarin, it would be an AI.

Also, the final-syllable plural form for A used to be EI, so when this diphthong change swept through, the plural form for final-syllable A's changed too.

---

[323] If you don't recall, review 4.1.2.3.3.

10.2 The Dialects of Beleriand

We've been learning about the language of Beleriand as if it were one homogeneous thing, but in actuality, it was far more diverse. We know that there were at least four dialects spoken in Beleriand before the Noldor came.

The Northern (Mithrim) dialect was so different from Sindarin that it's just about a different language. We also know so little about it – other than a few scattered words like **Hithlum**[324] and **Dorlomin**[325] and a vague view of its phonology – that it's fruitless to do anything except make names from it. To translate in it, you'd have to do so much reconstruction that any generated phrase would have to be viewed with heavy skepticism.

Of the Western, Central (Doriath), and Southern (Lindon/Ossiriand) dialects we know much, much more. For one, we know that they are almost identical, other than a few small differences in the way the sounds developed.

10.2.1 The West versus Doriath

These two dialects were almost exactly the same and only had a few small differences. These differences arose with the Girdle of Melian. They were the same until Doriath was sealed off, and hardly anyone could come in or out. Slowly, the speech inside and outside the magic wall began to diverge. Tolkien described the language as being preserved and left unchanged in Doriath (likely due to Melian's power) and outside, it was influenced by the Noldor. The Western dialect that we'll cover in this lesson is the dialect just before the Noldor start to influence it.

If you look back through the lessons, you will find that I've mentioned this before several times. I'll go over these differences again for you, but leaving the Noldorin changes out until we get to the section devoted to them.

---

[324] **Hithlu** in the other Sindarin dialects
[325] **Dorloven** in the other Sindarin dialects

10.2.1.1 Phonological Differences

If you go back to the lesson on Prestanneth,[326] you'll recall annotations marking a series of differences, all focused around N+R combinations. In the Doriath dialect, the NR is no problem. In the Western dialect, N+R=DHR. This is important to remember when making class plurals with -rim as well.

Another thing you may recall from the Prestanneth chapter was how M mutated to Ṽ.[327] After the Girdle of Melian was made, the Ṽ in Western Sindarin became just a V. In Doriath, the Ṽ didn't become a V until after Doriath fell. This means that Lúthien's pet name which was given to her by Beren would be "Tinúṽiel" while Doriath lasted. Watch out for words with Vs in them that come from Ms. Those also would need to be Ṽs when spoken in Doriath.

10.2.1.2 Grammatical Differences

The most marked difference is Central and Western Sindarin would be the pronouns. Outside of Doriath, another pronoun for "you" was adopted from Quenya, which you should recall from chapter 7. Until the Noldor come, they used the D-root for the plural and singular formal "you."

10.2.2 The South

Unlike Doriath with its wall, Ossiriand was separated from the center of Beleriand by simple distance, being at the far southeastern end of the region. Its elves were culturally Lindarin (as evidenced by their fondness for treehouses), but spoke a dialect of Sindarin.

In Mirkwood, the dialects adopted would be the Southern with traces of the Western, and the Sindar who fled Beleriand to join the Lindar tried to blend in with their Lindarin cousins and adopted their speech-styles. Tolkien took care to note that Legolas' lineage was Sindarin, but his name had been Woodelvenized.[328] Also, the way his clothing and

---

[326] Chapter 5

[327] Review how to pronounce this sound in 2.2.3.

[328] *The Letters of J.R.R. Tolkien*, letter #211

appearance is described in the Council of Elrond is virtually identical to the description of the Lindar in *The Silmarillion*.

This dialect has only two differences with Western Sindarin, as far as we know. The first one has to do with a certain set of sounds. This is best illustrated with a chart.

Old Sindarin	West/Doriath	South
an MP between vowels	became MM	became MPH
an NT between vowels	became NN	became NTH
an ÑC between vowels	became ÑG	became ÑCH
an LT between vowels	became LL	became LTH

Think back to all of the places you've used this. When a suffix starting with a vowel is added; when the past tense is conjugated; when a past participle is made... those are a lot of contrasting sounds. Also look out for this in the words themselves. For example, Western Sindarin "to give" **anna-** would be **antha-** in Southern Sindarin. This is because the ancient word is **antā-**. This will take a lot of careful research into the roots of the words you're using. I will help with this until you can figure it out on your own.

10.2.3 Examples

Now that we have covered the three dialects of Beleriand, we can apply them.

> Doriath: **Haṽathodh**?
> West/South: **Havathol**?
> *Would you please sit?*

The word "to sit" has the ancient root **kham-**, so the resulting verb root in Doriath would be **haṽ-**, not **hav-/haf-**, as it is elsewhere. For "you," I used the L- root for outside of Doriath, and the D-root for Doriath.

Doriath/West:	**Dollanneb**	i	mîr	'wîn	mi	'athrod.
South:	**Dolthantheb**	i	mîr	'wîn	mi	'athrod.
	hid-we	the	treasures	our	in	cave

> *We hid our treasures in a cave.*

In the Southern version, the ancient form of the verb "to hide" makes the verb take a different form. The ancient verb was **dultā-**, so the resulting form in Southern Sindarin is **doltha-**, not **dolla-**.[329]

The past tense conjugation is different too! The A-verb suffix is **-nt**, so when **-eb** is added, it becomes **-ntheb**, not **-nneb**, as it would in the other dialects.

---

[329] In dictionaries, **doltha-** will be the verb listed. We take it from Tolkien's earlier draft of Sindarin, Noldorin, and have to adjust it to fit Tolkien's later Sindarin.

10.3 The Exiles

As you should recall, the Noldor who pursued Morgoth to Middle-earth (on the ships of the Teleri of Alqualondë, whom they slew to obtain) were barred from returning to Valinor. Some of them, like Galadriel, came to Middle-earth because they wanted to make settlements for themselves far from the rule of the Valar, and to be rulers of these settlements. Either way, there was a wave of Noldorin settlers in Beleriand.

10.3.1 History

The Noldor came through the north, and learned first the language of the Mithrim, but continued south as the war with Morgoth raged on. The Northern language was too different to converse with the Sindar, so they started learning Sindarin. They also tried to homogenize Sindarin to some extent, building from the Western and Central dialects of Sindarin a sort of "normalized" Sindarin that they taught to fellow Noldor, but didn't entirely mesh with the Sindarin being spoken.

At first, the Sindar of Beleriand welcomed the Noldor, fighting beside them against the sudden invasion of Orcs. But then Elu Thingol, King of the Sindar, heard about the Kinslaying at Alqualondë. He banned the use of Quenya in his realm and ordered that those who spoke it openly be shunned. Melian, the Queen, had built a magical wall around Menegroth (thus making Doriath the Fenced Realm) to make a haven for the Sindar from the rampaging Orcs. Thingol then used this wall to keep the Noldor out as well – save Galadriel.

Outside the wall the Noldor stayed and founded settlements. First there was Nargothrod, which was made with the help of the Dwarves underground. It was between the lands of Círdan and Doriath – squarely where the Western Sindarin dialect was used. In the far north, many Noldor settled with the Mithrim to aid in the watch of Angband. They used the mysterious language of the Mithrim, but we won't deal with them. Then there was Thargelion, which was just north of Ossiriand. There was Gondolin, ruled by Turgon, where Sindarin and Quenya were spoken side by side. Many Quenya words were simply "Sindarinized" instead of translated there, like the name "Gondolin" itself. In fact, because it wasn't completely translated, the Sindar assumed that it meant "Hidden Stone" instead of "Singing Stone." The stronghold was named for the underground caverns carved by water running beneath the city, which echoed with the water still flowing through them.

So what do we get from this? We know the Noldor took the Western dialect of Sindarin and spread it amongst each other as the "correct" way to speak Sindarin. The Southern dialect remained mostly un-touched by the Noldor because little mixing between the Noldor and the Lindar took place.

10.3.2 Borrowing from Quenya

I first introduced this in 3.2.4, in the section about conjunctions. If you think back there are several often-used words that are borrowings from Quenya.

D's become L's. You'll notice this with a lot of Sindarin words that start with the letter D. This D developed into an L in Quenya. Because the sounds are different, and a Noldo trying to translate their name would want their new name to sound as much like their old one as possible, or they're just having a hard time thinking of the proper Sindarin word, the Quenya word starting with an L will be Sindarinized.

> You see this in words like formal singular second person **le** to contrast with the Sindarin **de**. Because of Noldorin influence, Sindarin outside of Beleriand adopted the L-based pronoun for the singular, and used the D-based pronoun for the plural.

> You see this influence in "fall," which is **dant** to the Sindar but **lant** to the Noldor, and "journey," which is absent to the Sindar but **lend** to the Noldor, borrowed from the Quenya word **lenda**.

> You also see it in "Elda" which is **edhel** to the Sindar but **eledh** to the Noldor. The last one, because of its use by the Noldor, became a term for Noldorin Elves.

DH's become R's. Sometimes where in Quenya you have **-r**, in Sindarin you have **-dh**. Watch out for this. It's pretty rare as far as borrowings go, but it does show up from time to time.

aníra- "To want/desire" to contrast with Sindarin ídha- (and variant ídhra-).[330]

Vanishing or extra G's. In the ancient Eldarin, there were words that started with G. These G's vanished in Quenya, but stuck around in Sindarin. So, the Noldor made many errors when trying to remember which words had G's on them – adding G's to some words, losing G's on others.

> We see this in words like **anglenna**- "to approach," This one is interesting. I think that it was made by putting a verb marker -**a** onto **lend** – an adaption of a Quenya word, as you'll remember, then adding a G before adding the prefix **an**-.

> We also see it in "to laugh" **lal**- (from the Quenya word **lala**-). Compare it to the Sindarin **gladh**-.

> This is why we also get dual entries for words like **glîr** and **lîr**, and **glaer** and **laer**, **gaear** and **aear** where the G was left out by the Exiles.

All of this makes translating quite tedious and full of lengthy research and some haphazard guesswork, as I think I've demonstrated here. I'm trying to cut down your time spent muddling around with this, but I expect that it will take some experimenting, trial, and error on your part. Don't be afraid to consult other Neo-Sindarin translators for help if you get stuck.

10.3.3 Researching Word Roots

I started you on this way back in Chapter 5, and after hinting at it, it's time for you to dive into it. You're going to be doing a lot of this as a Neo-Sindarin translator.

By now, there are several books that you should have in your possession. If you don't have them, GET THEM AS SOON AS POSSIBLE.

---

[330] That it applies to **aníra-/ídha-** is actually a theory of mine. Tolkien toyed with the idea of the root NIR- for "desire," and even made a Quenya word to match, but by the time he was writing "Words, Phrases, and Passages" he seems to have settled on using the root **ID** for "desire."

The Lost Road and Other Writings (History of Middle-earth Vol. 5)

> This is the book with the Etymologies in it. The Etymologies
> date back to a time before Sindarin was for the Sindar, which
> is important to remember. It's still the greatest collection of an-
> cient roots, and it is largely unchanged after Noldorin became
> Sindarin.

The Collected Vinyar Tengwar – vol. 5

> In here are the Addenda and Corrigenda to the Etymologies.
> These entries date back to the same era as The Etymologies,
> but have in them all of the entries left out, left incomplete, or
> possibly misread.

Parma Eldalamberon issue 17 "Words, Phrases and Passages in Various Tongues in The Lord of the Rings" and "Eldarin Roots and Stems"

> I've been talking about this book all throughout the lessons,
> and with a good reason. It has detailed LotR-era notes on the
> translations that Tolkien devised for LotR and most im-
> portantly, a glossary of ancient roots. In this book, you can see
> Tolkien mulling about and experimenting with his languages,
> as he was first making phrases that sounded cool, then bending
> the vocabulary and grammar to match. To see his process in
> such great detail is a lot of fun.

The War of the Jewels (History of Middle-earth Vol. 12)

> Herein lies "The Quendi and the Eldar," a detailed look at the
> evolution of a small set of roots through many of the Elven lan-
> guages. This is Post-LotR-era Sindarin, and those who use this
> for Neo-Sindarin texts generally agree that where there is a
> conflict in root or word meaning, this later version is preferred.
> It is quite valuable when it comes to understanding the use of
> roots to build new words.

Now that you have these very useful tomes, it's time to use them.

Step One

Find the possible words you're looking for. Do this by using these two
dictionaries:

Parf Edhellen[331] – This is a compilation of Elvish dictionaries that other people have put together. This makes it really fast and easy to find words that you need and to find cognates. It also has people still working on it, so that you know that its contents haven't started to molder like a lot of other online Tolkien-Elvish dictionaries. It also marks deduced and possibly fan-coined words clearly, as well as the sources of the words.

Eldamo[332] – This is a work in progress, but it is a very useful tool for us. It organizes the words according to when Tolkien made them, and what other words are related to them, are cognates, or if it's part of a phrase or compound word. This makes it easy (once you know which word you're looking for) to trace back its history and see if there are any more recent versions of the word. But since this isn't complete yet, it's really handy to know how to do this research on your own.

For example's sake, let's say that we're looking for a word for "journey." On *Parf Edhellen*, we find it from two different sources. *Hiswelókë* gives us **lend**. It's a word that has been derived from another, **lembas**, and we can find reference to it in *The Peoples of Middle-earth*, page 404.

PE17 Sindarin Corpus gives us only **lembas**, and a brief mention of a Quenya word, **lerembas** and a possible alternate translation, **ledhbas**. There is a reference to pages 51 and 60.

Step Two

Look up the roots of the words, in ALL of the collections of word roots. That way, if there are conflicting entries, you can choose the later entry.

This is where looking for a word for "journey" becomes more interesting. If you go by the page references alone, you'd think that the ancient root is surely LED-.

Open "The Etymologies" and you find the roots ELED and LED, and a mention of something that Tolkien was considering: using the root EDEL for Middle-earth, but he hadn't quite decided on it yet.

---

[331] https://www.elfdict.com/
[332] http://eldamo.org/

The "Addenda and Corrigenda" support this conclusion, and add another possible root: LEN, meaning "road" or "way."

In "Eldarin Roots and Stems" from *Parma Eldalamberon* issue 17, we once again meet the roots LED and LEN, but with little elaboration.

And finally, in "The Quendi and the Eldar," we get the full flowering of the roots. There, we learn that the ancient root was in fact DELE, that it became LED in Quenya due to metathesis.[333] This meant that Quenya speakers would assume that the ancient root was LED. In Sindarin, however, the word vanished all together, replaced by other words with similar meanings. The only remnant of it is in the original meaning of **Edelī**: Those of the Journey, which lost its meaning to just be a generic term for "Elf."

Step Three

Based on the entries, figure how the words would be the same or different in the various dialects of Sindarin.

So, depending on the dialect that I'm aiming for, I've got several options. If I wanted a word for the Doriathren or Southern dialects, I'd be better off hunting down another root. For the Exilic dialect and those who were influenced by them, **lend** is a viable option. Also, this marks **lembas** as something brought in by the Exiles and not something native to the Elves of Middle-earth.

10.3.4 Examples

Doriath:	**Ídhrodh**	i	'wend	*'ladhweg?
Exile:	**Anírol**	i	'wend	*lalweg?
	desire-you	the	maiden	cheerful?

Do you desire the cheerful maiden?

I used **aníra-** instead of **ídhra-**, the Exilic pronoun for "you," and for the word "cheerful" I used the word derived from Quenya, **lalweg**.

---

[333] I won't try to give a lengthy linguistic explanation for this, but it means that the L and D switched places, something rather common in romance languages when dealing with Ls and Rs, which Tolkien was no doubt familiar with when he devised this solution.

> South: **Glirin 'lîr a glind; a ni**   **'Linnel!**
> Exile: **Lirin lîr ar lind; ar ni *law 'Linnel...**
>   sing-I songs and chants and I (not) Lindarin elf
>
> *I sing songs and chants, and I am (not) a Lindarin Elf.*

Some more vanishing G's here, in "I sing," "song" and "chant." I also used different words for "and."

> West: **In eledhis echedir gram i lembas estannen.**
> Exile: **In ellith echedir gram i lembas estannen.**
>   the elf-women make cake that lembas called
>
> *The (Noldorin) women make a cake that is called lembas.*

This one has most of its differences from culture. **Eledhes** is one feminine version of **eledh**, which I mentioned in the borrowings from Quenya section. This term would only be used by someone trying to mark the elven woman being referred to as a Noldorin settler, as the feminine version used by the Exiles is the same as the version used by the Sindar: **elleth**.

10.4 Post-Beleriand

After Beleriand fell the Sindarin dialects became all mixed together, and we know very little about the differences between them beyond Tolkien's vague descriptions.

10.4.1 History

When Beleriand fell, the elves fled East. Some, mostly Exiles, stayed West of the Misty Mountains, in Mithlond, Lindon, and Eregion. There we expect to see the most Noldorin influence on the Sindarin language, and you can translate in Exilic Sindarin for that group. Some elves (mostly Sindar) went East of the Misty Mountains, to Lórinand and Greenwood (later called Mirkwood). These elves spoke a mixture of Southern and Western Beleriand dialects, probably rejecting Noldorin influences because of their mistrust of the Kinslayers.

Galadriel was an important character here, as she had followers. She was a charismatic leader, and she brought with her the Doriathren dialect of Sindarin, which was the dialect with the most prestige. Because of her long years spent in the company of Thingol and Melian, she was trusted by the Sindar, who would otherwise be wary of her because she was a Noldorin Exile. She stayed in Eregion for a while, then moved to Lórinand. After the current ruler of Lórinand left, Galadriel became the new ruler, though she refused that title. She renamed the land **Lothlórien**, in memory of the gardens of Lórien in Valinor. It is because of her that when I translate Sindarin spoken in Lothlórien, I make it very much like the Sindarin of Doriath.

The Woodelves whose forests became the new homes of the fleeing Sindar very quickly adopt the Sindarin language as their own. Tolkien writes that they probably speak with an accent and would sometimes Sindarinize their Woodelven speech, but Tolkien never goes into detail about what the Woodelven accent sounds like or what words and grammatical elements are brought into Sindarin. So, for the Woodelven of Lothlórien, I give it a Doriathren flavor. For the Woodelven of

Greenwood/Mirkwood, I give it a Southern Beleriand flavor, with one addition.[334]

10.4.2 One Lost Diphthong

Legolas' name is a great example of what Sindarin in Mirkwood sounds like.[335] The diphthong AE merged with the vowel E in the Woodelven dialect. We can't be certain when it occurred, but we can guess that it was around the time they crossed back over the mountains to settle in Greenwood – perhaps an influence of the Nandorin language, which as far as we know, doesn't have the AE diphthong.

Because of this change, we need to learn a phonological trait of Sindarin that may further change the words. If a monosyllable word is stressed, the vowel is lengthened. So, Woodelven **leg** would be **lêg** when used in a sentence. This doesn't apply when the end of the monosyllable is long – with double consonants at the end of the word – it isn't lengthened.

10.4.3 Examples

Western:	**Ae**	**mellyn!**	**Ledhidh**	**na Velegaer?**
Lothlórien:	**Ae**	**mellyn!**	**Trevedidh**	**na Velegaer?**
Greenwood:	**Ai**	**mellyn!**	**Trevedidh**	**na Veleger?**
	Hail	friends!	Travel-you	to Belegaer?

Hail friends! Are you traveling to the Great Sea?

For the western speaker, I used **ledh-**, a loanword from Quenya for "to travel."

For the Lothlórien speaker, I did a pretty generic western-Beleriand dialect. I used **trevad-** instead of **ledh-**.

---

[334] *Unfinished Tales*, "The History of Galadriel and Celeborn"

[335] To quote Tolkien on the topic of Legolas' name: "Legolas means 'green-leaves', a woodland name – dialectal form of pure Sindarin laegolas: *lassē (High elven lasse, S. las(s) 'leaf'; *gwa-lassa/*gwa-lassiē 'collection of leaves, foliage' (H.E. olassiē, S. golas, -olas); *laikā 'green' - basis LAY as in laire 'summer' (H.E. laica. S. laeg (seldom used, usually replaced by calen), woodland leg)." *The Letters of J.R.R. Tolkien*; Letter #211

For the Greenwood speaker, I used Ai in place of Ae, as we have an example of Legolas using it. Other than that, it's the same as the Loth-lórien-speaker, except for the AE>E in **Belegaer**.

Elrond: **Aníron Laer! Los ar cheleg 'we mbauglanner anan.**
Galadriel: **Ídhon Laer! Loss a heleg   'we mbauglanner anand.**
Thranduil: **Ídhon Lêr!   Los a cheleg 'we mbauglanther anan.**
       I long for summer! Snow and ice have oppressed us for a long
       time.

For Elrond, I gave his speech a very Exilic flavor. I used **aníra-** and **ar**. Also, I marked it as later Sindarin, with shortened final consonants for **loss** and **anand**.

For Galadriel, I gave her speech an archaic-Doriath flavor. I kept the long final consonants long and used H-mutation with **ah**.

For Thranduil, I made AE>E, then lengthened it because it's a single syllable word that's stressed. He's speaking later Sindarin, with the long consonants shortened. You'll notice that I gave him a southern-Beleriand accent as well, with -NTH- instead of -NN-. I had him drop H-mutation and use vocalic mutation in its place.

10.5 The Men of the West

Humans have their own languages, and most don't speak any Sindarin. The Númenóreans, however, have a unique history as a bilingual culture. The high classes use Sindarin as a symbol of their status, and use Quenya as a symbol of royalty. For the most part, things that need to be officially written down are written in Sindarin or Quenya, and court is held in Sindarin, which made the Westron-speaking hobbits quite a curiosity in Gondor! We don't actually have very much in the way of data or examples of Númenórean-Sindarin, so we'll be focusing on Sindarin as used in Gondor in the 3rd age.

10.5.1 History

When a group of humans helped the Elves get rid of Morgoth, the Valar rewarded them with an island of their own. These men became the Númenóreans. They were accomplished mariners, and they traded with the Elves on the coasts of Middle-earth. Then they tried to conquer Valinor, and they lost their island (along with all of the people on it) and the survivors fled to Middle-earth. For full details, read *The Akallabêth*.

They established kingdoms in Middle-earth, bringing their technology and wisdom with them, as well as their own dialect of Sindarin. This dialect was mainly based on Exilic Sindarin, but as their trading went far, words from other dialects of Sindarin could sneak in.

10.5.2 Phonological Changes

Besides Elven languages, the Gondorians spoke Adûnâyê, which has a definite effect on their use of Sindarin. Much of this you will recognize from earlier lessons.

You'll remember that certain sounds are difficult for them to use: CH and Y (pronounced as H before vowels and C elsewhere, and I respectively). This leads to changes to vocabulary like:

Rochan   → Rohan
Rochir   → Rohir
Elrochir → Elrohir

Tylys   → **Tilis**

10.5.3 Plurals

Human speakers made a few changes to plurals in Sindarin.[336]

- All O's are changed to E's.
- AI and EI are ignored.
- All A's are treated like normal A's.
- U is changed to I, instead of Y.

10.5.4 Prestanneth

And when using Prestanneth, use it as though you are the character who is doing the speaking. Think – would the character be familiar enough with Sindarin to know "star" **gail** is mutated differently than "stone" **gond**? Some words would be common enough that people would be able to remember their unique Prestanneth (like man and woman, which are both ND words in Sindarin.)

The past tense of "to kill" **dag-** would end up as **adhanc**, rather than **ananc**.

The lenition of "bread" **bast** would end up as **vast**, rather than **mast**.

The lenition of "wolf" **gaur** would end up as **'aur**, rather than **ñaur**.

Another thing to remember is that many of the forms of Prestanneth aren't used by humans, and instead are replaced by Lenition. Here's a list, as a basic reminder:

- L/R-Mutation → Lenition
- D-Mutation   → Lenition, no deletion of -D's.
- H-Mutation   → Lenition, H lost entirely.
- DH-Mutation   → Lenition, no deletion of -DH's

Lenition and Nasal Mutation would be untouched, and Mixed Mutation would be remembered to varying degrees. It is plausible that **en** could be reduced to **e** before consonants and Lenition used with it, and **an** be

---

[336] Review this in greater depth in 4.1.2.4.

used with Nasal Mutation, if the speaker is particularly unfamiliar with mutation rules in Sindarin.

10.5.5 A Few Last Words

Flipping back through the lessons, there are a couple words that ended up different in the Gondorian's dialect that you may recall. The first is the shortened **anin → 'nin**, and the last is "and" **ar/a**.

For Gondorians, there are 3 possible uses of "and."

1. Use **ar** alone, with Lenition.
2. Use **a** alone, with Lenition.
3. Use **ar** before vowels, and **a** before consonants, with Lenition.

10.5.6 Examples:

Exilic:	I	chîr	nîn	reviasser	anin	lond.
Gondorian:	I	hîr	nîn	reviasser	'nin	lond.
	the	ships	my	sailed		to-the harbor.

My ships sailed to the harbor.

For the Nasal mutation, since the C→CH, and they have difficulty with CH, I made it an H. Lastly, I changed **anin** to **'nin**.

Doriath:	I	ningloer	ledir	erin	aelin	ned	Laer.
Gondorian:	I	ningler	lodar	erin	aelin	ned	Nórui.
	the	water-lilies	float	on-the	lake	in	June.

The water-lilies float on the lake in June.

The singular of "water-lily" is **ninglor**, so I pluralized it the way a Gondorian would – ignoring the O which comes from **nin+glaur**. The verb **lod-** is an I-verb, but because a Gondorian would be unfamiliar with its proper conjugation, it is turned into an A-verb. Gondorians have a different calendar than Elves do. A Gondorian's "June" is "Summer" to an Elf. And lastly, Lenition is used in the place of Stop-Mutation on **ned+Nórui**.

Woodelf:	Ídhrassen	a-chened	Eryn-Lasgalen	'alol.
Gondorian:	Anírassen	ad-genad	Nimloth	'alol.
	wanted-I	again-seeing	Nimloth	growing

I wanted to see again a growing Nimloth/Mirkwood.

I used different words for "want" to highlight the Sindarin versus Exilic dialects. I used vocalic mutation on **ad-** + **cen-** and the A-verb suffix to make the gerund of **cen-** as a probable mistake that a Gondorian could make. Then I used **Nimloth**[337] in opposition to **Eryn-Lasgalen**.[338]

---

[337] The name of the White Tree that White Tree of Minas Tirith is said to have descended from.

[338] The name that the Elves use for Mirkwood – it means "forest of green leaf."

A Special Last Message for You:

Ae meldir/meldis! Avo veno *aden cheniol i naw vedui hen.

Avo *nevio bith. *Nevio noe.

Heniol? Se i *ñollanneth roveleg i *belin aned anlen. *Pi hedh *renil, *neviol vae.

*Novaer!

Answer key

2.1.5 Review

1. Hollow
2. Hobbit
3. Slimy
4. Comfort
5. Cat
6. Late
7. Challenge
8. Wreathe
9. Wreath
10. Of
11. Shiny
12. Read, Reed
13. Treasure
14. Linguistics
15. When

Part 2

1. /ɹˈop/
2. /kˈek/
3. /ˈsɪm.pəɫ/
4. /ˈfi.lɪŋ/
5. /ɹˈiɫ/
6. /ˌən.ˈfɪ.nɪʃt/
7. /ˈmun.ˌɹe.kəɹ/
8. /ˈdʒu.wəɫz/
9. /ˌdi.ˈfi.tɪd/
10. /ˈʃɪŋ.gəɫ/
11. /ˈli.ʒəɹ/ or /ˈlɛ.ʒəɹ/
12. /ɹˈaŋ/
13. /fˈɪfθ/ or /fˈɪθ/
14. /dʒəˈpæn/
15. /ˈɹɪ.dəɫ/
16. /ˈʍɛ.ðəɹ/

2.2.6 Review

1. /ɑlf/
2. /byːr/
3. /biːr/
4. /kɑw/
5. /xɑɛ/
6. /xɛ/
7. /hɑɛ/
8. /diːɟ/
9. /dujn/
10. /ɛrx/
11. /ɛrk/
12. /fiːr/
13. /gɑɛ/
14. /gɛ/
15. /gejɟ/
16. /gwiŋ/
17. /hɛɟx/
18. /hɛɟk/
19. /hɔɛð/
20. /ʍiːn/
21. /jɔːn/
22. /limp/
23. /ɫaw/
24. /mɑur/
25. /ŋɔll/
26. /nuːr/
27. /pɑjx/
28. /pɑjk/
29. /rɑɛv/
30. /rɛv/
31. /r̥ɔss/
32. /siˑ/
33. /suːl/
34. /tɑɛn/
35. /tɛn/
36. /tɑlv/
37. /θɛnt/
38. /wɑjθ/

2.3.1.1 Exercise

1. /gɔˑðɛɟlim/
2. /pɛrhɛɟ/
3. /ɛɟhɑɛɟ/
4. /tejliassɛv/
5. /rɔxwɑjθ/
6. /nɛdiɑθɔn/
7. /ejliɑnt/
8. /mɛɟdir/
9. /lɑθrɑdɑssɛb/
10. /ɑfɑrk/
11. /fɑŋgɔrn/
12. /ɑŋgwɛð/
13. /glɑmdriŋ/

2.3.2.1 Exercise

1. /gɔˑ.ðɛɟ.lim/
2. /pɛr.hɛɟ/
3. /ɛɟ.haɛɟ/
4. /tej.li.as.sɛv/
5. /rɔx.wajθ/
6. /nɛ.di.a.θɔn/
7. /ej.li.ant/
8. /mɛɟ.dir/
9. /laθ.ra.das.sɛb/
10. /a.fark/
11. /faŋ.gɔrn/
12. /aŋ.gwɛð/
13. /glam.driŋ/

2.3.3.1 Exercise

1. /gɔˑ.ˈðɛɟ.lim/
2. /ˈpɛr.hɛɟ/
3. /ˈɛɟ.haɛɟ/
4. /tej.li.ˈas.sɛv/
5. /ˈrɔx.wajθ/
6. /nɛ.ˈdi.a.θɔn/
7. /ˈej.li.ant/
8. /ˈmɛɟ.dir/
9. /laθ.ra.ˈdas.sɛb/
10. /ˈa.fark/
11. /ˈfaŋ.gɔrn/
12. /ˈaŋ.gwɛð/
13. /ˈglam.driŋ/

2.3.4.1 Exercise

1. /iŋ ˈgwɔɛn/
2. /aŋ ˈguːl/
3. /ˌni ŋɔ.ˈhɛ.na.θɔl/
4. /in ˈdajm/
5. /im ˈbɛ.xyr/

2.3.4.2 Exercise

1. /iˑ ˈaw/
2. /a ˈhi.aw/
3. /ˈiˑ.vɔr/
4. /a ˈhi.vɔr/

2.3.5 Review

1. /a.ˈdɛr.θad/
2. /a.ˈduj.al/

3. /ˈaɛ.a.rɔn/
4. /ˈɛ.a.rɔn/
5. /a ha.ˈda.na.dar/
6. /a hi.ˈaθ.rim/
7. /an.ˈnuˑ.najd/
8. /am ˈbaːr/
9. /an ˈdag.nir/
10. /aŋ ˈga.rav/
11. /ˈbaug.lir/
12. /kɛ.ˈnɛd.riɟ/
13. /ˈdriŋ.gɔ/
14. /ɛ.ˈðɛɟ.lɛn/
15. /ˈfim.brɛ.θiɟ/
16. /ga.lað.ˈrɛm.mɛn/
17. /ˈga.lu/
18. /ˈgɛ.lir/
19. /gi.ˈriθ.rɔn/
20. /ˈgu.ru.θɔs/
21. /ˈʍi.ni.ɔl/
22. /ˈja.lað/
23. /iˑ ˈɛɟɟ/
24. /i ˈŋan.nɛɟ/
25. /i ˈfɛ.lajθ/
26. /ˈiˑ.θ.rɔn/
27. /i ˈŋɛn.drajm/
28. /ˈiˑ.ni.as/
29. /ˈɬɛ.wig/
30. /ˈmɛɟ.lyrn/
31. /ˈmɛɟ.lirn/
32. /ˈŋiɟ.hɛr/
33. /ˌni ˈŋɛ.riɟ/
34. /ˌni ˈfɛ.dir/
35. /ˌniŋ gaw.ˈas.sɛr/
36. /ˈpɛ.li.ɔ/
37. /ɼuˑ.nɛn/
38. /ˈrɔx.bɛn/
39. /ˈrɔk.bɛn/
40. /ˈtal.raf/
41. /ˈθɛnd.rim/
42. /ˈθɔ.rɔ.naθ/
43. /tej.ˈθan.nɛn

3.1.1.1 Exercise

1. I chû vaer
2. Rych gelig
3. Nâr nenui

4.   I chû nenui gîn
5.   Aew vaer gelig.
     Aew gelig vaer.

3.1.2.1 Exercise

1.   Brastar am.
2.   Delio ennas!
3.   Grogab hîr.
4.   Delio hí!
5.   Sir, lathrassen.

3.1.2.2 Exercise

1.   Ath-alólef.
2.   Tre-deiliasser.
3.   Tre-nestathon.
4.   Ad-iestassedh.
5.   Ui-alólef.

3.1.2.3 Exercise

1.   I naneth eno fael
2.   I adar edregol vilui
3.   Muindor anand 'ladhweg
4.   Muinthel dhae vilui
5.   Muindor eno raen

3.1.4.1 Exercise

1.   Roch bo râd
2.   Padras bo râd
3.   Agarphassen hui chên
4.   Thîr hui chên
5.   Teiliar vin gaearon

3.2.1.1 Exercise

1.   I barf golas
2.   I barf 'wain tegilbor
3.   I 'olas 'wain tawar
4.   Tegilbor tawar
5.   I dawar pairf

3.2.2.1.1 Exercise

1.   Gwend na choll
2.   Coll na lyth
3.   Sant na lyth
4.   Sant nañ gwend
5.   Gwend na lyth

3.2.2.2.1 Exercise

1.   I mâr iñ-gwilwilith
2.   I 'wilwileth e-dawar
3.   I dawar in-droeg
4.   I mâr en-draug
5.   I dawar iñ-gwilwilith

3.2.3.1 Exercise

1.   The frog is green.
2.   The little child of a frog.
3.   The frog is a child.
4.   A green fish is a child of a frog.
5.   The little green fish.

3.2.3.2.1 Exercise

1.   Lhûg *law lim.
2.   I adan *ce fern.
3.   I thlûg *law fern.
4.   I lim *ce galen.
5.   I thlûg *law galen.

3.3.1.1.1 Exercise

1.   Lothuial athrant i hîr.
2.   I gabor labant i 'olf.
3.   Lothuial ant gabor.
4.   I hîr ant 'olf.
5.   I gabor ant i 'olf.

3.3.1.2.1 Exercise

1.   Nin awarthanner.
2.   Ven egleriog.
3.   Din orthof.
4.   Nin egleriog.
5.   Ven awarthanner.

3.3.1.3.1 Exercise

1.   Glaewen aun graim an Lothuial.
     Glaewen aun graim Lothuial.
2.   Ónen barf añ Glaewen.
     Ónen barf Glaewen.
3.   Tangadar i inc ammen.
4.   Den aun ammen.
5.   Den ónen an Lothuial.

3.3.4.1.1 Exercise

1. *Ce buia erin gae.
2. I vírdan *law achant i goron annin.
3. I ñollor *ce luitha i vîr.
4. I ñollor *law den achant.
5. I vírdan *law buia.

3.3.2.0.1 Exercise

1. In eryd bronar anand.
   Bronar in eryd anand.
2. Cuion eno.
3. I chui thuiar eno.
   Thuiar i chui eno.
4. Calad *ce thinna.
   *Ce thinna calad.
5. Nern *law 'wannar.
   *Law 'wannar nern.

3.3.2.1.1 Exercise

1. Linnassef angin.
   Gi linnassef.
2. Ivreth rithas angin.
   Ivreth gidh rithas.

3.3.3.1.1 Exercise

1. Amathon berthas tired 'Laewen.
2. Edain anírar andin bronad.
   Edain anírar bronad andin.
   Edain den anírar bronad.
3. Anírar an Amathon ve *chethed.
   Anírar ve *chethed an Amathon.
   An Amathon anírar ve *chethed.
4. Ava *istaned andin.
   Ava din *istaned.
5. Glaewen *law ava bronad.

3.3.3.2.1 Exercise

1. Nimphiel ebent an Nana: I dâl nîn harn.
2. Ebennin an Nana: I dâl nîn harn.
3. Ebennin anden: I dâl nîn harn.
   Den ebennin: I dâl nîn harn.

3.4.2.3.1 Exercise

1. Dandolo ammen!
2. No ilaurui fair!
3. Nathlo len pin!
4. Teitho barf ammen.
5. Goro nin o sen.

3.4.3.1 Exercise

1. Uil erin eryd.
2. Ollas annin o lhen.
   Ollas nin o lhen.
3. *Glosta erin eryd.
4. Herias anin hoth.
5. *Law moe annin darthad.
   *Law moe nin darthad.

3.4.4.3.2.1 Exercise

1. I ranc dîn osgarnen.
2. Le mae guiassen.
3. Im Olodhin estannen.
4. Le tollannen si.
5. I noss lîn beriannen.

3.5.1.2.1 Exercise

1. neledh a lephaen
2. canad a dolophaen
3. nederph
4. eneg a gambaen
5. tâd ar enebaen

3.5.2.2.1 Exercise

1. odog a odobaenui
2. enebui
3. neledh a daphaenui
4. leben a enebaenui
5. tolodh a gambaenui

3.5.3.1.1 Exercise

1. Tirn nelebui
2. Ruin neder a daphaenui
3. Tolodh a dolophaen moe
4. Inc baenui
5. Odog a lephaen gynd

4.1.3.1.1 Exercise

1. ael
2. oer
3. coel
4. coe
5. cîr
6. cyth
7. firyn
8. firith
9. lim
10. lhŷ
11. nuir
12. pin
13. remmeis
14. seirn
15. teweir
16. tylys
17. úthaes
18. elw
19. fergeim
20. ipheint
21. nerw
22. sauthennin
23. teiri

4.1.3.2.1 Exercise

1. ael
2. oer
3. coel
4. coe
5. cîr
6. cyth
7. firyn
8. firith
9. lim
10. lhŷ
11. nuir
12. pin
13. remmais

14. sairn
15. tewair
16. tylys
17. úthaes
18. ely
19. fergaim
20. iphant
21. nery
22. sauthennin
23. teiri

4.1.3.3.1 Exercise

1. ael
2. oer
3. coel
4. coe
5. cîr
6. ceth
7. firien
8. firith
9. lim
10. lhê
11. nuir
12. pin
13. remmais
14. sairn
15. tewair
16. tilis
17. úthaes
18. eli
19. fergaim
20. iphaint
21. neri
22. sauthennin
23. terai

4.2.3.1 Exercise

1. Gworath - all dirty
   ones/things
2. Nawagath - all Dwarves
3. Bassath - all bread
4. Narwath - all red
   ones/things
5. Lothath - all flowers

4.2.4.1.1 Exercise

1. Gworrim - dirty folk
2. Nawagrim - Dwarf folk
3. Bathrim - a group of bakers
4. Narurim - red folk
5. Lothrim - flower people

4.2.4.2.1 Exercise

1. Gwaurhoth - dirty horde
2. Nawaghoth - dwarf horde
3. Bassoth - bread-rioters/horde of bakers
4. Agarwaenhoth - blood-stained horde
5. Ívoth - cliff-folk horde

4.2.4.3.1 Exercise

1. Glaewenwaith
2. Cirionwaith
3. Ívwaith
4. Maeaswaith
5. Aelwaith

5.1.2.4.1 Exercise

1. Valan
2. maur
3. vrethil
4. grist
5. gugu
6. nôr
7. dhû
8. 'alenas
9. ñail
10. 'lad
11. 'roth
12. 'wass
13. charu
14. iaeth
15. thlewig
16. vinuial
17. baur
18. brestad
19. thrach
20. holch
21. drenarn
22. dum
23. vell
24. dholl
25. dhrammen
26. 'ael
27. 'wathui
28. chae
29. chwiniol
30. daer
31. dhadben
32. vae
33. balan
34. vi
35. ven

5.1.3.3.1 Exercise

1. I melain
2. I mboer
3. I mrethil
4. I christ
5. I chygy
6. I ndŷr
7. I nui
8. I ñelenais
9. I ñgîl
10. Iñ glaid
11. Iñ gryth
12. Iñ gwaiss
13. I chery
14. In iaeth
15. I laich
16. Ith law
17. I minuiail
18. I nyss
19. I phoer
20. I phrestais
21. Ith raich
22. I sylch
23. I thaim
24. I threnairn
25. I thym

5.1.4.1 Exercise

1. e-Balan
2. e-mbaur

3. e-brethil
4. e-grist
5. e-gugu
6. e-ndôr
7. e-dû
8. e-galenas
9. e-ñgail
10. eñ-glad
11. eñ-groth
12. eñ-gwass
13. e-charu
14. en-iaeth
15. e-lach
16. e-'lewig
17. e-minuial
18. e-baur
19. e-brestad
20. e-'rach
21. e-holch
22. e-tham
23. e-drenarn
24. e-dum

5.1.5.1 Exercise

1. Am Balan
2. Am baur
3. Am brethil
4. Añ grist
5. Añ gugu
6. Añ galenas
7. Añ gail
8. Añ glad
9. Añ groth
10. Añ gwass
11. An haru
12. An iaeth
13. An 'lewig
14. Am minuial
15. Am baur
16. Am brestad
17. An 'rach
18. An holch
19. An drenarn
20. An dum

5.2.1.5.1 Exercise

1. il-valan
2. il-vrethil
3. il-christ
4. il-chugu
5. il-dhu
6. il-'alenas
7. il-'lad
8. il-'roth
9. il-'wass
10. il-charu
11. il-iaeth
12. il-'lewig
13. il-vinuial
14. il-phor
15. il-phrestad
16. il-'rach
17. il-threnarn
18. il-thum

5.2.2.3.1 Exercise

1. o Balan
2. o mbaur
3. o brethil
4. o christ
5. o chugu
6. o ndôr
7. o dû
8. o galenas
9. o ñgail
10. o glad
11. o groth
12. o gwass
13. o charu
14. od iaeth
15. o thlewig
16. o minuial
17. o noss
18. o phaur
19. o phrestad
20. o thrach
21. os solch
22. oth tham
23. o threnarn
24. o thum

5.2.3.1 Exercise

1. a christ
2. a chugu
3. ah iaeth
4. a lhach
5. a phaur
6. a phrestad
7. a rhoch
8. a solch
9. a threnarn
10. a thum

5.2.4.1 Exercise

1. a christ
2. a chugu
3. adh iaeth
4. ad lach
5. ath lewig
6. a phaur
7. a phrestad
8. ath rach
9. a threnarn
10. a thum

6.1.1.1.1 Exercise

1. al-geleb
2. al-lagor
3. al-nen
4. al-vinai
5. al-rend

6.1.1.2.1 Exercise

1. "The maiden isn't young." I 'wend *law 'wain.
2. "The orcs aren't coming." In yrch *law delir.
3. "She isn't a traitor." Te *law 'warth.
4. "I didn't choose the red cloak." *Law *igílen i goll garan.
5. "The book wasn't on the floor." I barf *law erin banas.

6.1.1.3.1 Exercise

1. *Laenc
2. *Laen
3. *Laef
4. *Law
5. *Laer

6.1.2.1 Exercise

1. ú-istadui "unknowable"
2. Ú-bladon i lass han. "I can't touch that leaf."
3. ú-bladadui "untouchable"
4. Na dhû, ú-genin. "At night, I can't see."
5. ú-genui "invisible"

6.1.3.1.1 Exercise

1. Avo noro o nin! "Don't run from me!"
2. Av-aphado nin! / Avo aphado nin! "Don't follow me!"
3. Avo blado i genedril *ra-gui! "Don't touch the fragile mirror!"
4. Avo 'wanno! "Don't die!"
5. Av-erio! / Avo erio! "Don't stand! (Don't arise!)"

6.1.3.2.1 Exercise

1. Avon. / Avon *oled dhínen.
2. Avon. / Avon len aphadad.
3. Avof. / Avof peded i cherdir vîn.
4. Ava. / Ava le ñovaned.
5. Avar. / Avar lastad i in-nas lîn

6.1.4.1.1 Exercise

1. Pen-gae
2. Pen-'ond
3. Pen-thar
4. Penin.

5. Penif.

7.1.1.1 Exercise

1. That = far demonstrative singular
2. She = feminine third person singular
3. We = first person plural
4. You = second person singular
5. These = close demonstrative plural

7.1.2.1 Exercise

1. Si 'elaidh.
2. Me noeg.
3. Le nu delu.
4. Ni him.
5. Te elleth. / T'elleth

7.1.3.1 Exercise

1. Ni meria nef len.

2. He chebin vi 'wen.
3. Dhe ñostof hui hain.
4. Hin aderthathanc a then.
5. Din eglerianc or san.

7.1.4.1 Exercise

1. Tollo i vuindor gîn an-hain.
2. Anna gyll andin.
3. Padrog anhen.
4. Reinor tôl demened angwen.
5. Eithannen i vuinthel lîn anlen.

7.1.5.1 Exercise

1. I gyll hin
2. I masgorn 'wîn
3. I vôr gîn
4. I gabor dîn
5. I ndîr hain

7.1.6 Where the Pronouns Come From

	Nominative	Oblique	Dative	Poss./Adj.
1.sing.	**ni**	nin	annin	nîn
1.ex.pl.	**me**	men	ammen	mîn
1.inc.pl.	**gwe**	**gwen**	**angwen**	**gwîn**
2.fam.sing.	ci	**cin**	**angin**	**cîn**
2.rev.sing.	**le**	le(n)	**anlen**	lîn
2.pl.	**de**	de(n)	**anden**	**dîn**
3.sing.	**te**	ten	**anden**	tîn
3.pl.	ti	**tin**	andin	**tîn**
clo.dem.sing	**se**	**sen**	**anhen**	sen
clo.dem.pl.	**si**	**sin**	**anhin**	sin
far.dem.sing.	**sa**	san	**anhan**	**san**
far.dem.pl.	**sai**	sain	**anhain**	**sain**
Interrogative	**ma**	man	**amman**	**man**

7.2.1.1 Exercise

ebenni- "said"	Singular	Plural
1st exclusive	ebennin	ebennif
1st inclusive	ebenninc	ebennib
2nd familiar	ebennig	████████
2nd reverential	ebennil	ebennidh
3rd	ebent	ebennir

padra- "walk"	Singular	Plural
1st exclusive	padron	padrof
1st inclusive	padranc	padrab
2nd familiar	padrog	████████
2nd reverential	padrol	padrodh
3rd	padra	padrar

7.2.2.1 Exercise

ant "gift"	Singular	Plural
1st exclusive	annen	annef
1st inclusive	annenc	anneb
2nd familiar	anneg	████████
2nd reverential	annel	annedh
3rd	anned	annent

lanc "throat"	Singular	Plural
1st exclusive	langen	langef
1st inclusive	langenc	langeb
2nd familiar	langeg	████████
2nd reverential	langel	langedh
3rd	langed	langent

7.2.3.4.1 Exercise

1. Im Barawen.
2. Im medhiannef i *vaeas.
3. Gweriannel im.
4. Im i iôn nîn gannada vae.
   Im i ionen gannada vae.
5. Teithanneg i phith hin anim.

7.3.1.1 Review

1. Sinnin i udul dess anin fen.
2. Sinnin i ilaurui Anor eria a dhanna.
3. Sinnin i yrch enengir i adarel.

  4. Sinnin i ni faug.
  5. Sinnin i dír-vudassel / Sinnin i dhír-vudassel.

7.3.2.0.1 Exercise

  1. Iôn i aun 'lî annin udul. / Iôn i udul aun 'lî annin.
  2. Anno vant anin hell han i ruthra.
  3. Critho i luith ai 'alar dhae orchal. / Critho i luith i ñalar dhae orchal.
  4. I chui i thirion gawar./I chui ai dirion gawar. / Tirion i chui in gawar. / Tirion i chui ai ñawar
  5. Gosto i naen i chuiar. / Gosto i naen ai guiar.

7.3.2.2.1 Exercise

  1. Throw the stone when the gate opens.
  2. I know for whom the bells toll.
  3. We will sing while you eat.
  4. I saw you where my friends live.
  5. The man runs from where orcs come.

7.3.3.1 Exercise

  1. Ma tôl?
  2. Man evening?
  3. Mivan den *ichírel?
  4. Pen van dhen aphadant?
  5. Naman hen echant?

7.3.4.4 Exercise

  1. Q. Gostol? "Are you afraid?"
      A. *Laen. "Not I."
  2. Q. Sevil i 'aud i echennin? "Do you have the machine that made?"
      A. No. "I hope so."
  3. Q. Mudathol hîr? "Would you please work today?"
      A. Athon. "I will."
  4. Q. *Ce gi mibin? "Might I kiss you?"
      A. Baw!/Avo! "Don't!"
  5. Q. *Devil annin le muiad? "Do you permit me to serve you?"
      A. No. "Make it so."

8.1.1.1 Exercise

thuia- "breathe"	Singular	Plural
First person Exclusive	thuion	thuiof
First person Inclusive	thuianc	thuiab
Familiar second person	thuiog	███████
Reverential second person	thuiol	thuiodh
Third person	thuia	thuiar

haf- "sit"		
First person Exclusive	hevin	hevif
First person Inclusive	hevinc	hevib
Familiar second person	hevig	
Reverential second person	hevil	hevidh
Third person	hâf	hevir
***(n)dadhren- "forget"**		
First person Exclusive	dedhrenin	dedhrenin
First person Inclusive	dedhreninc	dedhrenib
Familiar second person	dedhrenig	
Reverential second person	dedhrenil	dedhrenidh
Third person	dadhren	dedhrenir

8.1.3.1 Exercise

1. thuio
2. havo
3. *dadhreno
4. iuitho
5. goro

8.1.4.1 Exercise

1. thuiad
2. haved
3. *dadhrened
4. iuithad
5. gored

8.1.5.1.1 Exercise

1. tolen thuiad
2. tolen haved
3. tolen *dadhrened
4. tolen iuithad
5. tolen gored

8.1.5.2.1 Exercise

1. nidhin thuiad
2. nidhin haved
3. nidhin *dadhrened
4. nidhin iuithad
5. nidhin gored

8.1.5.3.1 Exercise

1. thuiatha

2. havatha
3. *dadhrenatha
4. iuithatha
5. goratha

8.1.5.4.1 Exercise

1. avon thuiad
2. avon haved
3. avon *dadhrened
4. avon iuithad
5. avon gored

8.2.1.0.1 Exercise

1. Narchant, Narchannen
2. Hwinias(t), Hwiniassen
3. Grogas(t), Grogassen
4. Crithant, Crithannen
5. *Glostas(t)

8.2.2.2.1 Exercise

1. Avlamp, Evlemmin
2. Achant, Echennin
3. Ananc, Enengin
4. Ununt, Ynynnin
5. *Aranc, *Erengin

8.2.2.3.1 Exercise

1. Edhiw, Edhíwen
2. *Erin, *Erínen
3. Avodh, Avódhen
4. Udhul, Udhúlen

5. Îr, Íren

8.3.1.1 Exercise

1. Cab
2. Dew
3. Breniad
4. Echad
5. Farad

8.3.2.1 Exercise

1. Giriel
2. Teiliol
3. Pennol
4. Norel
5. Havel

8.3.3.1 Exercise

1. Mellen
2. Teiliassen
3. Gweriannen
4. Nornen
5. Hammen

8.3.4.1.1 Exercise

1. Bethiel
2. Dregiel
3. Ristiel
4. Telliel
5. Luithiel

8.3.4.2.1 Exercise

1. Buiel
2. Dóriel
3. Míniel
4. *Píliel
5. Núdiel
6. Ostúliel
7. Róniel
8. Fíriel
9. Díliel
10. Úriel
11. Dúliel

8.3.4.2.2 Exercise

1. I vess mâd vae mudiel ned i aur min barth.
2. Dógiel valrog ydyngin i chiril anin ost nîn.

9.1.1.1 Exercise

1. Melweg "lovey-dovey, amorous, romantic"
2. Pedweg "talkative, chatty"
3. Lalweg "cheerful"
4. Gweriadweg "untrustworthy, likely to cheat/betray"
5. *Hannadweg "thankful"

9.1.2.1 Exercise

1. Dregui "able to flee"
2. Egleriadui "praise-able"
3. *Renui "memorable"
4. Uanui "monsterous"
5. írui "desirable"

9.1.3.1 Exercise

1. Caeleb/caelphant "sick, bedridden with sickness"
2. Uireb/uirphant "eternal"
3. Neneb/nephant "watery"
4. Úreb/úrphant "hot, fiery"

5.   Finneb/Fimbant "hairy"

9.1.4.1 Exercise

1.   Mírren "made of jewels"
2.   Hadhodren "dwarven"
3.   Madharen "muddy"
4.   Periandren "hobbitish"
5.   Collen "golden, made of gold"

9.2.3.1.1 Exercise

1.   Tríwas "slenderness"
2.   Rhosgas "brownness"
3.   Merenas "festiveness"
4.   Ioras "ancientness"
5.   Bruias "noisiness"

9.2.3.2.1 Exercise

1.   Úras "inferno"
2.   Leinas "ball of thread"
3.   Lassas "leaf-pile"
4.   Halas "school/net of fish"
5.   Naglas "mouthful of teeth"

9.2.3.3.1 Exercise

1.   Badhas "judgment"
2.   Goras "advice"
3.   *Mibas "kiss"
4.   Northas "charge"
5.   Ovras "crowd, heap"

9.2.4.1 Exercise

1.   Tirith "guard, watch"
2.   Cetheth "examination, interrogation"
3.   Gohenanneth "forgiveness"
4.   Nídhasseth "determination"
5.   Osgareth "amputation"

9.2.5.1 Exercise

1.   Naror, narron, nerril "narrator"
2.   Goror, gorron, gerril "advisor"
3.   Leinor, leidhron, leidhril "spinner, tailor, seamstress"

9.2.5.2.1 Exercise

1.   Achardir, Achardis "avenger"
2.   Cendir, cendis "seer"
3.   Crithedir, crithedis "reaper"
4.   Dewedir, dewedis "failure"

5. Mudedir, mudedis "laborer"

9.2.6.1.1 Exercise

1. Talagannion "Son of Harper" Talagannien "Daughter of Harper" Talaganniel "Daughter of Harper"
2. Redhrion "Son of Planter" Redhrien "Daughter of Planter" Redhriel "Daughter of Planter"
3. Candission "Son of Commander" Candissien "Daughter of Commander" Candissiel "Daughter of Commander"

9.2.6.2.1 Exercise

1. Tanor "male smith" Taneth "female smith" Tanel "female smith" Tenil "female smith"
2. Arasson "buck" Arasseth "doe" Arassel "doe" Eressil "doe"
3. Tonnor "tall man" Tonneth "tall woman" Tonnel "tall woman" Tennil "tall woman"

9.3.4.1 Exercise

1. Ronis "Lion Woman"
2. Dínil "Friend/Lover of Women/Lesbian/Feminist"
3. Losser "Snow Lover"
4. Sarnhel "Stone Girl"
5. Lothwen "Flower Maiden"
6. Sídhil "Heir(ess) of Peace"
7. Rochben "Knight (gender-neutral)"

9.3.5.1 Exercise

1. Sannion "Vast Garden"
2. Lhonor "Marsh Land"
3. Galadhian/Galadhan "Expanse of Trees"
4. Calembar "Green Home"
5. Lithien "Expanses of Sand/Ash"

Neo-Sindarin Wordlist

This is a list of Neo-Sindarin words appearing in this book, not a complete dictionary. Here are the dictionaries I listed in chapter 5.

- *Parf Edhellen* - https://www.elfdict.com/
- *Eldamo* - http://eldamo.org/
- *Hiswelókë's Sindarin Dictionary* - https://www.jrrvf.com/hisweloke/sindar/online/
- *Parviphith Edhellen* - http://www.uib.no/people/hnohf/parviphith.doc

Abbreviations

&	and
*	reconstructed, made by fans
4adj.	for adjectives
4Av.	for A-verbs
4Iv.	for I-verbs
4n.	for nouns
4v.	for verbs
adj.	adjective
adv.	adverb
agent.	agentive
arc.	archaic
art.	article
AU	O from AU
car.	cardinal number
compl.	complementizer
con.	conjunction
dem.	demonstrative
D.	Doriathren dialect
dat.	dative
E.	Exilic dialect
ex.	exclusive
fam.	familiar
fem.	feminine
G.	Gondorian dialect
ger.	gerund
imp.	impersonal
inc.	inclusive
ind.	indefinite
int.	interjection
interr.	interrogative
intran.	intransitive
irr.	irregular
LT	LL from LT
masc.	masculine
MP	MM from MP
n.	noun
NC	NG from NC
NT	NN from NT
O	suffix makes verb -A to -O
obl.	oblique
ord.	ordinal number
pa.	past
par.	particle
part.	participle
per.	perfect
pl.	plural
poss.	possessive
pref.	prefix
prep.	preposition
pres.	present
pro.	pronoun
p.	past
pt.	past tense for pronoun affixes
pt3.	past tense 3rd person singular
ref.	reflexive
rel.	relative
rev.	reverential
sing.	singular
suf.	suffix
sun.	sundóma
TA	TA-verb
tran.	transitive

v.   verb

Suffixes

-as abstract n. suf. 4v. 4n. 4adj. -ness

-ath pl. suf. all

-atha future suf. 4v. willing to...

-b 1) nom. inc. pro. suf. 4v. we *2) pos. inc. pro. suf. 4n. our

-d 1) pos. pro. suf. 4n. his, her, its 2) ger. suf. 4Av.

-dh 1) [O] nom. rev. pl. pro. suf. 4v. you *2) pos. rev. pl. pro. suf. 4n. your

-eb adj. suf. 4n. -ful

-ed ger. suf. 4Iv.

-eg diminutive suf.

-el 1) pres. part. suf. 4Iv. 2) fem. agent. suf.

-en pa. part. suf. 4v.

-eth fem. agent suf.

-f 1) [O] nom. ex. pro. suf. 4v. we *2) pos. ex. pro. suf. 4n. our

-g 1) [O] nom. fam. sing. pro. suf. 4v. you 2) pos. fam. sing. pro. suf. 4n. your

-hoth pl. suf. group of mistrusted people

-iel 1) perfect part. suf. 4v. 2) fem. agent. suf. daughter of...

-ien fem. agent. suf. daughter of...

-ig diminutive suf.

-il fem. agent. suf.

-ion masc. agent. suf. son of...

-l 1) [O] nom. rev. sing. pro. suf. 4v. you 2) pos. rev. sing. pro. suf. 4n. your

-n 1) [O] nom. pro. suf. 4v. I 2) pos. pro. suf. 4n. my 3) pa. suf. 4Iv.

-nc 1) nom. dual inc. pro. suf. 4v. you and I 2) pos. dual inc. pro. suf. 4n. mine and your

-nt 1) pos. pro. suf. 4n. their 2) tran. pa. suf. 4Av.

-o imperative suf. 4v.

-og diminutive suf.

-ol pres. part. suf. 4Av.

-on masc. agent. suf.

-r 1) nom. pro. suf. 4v. they 2) agent. suf. -er, doer, one who...

-ren adj. suf. 4n. of, made of, from, made from

-rim pl. suf. group of people

-s intran. pa. suf. 4Av.

-st intran. pa. suf. 4Av.

-th n. suf. 4v. -ion

-ui adj. suf. 4v. 4n. -ful, -like, -able, -ible

-weg adj. suf. 4v. often, habitual action

A

a 1) int. Oh!, Hi! 2) con. and

ab- pref. prep. after

ab prep. after

ach 1) con. but 2) n. neck

achar- v. avenge, requite, react

achared n. vengeance

acharn n. vengeance

achas n. dread, fear

ad adv. again

ad- pref. adv. re-,

ada n. daddy, papa

adab n. building, house

adan n. human

adanadar n. father of man

adar n. father

adel prep. behind

*aden prep. until

adertha- tran. v. reunite

aderthad n. reunion

adh 1) con. and 2) prep. with, by, near, beside, alongside

adleg- v. loose, release, let loose

aduial n. evening twilight

ae int. Oh!, Hi!

aear E. n. sea

aearon E. n. ocean

aeglos n. icicle

ael n. lake, pool, mere

aelin n. pool, lake

aen 1) adj. holy 2) meaning unknown

aew n. small bird

agarwaen adj. bloody

aglar n. glory, brilliance, splendor

aglareb adj. glorious, full of glory, brilliant

ah 1) con. and 2) prep. with, by, near, beside, alongside

ai 1) int. Oh!, Hi! 2) pl. rel. pro. who, that, which

al- pref. no, not

alae v. look, behold

***alben** ind. pro. no one

alfirin 1) n. a species of flower 2) adj. immortal

***alhad** ind. pro. nowhere

***alnad** ind. pro. nothing

alph n. swan

am 1) adv. up, upward 2) prep. above, upon

am- pref. adv. up, upward

Amar n. settlement, inhabited lands

amartha- tran. v. define, decree, destine

amath n. shield

ambenn adv. uphill, upwards

***amman** interr. dat. pro. to/for whom/what

ammen dat. ex. pro. to/for us

amrûn n. east

an- pref. adv. forth, movement towards somewhere

an prep. to, for

anand adv. for a long time

anc n. jaw, row of teeth

***anden** 1) dat. rev. pl. pro. to/for you 2) dat. pro. to/for him/her/it

***andin** dat. pro. to/for them

andrand n. Age

ang n. iron

***angin** dat. fam. sing. pro. to/for you

anglenna- tran. v. approach

angren adj. made of iron

angwedh n. iron chain

***angwen** dat. inc. pro. to/for us

***anhain** dem. dat. pro. to/for those

***anhan** dem. dat. pro. to/for that

***anhen** dem. dat. pro. to/for this

***anhin** dem. dat. pro. to/for these

***ani** dat. rel. pro. to/for whom/which

anim dat. ind. ref. pro. to/for self

anin prep. to, for the

aníra- tran. intran. v. desire

***anlen** dat. rev. sing. pro. to/for you

anna- [TA] tran. v. [irr. ger. **aned**] give

annin dat. pro. to/for me

annon n. great gate, door

ann-thennath n. accentual verse

annui adj. western

annûn n. west

annúnaid n. Westron

Anor n. The Sun

ant n. gift

anu adj. male

anwar n. awe

aphada- tran. v. follow

apharch adj. very dry

ar con. and

ar- pref. adv. without, outside

arad n. day

aran n. king

aranel n. princess

aras sing. n. deer

aronoded adj. uncountable

astor n. loyalty

Astoron n. Loyal Man

ath- 1) pref. adv. easily 2) pref. prep. on both sides, across

atha- v. be willing to

athae adj. healing, benifitial, helpful

athan prep. beyond

atheg n. daddy

athra- 1) intran. v. cross (to and fro) 2) pref. prep. across

athrabeth n. conversation

aur n. day, sunlight, morning

auth n. war, battle

av- pref. adv. don't

ava- tran. intran. v. refuse

avo adv. don't

Avon n. Aman

awarth n. abandonment

awartha- tran. v. forsake, abandon

B

bâd n. pathway, beaten track

badh- v. judge

badhas n. judgment

badhor n. judge

badhron masc. n. judge

baen adj. blond

bain adj. beautiful

Balan n. Vala

Balannor n. Valinor

balrog n. demon of might

barad n. tower, fortress

barah adj. eager

***barf** n. armor

batha- tran. v. trample

bauglir n. oppressor

Baw! int. No don't do that!

be prep. according to

***bedhril** fem. n. judge

beleg adj. great, large, big, mighty

Belegaer n. Great Sea

Belegast n. Vast Void

beleglind n. long chanted epic poem or song

Belego n. Vast Void

Beleriand n. Expanse of Balar

bellas [LT] n. strength

belt adj. strong

ben prep. according to the

benn n. husband, man, male

beren adj. bold

beria- [sun. A] tran. v. protect

bertha- intran. v. dare

bess n. wife, woman

blab- v. beat, flap (wings), batter

bôr n. vassal

brasta- intran. v. tower up, loom

breitha- intran. v. break out suddenly, burst forth

brenia- [sun. O] intran. v. endure

breth n. queen

brethil n. birch

brith n. gravel

brona- intran. v. last, survive

bronadui adj. surviving

brui adj. loud, noisy

budhu [irr. pl. **bydhu**] n. large insect

buia- tran. v. serve, hold allegiance to

bŷr n. follower, vassal

[m]B

[m]bach n. article for exchange, ware, item, thing

[m]bachor [arc. **[m]bachr**] n. pedlar, merchant

[m]band n. duress, prison, custody, safe-keeping

[m]banga- [NC] tran. intran. v. trade

[m]Bannos n. place the spirits of the dead are collected by Badhron

[m]bâr n. home

 [m]bardh n. home

[m]bardor n. homeland

[m]bartha- tran. v. doom

[m]basgorn n. loaf of bread

[m]bass n. bread

***[m]basta-** tran. intran. v. bake bread

[m]baugla- tran. v. oppress

[m]bauglir n. tyrant

[m]baur n. need

[m]boe imp. v. must, need, be necessary

C

cab- v. leap, hop, jump

cabor [arc. cabr] n. frog

cae n. earth

cael n. sickness

caeleb adj. bedridden, sick

cair n. ship

calad n. light

calen adj. green, fresh, vigorous

callon masc. n. hero

*cambaen car. 40

can- v. cry out, call, shout

*canab car. 14

canad car. 4

canath n. tharni, a fourth of a castar

candis n. fem. commander

cannui ord. fourth

câr n. building

car- v. do, make, build

carab n. hat

caran adj. red

caras n. city

carpha- tran. intran. v. [irr. pt3. agramp irr. pt. egremmi- irr. tran. pt3. agarfant irr. intran. pt3. agarfas(t) irr. p. part. crammen] talk, speak, pronounce

caul n. great burden, affliction

caun 1) [irr. pl. cónin] n. prince, commander, ruler 2) n. outcry, clamour 3) adj. empty, void 4) n. valor

caw n. top

caw- v. [irr. p. part. caun] taste, select, choose

*ce par. may, might

celair adj. brilliant

celeb n. silver

celebren adj. made of silver

Celebrimbor n. Silver Hand

celeg adj. swift, agile, hasty

cen- v. see

cenedril n. mirror

cenui adj. visible

ceredir masc. n. crafter

*ceredis fem. n. crafter

cerin n. mound

certh n. rune

certhas n. runic alphabet

Cerveth n. July

*cesta- tran. v. seek, search for, look for

*ceth- v. examine, search, interrogate

Ceven n. Earth, the ground

ci nom. fam. sing. pro. you

*cí par. may, might, maybe, perhaps, if

cîl 1) n. renewal 2) n. cleft, pass between hills, gorge

*cil- v. choose

*cin obl. fam. sing. pro. you

*cîn poss. fam. sing. pro. your, yours

côl n. gold

coll 1) n. coak, mantle 2) adj. red, scarlet 3) adj. hollow

*corf n. ring

coron 1) n. globe, ball 2) n. mound

*Corvor *n. Ring Day

coth n. enemy, foe, enmity

cram n. waybread, cake made of compressed flour or meal with milk and honey

crann adj. red-faced

crist n. cleaver, sword

critha- tran. v. reap

cû n. bow

cugu n. dove

cuia- intran. v. live

cuina- intran. v. be alive

curu n. skill

D

dad adv. down, downwards

dadbenn adv. downhill, downwards

dae 1) adv. very, exceedingly 2) n. shadow

daen n. corpse

danna- [TA] intran. v. fall

dant n. fall

dar- v. halt, stop, wait, remain

dartha- intran. v. wait, stay, last, endure, remain

dath n. hole, pit, abyss

*** dav-** v. allow, yield, permit

de nom. rev. pl. pro. you

del n. fear, disgust, loathing, horror

deleb adj. horrible, abominable, loathsome

delia- [sun. U] intran. v. hide, conceal

delos n. abhorrence, detestation, loathing

dem adj. sad, gloomy

den obl. rev. pl. pro. you

dew- v. fail, miss mark, go wrong

di- pref. prep. beneath, under, sub

dîl n. stopper, stuffing, stopping

dilia- tran. v. stop up, plug

dim 1) n. stair 2) n. sadness

dîn *1) poss. rev. pl. pro. your, yours 2) n. silence

dínen adj. silent

dír- pref. adv. with difficulty from physical hardships or lack of trying

dolen adj. hidden

doll adj. dark

dolla- [sun. U] [TA] tran. v. conceal

donn 1) adj. dark skinned 2) adj. shady, shadowy 3) n. fist, hand

dorn 1) adj. tough, stiff, thrawn, obdurate 2) n. dwarf

drambor [AU] n. fist

draug n. wolf

drav- v. hew

drega- intran. v. flee

dringa- tran. v. beat, hammer

drû [irr. pl. **drúin**] n. woodwose

dû n. darkness, night

duin n. river

dûr adj. dark

dý- pref. adv. mistakenly

dýgar- v. make a mistake

[n]Ð

[n]dad- pref. adv. re-, un-, back

*** [n]dadhren-** v. forget

[n]dadwen- v. return, go back

[n]dae- pref. adv. horribly, dreadfully, ghastly

[n]dag- v. kill, slay

[n]dagnir masc. n. killer, bain

*** [n]dagnis** fem. n. killer, bain

[n]dagor [arc. **[n]dagr**] n. battle

[n]dagra- tran. intran. v. battle

[n]dam n. hammer

[n]damen- v. return, go back

[n]damma- tran. intran. v. [irr. pt3. **dammint** irr. pt. **damminni-**] hammer

[n]dan- pref. adv. re-, un-, back

[n]dan prep. against

*** [n]dananna-** [TA] tran. v. give back, return

[n]dandol- [sun. U] v. return, come back

[n]daug n. soldier

[n]dess n. young woman

[n]dî n. woman, lady, bride

[n]dîl n. lover, friend

[n]dîr n. man (the gender)

[n]dírnaith n. wedge-shaped battle formation

[n]dîs n. bride

[n]dôl 1) n. head 2) n. hill, mountain

[n]dôr n. land

[n]Doriath n. Land of the Fence

[n]dortha- intran. v. dwell, stay

[n]dûn n. West

E

echad- v. make, fashion

Echuir n. Stirring

ed prep. out of, forth

edhel n. elf

edhellen 1) n. Sindarin language 2) adj. elven, elvish, of or from the elves

edledhia- [sun. E] intran. v. [irr. pt3. **eglant** irr. pt. **eglenni-** irr. pt3. **egledhas(t)**)] go into exile

edonna- [sun. O] [TA] tran. v. beget

edra- tran. intran. v. open

edregol adv. especially

êg n. thorn

egel [arc. **egl**] n. exile

egleria- [sun. A] tran. v. praise, glorify

ego int. v. Be gone!

egor con. or

eiliant n. rainbow

ein- pref. adv. well, properly

eitha- 1) tran. v. ease, assist, help 2) tran. v. prick, stab (with a sharp point), treat with scorn, insult

eithel n. well, spring, water fountain

eithro adv. also

êl [pl. **elin**] n. star

eledh E. n. elf

eledhes fem. n. Noldorin elf

eledhon masc. n. Noldorin elf

elia- [sun. A] tran. v. bless, help, cause to prosper

elleth fem. n. elf

ellon masc. n. elf

Elo! int. Wow!

elu 1) adj. pale blue 2) name Elu Thingol's name, lacks meaning

emig n. mommy, mama

en prep. of the

*enebaen car. 60

Enedhin n. Mid Year's Day

eneg car. 6

*enem car. 16

eneth n. name

engui [NC] ord. sixth

ennas adv. there, yonder

Ennor n. Middle-earth

eno n. still

ephel n. outer fence of a town, city, field

er car. 1

er- pref. adv. alone

erch n. prickle

erchammui adj. one handed

ereb adj. isolated, lonely

eria- [sun. O] intran. v. arise

erin prep. over the, upon the

ertha- tran. v. unite, make one

erui 1) ord. first 2) adj. single, alone

Eryn-Lasgalen n. Forest of Greenleaf

esta- tran. v. name, call

estent adj. very short

ethir 1) n. spy 2) n. mouth of a river, estuary

*ethog- [sun. U] v. lead out

Ethuil n. Spring

F

*faefelf n. soul-feeling

faeg adj. bad, mean, poor

fael 1) adj. fair-minded, just, generous 2) n. gleaming brilliance of the sun

faen 1) adj. white 2) adj. radiant

Faenor n. Spirit of Fire

faer n. soul

fair 1) n. mortal 2) n. right hand 3) adj. quick, ready, prompt

falas n. shore

falf n. foam, breaker

fang n. beard

Fangorn n. Treebeard

far adv. & adj. sufficient, enough, quite

fara- tran. v. hunt

faras n. hunting
farn adj. enough
faug adj. thirsty
*****faul** n. thirst
faun n. cloud
feira- intran. v. suffice
*****fel-** v. feel (an emotion or sensation)
fela [irr. pl. **fili**] n. cave
*****felf** n. feeling, sensation, emotion
fennas n. doorway, gateway
fêr [irr. pl. **ferin**] n. beech tree
fer- pref. adv. soon, promptly
feredir masc. n. hunter
*****feredis** fem. n. hunter
feria- [sun. E] tran. v. make ready (promptly)
fern 1) adj. dead 2) n. dead person
filig n. small bird
filigod n. a single small bird
fim adj. slender, slim
Fimbrethil n. Slender Beech-tree
find n. tress, lock of hair
*****fir-** v. die (a natural/mortal death)
firieth fem. n. mortal woman
firion masc. n. mortal man
Firith n. Fading
forgam adj. right-handed
forod n. north
Forodwaith n. North Folk
forvo 1) n. right 2) adj. northern
fuia- tran. v. feel disgust for, abhor

G

gad- v. catch
gador [arc. **gadr**] n. prison
gae n. dread
gaear n. sea
gaearon n. ocean
gael adj. glimmering
*****gal-** pref. adv. well, blessedly
gala- intran. v. grow
galadh n. tree
galadhremmen adj. tree-woven

Galadriel n. Woman Garlanded with Radiance
*****Galdol**! int. Welcome!
galenas n. pipeweed
galu n. blessing, good fortune
gamp n. hook, claw, crook
Gardhon n. the Realm, Arda
gas n. hole
gast n. void
gathrod n. cave
gaud n. device, contrivance, machine
gaw n. void
gelir n. happy person
gell n. joy, triumph
*****gella-** intran. v. rejoice, delight
gem adj. sickly
gilgalad n. starlight
gir- v. shudder
girith n. shuddering, horror
girithron n. December
glad n. wood
gladh- v. laugh
*****gladhweg** adj. cheerful
glaer n. long lay, narrative poem
glam n. noisy speech
Glamdring n. Foe Hammer
glamhoth pl. n. horde of orcs, noisy horde
glamog n. orc
glân 1) adj. white, bright 2) hem, border
glass n. joy
*****glassui** adj. happy
glavra- intran. v. babble
glawar n. sunlight
gleina- tran. v. bind, enclose limit
glî n. honey
glind 1) n. song, chant, singing, air, tune 2) n. singer
glinna- 1) tran. intran. v. sing, chant 2) [TA] tran. v. glance at
Glinnel n. Lindarin Elf
glîr n. song, poem, lay
glir- v. sing, recite a poem trill

gloss adj. snow white

***glosta-** imp. v. snow

go- pref. adv. together

gobel [AU] n. walled village, enclosed town

gobennathren adj. historical

Gódhel n. Noldorin Elf

goe 1) n. terror, great fear 2) n. envelope of air around the world

gohena- [AU] tran. v. forgive (an equal)

golas [AU] n. foliage

golf n. branch

gonathra- [AU] tran. v. entangle, enmesh

gond n. stone

gondram n. hewn stone

gondren adj. made of/from stone

gonedia- [sun. O] tran. v. reckon

gonod- [AU, sun. O] v. count, sum up, reckon, count up

gonodui adj. countable

gor- [sun. O] v. advise, counsel, warn

***goras** n. advice

gost n. dread

gosta- tran. intran. v. fear exceedingly

govan- [AU] tran. intran. v. meet

groga- intran. v. feel terror

groth n. tunnel

gruitha- tran. v. terrify

gûr n. heart, conscience see 4.1.4

guruthos n. shadow of death

gwador masc. n. sworn brother, associate

Gwaeron n. March

gwaew n. wind

gwain adj. young, new

gwaith 1) n. people, region 2) n. host, regiment, fellowship 3) n. manhood

gwanna- intran. v. depart, die

gwanûn dual pl. pair of twins

gwanunig n. one twin

gwanur n. relative

gwarth n. traitor

gwass n. stain

gwath n. shadow

gwathel fem. n. sworn sister, associate

gwathui adj. shadowy

Gwathuirim n. Dunlendings

gwaun n. goose

gwaur adj. dirty, soiled

***gwe** nom. inc. pro. we

gwedh- v. bind

gwelu n. air

gwelwen n. inner air

***gwen** obl. inc. pro. we

gwend 1) n. maiden 2) n. friendship, bond

gweria- [sun. A] tran. v. cheat, betray

gwesta- tran. intran. v. swear (an oathe)

***gwil-** v. fly

gwilwileth n. butterfly

***gwîn** poss. inc. pro. our, ours

gwing n. foam, spindrift, spray

gwinig n. little baby

Gwirith n. April

[n]G

[n]gail 1) n. star, silver spark 2) adj. light, bright

[n]gal- v. shine clearly, glow, radiate light

[n]ganna- intran. v. play a harp

[n]gannada- intran. v. play a harp

[n]gannel n. harp

[n]garaf n. wolf

[n]gaur n. werewolf

[n]gawa- tran. intran. v. howl

***[n]gelia-** [sun. O] tran. v. learn

[n]gilith n. firmament

[n]Gilthoniel n. Star Kindler

[n]gilwen n. firmament

[n]goll adj. wise

***[n]golla-** [LT] tran. v. teach

***[n]gollanneth** [LT, NT] n. teaching, lesson

[n]gollor n. magician

[n]golodhvir n. silmaril

[n]golovir n. Silmaril

[n]gor- pref. adv. with emotional pain, fear, or dread, and therefore difficult to do.

[n]gorgor n. extreme horror, terror, haunting fear

[n]gorn n. dread/awe from reverence

[n]gorog n. horror

[n]goroth n. horror

[n]gorth n. horror

[n]gortheb adj. horrible

[n]gûd n. foe

[n]gûl n. sorcery, magic lore, long study, knowledge, secret lore

[n]gurth n. death

H

habad n. shoe

had- v. hurl, throw

hâdh n. cleaver

hadhod n. dwarf

hadlath n. throwing sling

hador [arc. hadr] n. spear/dart thrower

hadron masc. n. spear/dart thrower

hae adj. distant, far away, far, remote

hal- v. lift

hâl n. fish

hall 1) adj. exalted, high 2) adj. veiled, hidden, shadowed, shady

ham n. chair

*hanna- [NT] tran. v. thank

harad n. South

haradren adj. from the South, Southern

harn 1) adj. hurt, wounded 2) adj. south, southern 3) n. helmet

harna- tran. v. wound

haru n. wound

harvo [AU] n. left hand, left side

hasta- tran. v. hack through

hathol [arc. hathl] n. broadsword blade, ax blade

haudh n. burial mound, grave, tomb

hav- v. sit

heb- v. retain, keep hold of, keep

*hedril fem. n. spear/dart thrower

helch adj. bitter cold

heleg n. ice

hên 1) n. eye 2) n. child

henia- [sun. A] tran. intran. v. understand

henneth n. window

hent dual pl. pair of eyes

herdir n. master

heria- [sun. O] imp. v. begin suddenly and vigorously, have an impulse, be feel compelled to do something

herth n. troop under the command of a hîr

hîl n. heir, heiress

him 1) adj. cold, cool 2) adj. steadfast, abiding, continually

hîr n. lord, master

*hir- v. find

hiril n. lady

Hithui n. November

honeg n. bro

horn adj. impelled, compelled

hortha- tran. v. urge on, speed, compell

hoth n. crowd

hû 1) n. dog, hound 2) n. spirit, shadow

hûr n. readiness for action, vigor, fiery spirit

HW

hwá n. breeze

hwand n. sponge

hwest n. puff, breath, breeze

hwîn n. giddiness, faintness

hwinia- intran. v. twirl, eddy, whirl

hwiniol part. adj. twirling, whirling, giddy, fantastic

I

i 1) sing. art. the 2) compl. that 3) rel. sing. pro. that, who, which

iaeth n. neck

ial n. call, cry

iand [irr. pl. **iend**] n. expanse

iant n. bridge

iâth n. fence

iathrim n. Elves of Doriath

iaun adj. vast

iaur adj. ancient

Iavas n. Autumn

*Iavor n. Harvest Day

iaw 1) n. corn 2) n. ravine

ídha- tran. v. desire, long for

ídhra- tran. v. desire, long for

idhrind n. year cycle

iell n. daughter, girl

*iesta- tran. intran. v. wish

îf n. cliff, sheer descent

il- pref. every, all

ilaurui adv. daily

*ilhad ind. pro. everywhere

*ilnad ind. pro. everything

*ilphen ind. pro. everyone

im ind. ref. pro. self

în 1) n. year 2) ind. ref. poss. pro. own

in 1) pl. art. the 2) rel. pl. pro. that, who, which 3) pl. prep. of the

inc n. guess, idea, notion

ind n. heart, intent see 4.1.4

ínias n. annals

innas n. will

inu adj. female

io adv. long ago

iôn n. son, boy

iphant adj. old, year-full

îr 1) adv. only 2) n. sexual desire

ir compl. when, while

írui adj. desirable

ist n. knowledge

ista- tran. intran. v. [irr. pt3. **sint** irr. pt. **sinni-**] know, have knowledge

istadui adj. knowable

*istanna- [TA] tran. intran. v. teach, give knowledge

Ithil n. The Moon

ithron n. wizard

iuitha- tran. v. use, employ

Ivanneth n. September

ivor [arc. **ivr**] n. crystal

L

laba- intran. v. hop

lach n. flame

lachenn adj. flame-eyed, Noldorin

*lae- v. be not

Laegel n. Green-elf

Laegolas n. Green Foliage

laer 1) E. n. long lay, narrative poem 2) n. Summer

laes n. baby

lagor [arc. **lagr**] adj. swift, rapid

lain 1) adj. free 2) n. thread

lal- E. v. laugh

lalaith n. laughter

*lalweg E. adj. cheerful

lam n. tongue, language

lanc 1) n. throat 2) adj. naked 3) n. sharp edge, blade

lang n. cutlass

*lann n. thin cloth, tissue

lant E. n. fall

lanthir n. waterfall

lass n. leaf

lasta- tran. intran. v. listen, hear

*lastor n. eavesdropper

lathra- tran. intran. v. listen in, eavesdrop

lathrada- tran. intran. v. listen in, eavesdrop

lathron masc. n. eavesdropper

laug adj. warm

lav- v. lick

lavan n. animal
*law par. not
le nom. rev. sing. pro. you
lebdas n. index-finger
*lebem car. 15
leben car. 5
lebenedh n. middle-finger
lebent n. ring-finger
leber n. finger
lebig n. pinkie
ledh- E. v. travel
ledhbas E. n. waybread
leithia- [sun. E] tran. v. release
lembas E. n. waybread
*lemmui ord. fifth
len obl. rev. sing. pro. you
lend E. n. journey
*lephaen car. 50
lest n. girdle
lethril fem. n. eavesdropper
leutha- tran. v. pick up or out with
    your fingers
lim 1) n. fish 2) adj. quick, swift 3)
    adj. clear, sparkling, light
limmida- [MP] tran. v. [irr. pt3.
    limmint irr. pt. limminni-]
    moisten
limp adj. wet
lîn 1) poss. rev. sing. pro. your,
    yours 2) n. pool, mere
lind 1) E. n. song, chant, singing,
    air, tune 2) E. n. singer
linna- E. tran. intran. v. sing, chant
linnod n. short poem
lîr E. n. song, poem, lay
lir- v. sing
lith n. ash, dust
lithui adj. ashen, dusty
loda- intran. v. float
lom adj. weary
lond 1) n. harbor, haven 2) nar-
    row pass
loss n. snow
loth n. flower
Lothlórien n. Flower of Lórien

Lothron n. May
lû n. hour, time, occassion
luitha- tran. v. enchant
lunt n. boat
lûth n. flower

LH

lhaew adj. sickly, sick, ill
lhaw dual pl. n. pair of ears
lhê n. thread
lhewig n. ear
lhing n. spider, spider web, cob-
    web
lhô n. shallow lake, fenland, marsh,
    flood
lhûg n. dragon, snake, serpent,
    reptile, worm

M

ma 1) int. Good!, Right!, Yes! 2)
    nom. interr. pro. who
*mabed- v. ask (a question)
mad- v. eat
madha [irr. pl. meidhi] n. mud
madui adj. edible
madweg adj. gluttonous
mae 1) adv. well 2) adj. soft, pliant
maeas n. dough
*Maedol! int. Welcome!
mael n. lust
maelui adj. lustful
maen adj. skilled
maenas n. skill
maer adj. good
maetha- 1) tran. v. fight 2) tran. v.
    handle, wield, manage, deal
    with, use
maethor n. warrior
magol [arc. magl] n. sword
magor [arc. magr] n. swordsman
maidh adj. pale skinned, pale, fal-
    low
main ord. first
mallen [LT] adj. golden

mallorn [LT] n. golden tree from Lothlórien

malt n. gold

malu adj. fallow, pale

man 1) interr. obl. pro. who, what 2) interr. adj. which

mant n. food

maur n. gloom

maw n. hand

*__me__ nom. ex. pro. we

*__medhia-__ [sun. A] tran. v. kneed, soften

medui adj. last, final

megil n. sword

*__meidhia-__ [sun. A] tran. v. kneed, soften

mel- v. love, like, be in love

meldir masc. n. friend

meldis fem. n. friend

*__melethor__ [arc. **melethr**] n. lover

melethril fem. n. lover

melethron masc. n. lover

mellon n. friend

mên 1) n. road, way 2) n. place

men obl. ex. pro. we

men- v. go

meneg car. 1000, myrriad

menel n. heavens, place of stars

*__mengui__ [NC] ord. 1000th

*__menna-__ [TA] tran. intran. v. send, make go

*__mer-__ v. be happy

meren adj. festive, gay, joyous

*__merifind__ adj. black-haired

merilind n. nightingale

mi prep. in, between

*__mî__ rel. pro. in where

*__mib-__ v. kiss

mibas n. kiss

milui adj. kind, friendly, loving

mîn 1) poss. pro. our/ours (excluding you) 2) prep. in the

min 1) car. 1 2) prep. in the, between the

minai adj. unique

minib car. 11

minna- tran. intran. v. enter

minui ord. first

minuial n. daybreak

mîr n. jewel, treasure

mírdan n. jewel smith

mirian n. silver coin used in Gondor, castar

mista- intran. v. stray

mith adj. grey

Mithrandir n. Grey Wanderer

*__mivan__ interr. adv. in where

mîw adj. frail, small, tiny

môr n. darkness, night, blackness

morn adj. dark, black

muda- intran. v. labor, toil

*__muia-__ intran. v. whine

*__muig__ n. cat

muil n. drear

muin adj. dear

muindor n. brother

muinthel n. sister

N

'nin G. prep. to/for the

n[a] prep. to, towards, at

*__n'i__ rel. pro. at where/when

na- intran. v. be

nad 1) n. thing 2) ind. pro. something

nadha [irr. pl. **neidhi**] n. fetter

naeg n. pain

naegra- tran. v. pain

naer adj. sad, lamentable

nag- v. bite

nagol [arc. **nagl**] n. tooth, fang

nail ord. third

*__naman__ interr. adv. with what, how

nan prep. with, included, possessing

nana n. mommy, mama

nand n. valley

naneth n. mother

nâr n. rat

nara- tran. intran. v. narrate, tell

Narbeleth 1) n. Fading 2) n. October

narcha- tran. v. rend

narn n. tale, saga, spoken story

naru adj. red

Narwain n. January

nasta- tran. v. prick, point, stick, thrust

natha- tran. v. help, bring help to, save, rescue

nathal n. guest

nathla- v. welcome, be kind to

naub n. thumb

naug 1) adj. stunted 2) n. dwarf

naur n. fire, flame

***navan** interr. adv. at where

naw 1) n. idea 2) adj. hollow *3) int. It is so!, Yes!

nawag n. dwarf

ned prep. in, during, referring to time

neder car. 9

***nederph** car. 19

***nederphaen** car. 90

nedh- pref. prep. in, inside, mid-

***nedi** rel. pro. during when

nedia- [sun. O] tran. v. count

nedrui ord. nineth

nef prep. on this side of

neithan adj. deprived, wronged

***neleb** car. 13

neledh car. 3

neledh- v. enter,

nella- intran. v. ring (a bell)

***nelphaen** car. 30

nelui ord. third

***neman** interr. adv. during when

nên n. water, lake, pool, stream, waterland

nenui adj. wet

nesta- tran. intran. v. heal

nestag- v. insert, stick in

neth 1) n. sister 2) n. teen girl 3) adj. young

nethig n. sis

***nevia-** [sun. E] tran. v. translate, localize

***ni** nom. pro. I

niben 1) adj. small, petty 2) n. little pinkie

nîd adj. damp, wet, tearful

nidh- v. will, intend

nídha- tran. v. be determined to, intend

niged n. pinkie

Nimloth n. White Blossom

nimmida- [MP] tran. v. [irr. pt3. **nimmint** irr. pt. **nimminni**-] whiten

nimp 1) adj. pale, pallid, white 2) adj. small and frail

nîn 1) poss. pro. my 2) adj. wet

nin obl. pro. me

ninglor [AU] n. waterlily

***nínia-** intran. v. weep, cry

níniel adj. tearful

Nínui n. February

No! int. May it be so!, Make it so!, Yes!

nobad [AU] n. thumb & pointer-finger

nod- [sun. U] v. tie, bind

nodui adj. countable

nor- [sun. O] intran. v. run

nordh n. 1) oak 2) cord

norn adj. twisted, knotted, crabbed, contorted

northa- tran. v. make run, ride (a horse or animal)

Nórui n. June

***norweg** adj. often running

noss n. family, kindred, clan, house

***Novaer!** int. Goodbye!

nu prep. beneath, under

nuin prep. under the

nûr 1) n. race, group of related people 2) adj. sad 3) adj. deep

O

od prep. from, of

***odi** rel. pro. from whom/where

***odob** car. 17

***odobaen** car. 70

odog car. 7

oh prep. about, around, concerning

ôl [irr. pl. **ely**] n. dream, vision

***ol-** [sun. O] v. become

olla- [LT] imp. v. be given a dream or vision

***oman** interr. adv. from where

onna- [sun. O] [TA] tran. v. beget

onod n. ent

or prep. over, above

orch n. orc, goblin

orchall adj. very tall

orod n. mountain

oron n. tree

***oronnad** n. birthday

oroth n. wrath, rage

ortha- tran. v. [irr. pt3. **oront** irr. pt. **erenni-**] raise

orthor- v. master, conquer

***Orvinui** n. New Years Day

os- pref. prep. around, about

osgar- v. cut round, amputate

osp 1) n. reek 2) n. smoke

ost n. fortified city or town, a fortress

***ostol-** [sun. U] v. come around, circumvent

oth- pref. adv. badly, improperly

othol n. stranger, guest

othrad n. city street

othui ord. seventh

ovor [arc. **ovr**] adj. abundant

ovra- v. abound, pile up

ᚹ

pad- v. walk

pâd 1) n. track, road, way 2) ford 3) n. step (the action of taking it)

pada- intran. v. walk, step

padra- intran. v. walk, step

pae car. 10

paenui ord. tenth

paich n. juice, syrup

palan- pref. adv. far and wide, afar

***palangened** [NC] n. television

***palangon** [NC, AU] n. telephone, cellphone

palath n. surface

pân n. wooden plank

panas 1) wooden floor

pant adj. full

parch adj. dry

parf n. book

parth n. field, enclosed grassland, sward

paur n. fist

ped- v. say, speak

pel- v. wither

pêl [pl. **peli**] n. fenced field, enclosure

pelia- [sun. A] tran. v. spread

***pell** adj. calm, quiet, still

pen 1) n. person 2) ind. pro. one, someone, somebody

pen- 1) pref. prep. without, -less 2) v. lack, have not

pendrad n. stairway

peng n. bow

penia- [sun. A] tran. v. fix, set

penn 1) adj. crested 2) n. slope

penna- intran. v. slant down, come down a slope, fall, slide down

pen-nediad adj. countless, innumerable

Penninor n. New Years Eve

***per-** 1) pref. adv. half 2) v. turn

Perhael n. Samwise

periand n. hobbit

pessa- imp. v. be changed, be affected, have one's heart moved (could be a good or bad feeling)

peth n. word

*pi compl. if

*pil n. robber, thief

*pil- v. steal, rob, thieve

pilinn n. arrow

pirind n. winking flower

plada- tran. v. feel (with one's palm), pass the sensitive part of the palm over a surface

pladadui adj. touchable

po prep. on

*pol- [sun. O] v. can, be physically able to

*posta- intran. v. rest

presta- tran. v. affect, disturb, trouble

prestanneth n. mutation

puia- intran. v. spit

R

râd n. path, track

rada- intran. v. make a way, find a way

raeda- 1) tran. v. catch (in a net) *2) intran. v. smile

raef n. net

raeg adj. crooked, bent, wrong

raen 1) adj. smiling, gracious, sweet-faced 2) adj. crooked 3) adj. nettled, enlaced

*rag- v. break

*ragui adj. fragile, breakable

rammas n. great wall

ran- v. wander

ranc n. arm

randir masc. n. wanderer

*randis fem. n. wanderer

râth 1) n. street 2) n. course, riverbed

raud 1) adj. tall, high, lofty, eminent, noble 2) n. metal

raw 1) n. lion 2) n. wing 3) n. bank [of earth]

redhor n. planter

reitha- 1) tran. intran. v. [irr. tran. pt3. **rithant** irr. intran. pt3.

rithas(t)] strive, try *2) tran. v. rescue, save (from ruin/peril/loss)

rem 1) adj. frequent, numerous 2) n. mesh, net

*ren- v. remember, have in mind

rend adj. circular

renia- 1) [sun. A] intran. v. stray, wander 2) [sun. A] intran. v. fly, sail

rev- v. ensnare, entangle

revia- intran. v. sail

rîdh n. sown field, acre

rîn 1) n. remembrance 2) n. queen, crowned lady

ring adj. cold

rista- tran. v. rend, cut, rip

ro- [AU] pref. adv. most, -est

roch n. horse

Rochand n. Horse Land

rochben n. horse rider

rochir n. knight, mounted warrior

rochon n. knight, horseman

Rochwaith n. People of Rohan

ross 1) adj. red-haired 2) n. foam, spindrift, spray 3) rain

ruin n. footprint

rûth n. anger, rage

ruthra- intran. v. rage

RH

rhach n. curse

rhae- pref. adv. awkwardly

rhaw 1) n. wilderness 2) n. body, flesh 3) adj. wild, untamed

rhib- v. scratch

Rhîw n. Winter

*rhofelf [AU] n. body-feeling

rhosg adj. brown

rhoss n. whisper, rustling sound

rhu- pref. adv. wickedly, evily

rhugar- v. do evil

rhûn n. East

rhúnen adj. eastern

S

*sa nom. dem. pro. that

sad 1) n. place, spot 2) ind. pro. someplace, somewhere

*saeb adj. hungry

*saeg n. hunger

*sai nom. dem. pro. those

said adj. private, separate, uncommon, excluded

sain 1) adj. new 2) dem. obl. pro. those *3) dem. adj. those

salph n. broth, liquid food, soup

san 1) dem. obl. pro. that 2) dem. adj. that

sant n. garden, field, yard, private space

sarn n. small stone

sarnas n. pile of stones

sautha- v. drain

sav- *1) v. believe in, accept as fact 2) v. [irr. pt3. aw irr. pt. awe-] have

*se nom. dem. pro. this

sell n. girl, daughter

sen *1) dem. obl. pro. this 2) dem. adj. this

sennui adv. instead

ser n. lover, friend

sí 1) adv. now 2) adv. here

si 1) adv. now 2) adv. here *3) nom. dem. pro. these

sîdh n. peace, tranquility

sigil 1) n. necklace 2) n. dagger, knife

síla- intran. v. shine white

silef n. white crystal

silivren adj. silver-white

sin *1) dem. obl. pro. these 2) dem. adj. these

sîr 1) adv. today 2) adv. now 3) n. river

soga- tran. v. drink

solch n. root

sui prep. as, like

suil n. greeting

suila- tran. v. greet

suilanna- [TA] intran. v. give greeting

suin prep. as the, like the

sûl 1) n. wind 2) n. goblet

T

*tab- v. stop, close, block

tâd car. 2

tadui ord. second

taen 1) n. height, summit of a high mountain 2) adj. long and thin, slender 3) n. sign

taer adj. straight

taetha- tran. v. fasten, tie

taid ord. second

tâl 1) n. foot 2) n. flat space, platform

talagand n. harper

talan n. tree-house

talath n. flat lands, plain; flat surface, plane

talf 1) n. palm of hand 2) n. flat field, flat land

talraph n. stirrup

talt adj. slipping, falling, insecure

tân n. smith

tang n. bowstring

tangada- [NC] tran. v. make firm, establish, confirm

*taphaen car. 20

tara [irr. pl. teiri] adj. tough, stiff

tarlanc adj. stiff-necked, obstinate

tas n. index-finger

tass 1) n. task, labor 2) n. trouble

taur 1) n. forest, great wood 2) n. king of a tribe 3) adj. mighty, vast, overwhelming, huge, awful, high, sublime

taw 1) adj. wood as material 2) n. wool 3) adj. woolen, made of wool

tawar n. forest

te nom. pro. it, he, she

tegilbor n. scribe

Tegilbor n. Pen Hand

teilia- [sun. A] tran. intran. v. play (a game)

teitha- tran. intran. v. write, inscribe, make marks or signs

telia- *1) [sun. E] tran. v. finish, conclude 2) [sun. A] tran. intran. v. play (a game)

tellen n. sole of a foot

telu n. roof, dome

ten obl. pro. him, her, it

ti nom. pro. they

tîn poss. pro. its, his, her, their

***tin** obl. pro. them

tinnu n. starry twilight

tinu n. star

tîr adj. straight, right

tir- v. watch, gaze, look at

tíra- tran. v. guard, see, watch

tiria- tran. v. watch, look at, gaze

tirn n. watcher

tithen adj. small

toba- tran. v. cover, roof over

tobas n. roof, roofing

tog- [sun. U] v. lead, bring

tol- [sun. U] v. come

tolch n. little prominent one

toleg n. little prominent one

tolla- [sun. U] [TA] tran. v. fetch, make come, summon

tollui ord. eighth

***tolob** car. 18

tolodh car. 8

tolog adj. stalwart, trusty

***tolophaen** car. 80

tond adj. tall

torog n. troll

tortha- tran. v. wield, control

Trann n. Shire

trasta- tran. v. harass, annoy, trouble

***trastadweg** adj. annoying

tre- 1) pref. adv. thoroughly 2) pref. prep. through

trenarn n. story

trevad- v. traverse travel

trî prep. through, throughout

trîw adj. slender

tûg adj. fat, thick

***Tuilor** n. Spring Day

tulus n. poplar tree

tum n. valley

TH

thala [irr. pl. **theili**] adj. stalwart, steady, firm

***thalieth** fem. n. heroine, dauntless woman

thalion masc. n. hero, dauntless man

tham n. hall

thammas n. great hall

thand 1) adj. firm, true, abiding 2) n. shield

thang n. compulsion, duress, need

thangail n. shield-wall

thâr n. stiff grass

thar- pref. adv. across, athwart, over

thar prep. across, thwart, over

thaw adj. corrupt, rotten

thel- v. intend, mean, purpose, resolve, will

thela [irr. pl. **thili**] n. spearpoint

thend 1) adj. grey 2) n. Sindarin Elf

Thennor masc. n. Sindarin Elf

thent adj. short

***ther-** v. sew

theria- v. dread

thia- tran. v. appear, seem

thilia- intran. v. glisten, sparkle, glitter

thinna- [NT] intran. v. fade, grow towards evening, turn grey

thîr n. face, look, expression, countenance

thôl n. [irr. pl. **thely**] helmet, helm

thora- tran. v. fence in, surround

thoron n. eagle

Thranduil n. Vigorous Stream

thu- pref. adv. badly, incorrectly
thuia- intran. v. breathe

U

ú- pref. adv. cannot
úan n. monster
uanui adj. hideous
ui- pref. adv. ever, always
uial n. twilight
uil 1) imp. v. rain 2) n. seaweed
uin prep. from the
uir n. eternity
uireb adj. eternal
ulund n. monster, deformed and hideous creature
um adj. evil

***ummas** n. evil
ûn n. creature
ûr n. heat, fire
urug n. bogey, monster
úrui adj. hot
Urui n. August
úthaes n. temptation

Y

ylf 1) n. cup, drinking vessel 2) n. brand
ýneg car. 12
yr- v. run

Index

About the author

Fiona Jallings has a BA in English-Linguistics and a minor in Japanese. She's been studying Tolkien's languages since she was 15, when the first *Lord of the Rings* movie came out. She uses her linguistic knowledge to teach free online classes about Neo-Sindarin and maintains the website Realelvish.net, which provides phrasebooks and name translations in a handful of Tolkien's languages.

She lives a quiet nerdy life in Northwestern Montana with her wife of many years, spending her free time taking photos of wildlife, sewing her own cosplay costumes, and talking to her cat Muior.

CPSIA information can be obtained
at www.ICGtesting.com
Printed in the USA
LVHW031555060420
652380LV00006B/39/J